STUPIDISM

————————

DAVID ELLSWORTH

HOW MUCH DO PEOPLE REALLY KNOW ABOUT THE THINGS THEY BELIEVE AND IF THEY DO KNOW, WHY DO THEY CONTINUE TO BELIEVE?

"Some would call it sacrilege but I call it a hilarious, eye-opening view of some of the world's major belief systems."

- International Review

"Ellsworth takes off the gloves and takes on some of our most wacky religions."

- Sunset Book Alerts

"Maybe the mother of all doctrinal writings."

- Mundo

DAVID ELLSWORTH

Table of Contents

INTRODUCTION

Our planet is inhabited by believers. If humanity was to be described in any singular form, certainly it would be that – we are believers. Confined and limited by the laws of physics surrounding us, we yet believe that supernatural elements maintain a shadowy place in our lives. We may be held firm by gravity yet believe that witches can fly. Half the people in the United States and England believe in ghosts. Seventy-seven percent of the people in the United States believe aliens have visited the earth, which is understandable when one considers the National Science Foundation poll showing that one in four Americans believe the sun moves around the earth.

Karma, intuition, fate, all fall within the realm of things many or most people believe in spite of the fact that not one is supported by any kind of evidence, and the result is that there are some very rich astrologers and mediums. But the implications of belief go much farther than that. Governments have been formed on the principles of belief, not fact. Laws have been based on the concepts of common belief, not fact. Countless universities have been founded to teach belief, not documented information. The world's religions dominate the politics of man and yet represent belief, not fact.

It has been said that there has been an ancient conflict between religion and science and yet, I maintain that the conflict was much broader than that. It is the conflict between belief and knowledge. Priests, ministers, parsons, all ask us to place belief above knowledge or even go so far as to assert that their belief is synonymous with knowledge, conveniently ignoring that there is no evidence to support their claim. They go so far as to suggest that to study one's belief creates knowledge, as if learning the details of ancient tales and legends contained within one's belief is equating that belief to the realities of our world. The study of one's belief does not alter it from being a belief and knowledge of a belief remains in the realm of belief.

Anyone maintaining that belief can be equal to knowledge should answer which is the most rewarding phrase, "I believe he/she loves me" or "I know he/she loves me." Belief cannot be equated to knowledge and yet the mechanisms of daily life are as dependent upon belief as they are knowledge. Things we are taught to believe become our imaginary facts. As children we accept the authority of parents as the most validated source and "If you keep crossing your eyes, they'll get stuck there forever" becomes a

7

fearful reality of life. As often as not, such mandates remain as truths well into adult life.

Like it or not, our world is composed of thinkers and believers, those in pursuit of knowledge and those locked in the mystical realm of mere belief. The difference between the two is that the world of the believer is far more dangerous and threatening.

Throughout the world, entire cultures are woven from beliefs finding their origin in the primitive mind long before recorded history. The man trembling in a cave, fearful of the dark that brought cold and a host of predators, easily perceived the sun as his god. The arrival of warmth and light came as gifts of a visible deity distributing its benefits equally to all. Religion had been born. The sun god would become the most enduring god of all time, practiced as Sol Invictus by the Romans into the time of Constantine, by the Egyptians and Aztecs and is still practiced by some in parts of the world.

Codes by which entire civilizations base their morals, goals and character are founded on what people have been taught to believe, regardless of truth, logic or intelligence. Instilled into the minds of young people are fantasies pretending to be fact, but enforced socially as if they were the standard of all that is good and right with the world. And it is belief – not knowledge – that is held as being righteous, admirable and the measure of the noble man.

Today, religion is no longer inflicted upon others through power or force, and yet the evolution of what man has created as representative of his spiritual self has taken some bizarre turns. Intelligence and perception have been suspended through various means. Articulate evangelists, an allegiance to the scripture as being absolute or a person simply being weak and vulnerable to the hawkers of faith have contributed to the formation of religious concepts challenging all rational thought.

It seems ironic that while legitimate geniuses or those with astounding talents should live in obscurity and forever forgotten, charlatans and frauds should be given their place in history and revered as prophets, holy men and those speaking not about God, rather for Him.

Herein we will explore but a few of these con men who carved out their place in history and the legacy of false faiths they left behind. We will also probe into those subscribing to the most pre-prosperous forms of belief in a study I have called Stupidism.

THE FACE OF FAITH

The near-universal existence of religion across cultures is surprising. Many people have speculated on what makes tribes around the world so fixated on believing in gods and propitiating them and so on. More recently people like Dawkins and Dennett have added their own contributions about parasitic memes and hyperactive agent-detection.

But I think a lot of these explanations are too focused on a modern idea of religion. I find ancient religion much more enlightening. I'm no historian, but from the little I know ancient religion seems to bleed seamlessly into every other aspect of the ancient way of life. For example, the Roman religion was a combination of mythology, larger-than-life history, patriotism, holidays, customs, superstitions, rules about the government, beliefs about virtue, and attempts to read the future off the livers of pigs. And aside from the pig livers, this seems entirely typical.

American culture has a lot of these features too. It has mythology and larger-than-life history: George Washington chopping down the cherry tree, the wise and glorious Founding Fathers, Honest Abe single-handedly freeing the slaves with his trusty hatchet. It has patriotic symbols and art: the flag, the anthem, Uncle Sam. It has holidays: the Fourth of July, Martin Luther King Day, Washington's birthday. It has customs: eat turkey on Thanksgiving, have a barbecue on Memorial Day, watch the Super Bowl. It has superstitions – the number 13, black cats – and ritual taboos – even "obvious" things like don't go outside naked needs to be thought of as taboo considering some cultures do so without thinking. It has rules about the government – both the official laws you'll find in the federal law code, but also deep-seated beliefs about the goodness of democracy or about how all men are created equal, and even customs that affect day-to-day governance like the President giving a State of the Union in January before both houses of Congress. There are beliefs about virtue: everyone should be free, we should try to be independent, we should work hard and pursue the American Dream.

People call the Jewish dietary code unusually strict, but it's important to realize the strictness of modern American kashrut. Absolutely no eating insects – remember, even Jewish kashrut allows locusts! Precious few birds outside of chickens, ducks, turkeys, and geese – remember, even Jewish kashrut allows pigeons! No dogs, cats, rodents, or horses. No reptiles or amphibians, no matter how much the French try to convince us that frog legs are great. No eating clearly obvious animal heads with eyes and stuff (even though dozens of advanced cultures do so happily). No blood products (eg black pudding). Mixing milk and soda in the same glass would be absurd and disgusting. Any tuna made with a process that cannot 100% exclude dolphins is impure. And this isn't even including all of the more modern health-oriented taboos like gluten, MSG, trans-fats, GM foods, et cetera.

If we were to ask the same New Guinea tribe to follow Jewish food taboos one week and American food taboos the next, I'm not sure they'd be able to identify one code as any stricter or weirder than the other. They might have some questions about the meat/milk thing, but maybe they'd also wonder why cheeseburgers are great for dinner but ridiculous for breakfast.

People get worked up over all of the weird purity laws and dress codes in Leviticus, but it's important to realize how strict our own purity laws are. The ancient Jews would have found it ridiculous that men have to shave and bathe every day if they want to be considered for the best jobs. One must not piss anywhere other than a toilet; this is an abomination (but you would be shocked how many of the supposedly strait-laced Japanese will go in an alley if there's no restroom nearby). I have been yelled at for going to work without a tie *and* for tying my tie in the wrong pattern; wearing sweatpants to work is right out. And once again, this gets even longer if you you let the more modern/rational rules onto the list – Leviticus has a lot to say about dwellings with fungus in them, but I recently learned to my distress that landlord/tenant law has a lot more.

Once again, if we made our poor New Guinea tribe follow Jewish purity laws one week and American purity laws the next, they would probably end up equally confused and angry both times. So when we think of America as a perfectly natural secular culture, and Jews as following some kind of superstitious draconian law code, we're just saying that our laws feel natural and obvious, but their laws feel like an outside imposition. And I think if a time-traveling King Solomon showed up at our doorstep, he would recognize American civil religion as a religion *much* quicker than he would recognize Christianity as one. Christianity would look like a barbaric mystery cult that had gotten too big for its britches; American civil religion would look like home.

Insofar as this isn't obvious to schoolchildren learning about ancient religion, it's because the only thing one ever hears about ancient religion is the crazy mythologies. But I think American culture shows lots of signs of trying to form a crazy mythology, only to be stymied by modernity-specific factors. We can't have crazy mythologies because we have too many historians around to tell us exactly how things really happened. We can't have crazy mythologies because we have too many scientists around to tell us where the rain and the lightning *really* come from. We can't have crazy mythologies because we're only two hundred-odd years old and these things take time. And most of all, we can't have crazy mythologies because Christianity is already sitting around occupying that spot.

But if America was a thousand years old and had no science, no religion, and no writing, we would have crazy mythologies up the wazoo. George Washington would take on the stature of an Agamemnon; Benjamin Franklin would take on the status of a Daedalus. Instead of centaurs and satyrs and lamia we would have jackalopes and chupacabras and grey aliens. All those people who say with a nod and a wink that Paul Bunyan dug the Great Lakes as a drinking trough for his giant ox would say the same thing nodless and winkless. Superman would take on the stature of a Zeus, dwelling beside Obi-Wan Kenobi and Bigfoot atop Mt. Whitney, helping the virtuous and punishing the wicked. Some American Hesiod would put succumb to the systematizing impulse, put it all together and explain how George Washington was the son of Superman and ordered Paul Bunyan to dig Chesapeake Bay to entrap the British fleet, and nobody would be able to say they were wrong. I mean, we already have Superman vs. Batman as canon, why not go the extra distance?

So in one sense our best analogy for ancient religion is American civil religion coupled to the sort of national mythology we might have gotten if we'd been a little bit more historically confused. But in another sense ancient religion was actually much stronger than this. America has its own individual culture, but it also partakes of the entire Western liberal industrial secular worldview. An American might not feel culture shock if she moved to Britain; she probably would if she moved to New Guinea.

The ancient world had far less trade and transportation than our own and was far less homogenized. If you want to get into the shoes of an ancient contemplating his religion, imagine you're an American in a world where even your closest neighboring countries are as different from you as New Guinea hill tribes, or Afghan chiefdoms, or Chinese party cadres. In a world like this, your identity as an American would be very salient – and the essence of being an American is impossible to separate from this whole set of national beliefs about celebrating the Fourth of July, not eating insects, wanting freedom and democracy, and believing that Superman lives atop Mt. Whitney. Outside the community of people who 100% believe all these things, there's just unreachable foreigners whose language you do not speak and whose customs seem somewhere between inscrutable and barbaric.

That was ancient religion – culture in a world where culture meant something. It was nothing like modern religion – which is why you never hear the Greeks complaining that the Egyptians were evil heretics who denied the light of Zeus and needed to be converted by the sword. But ancients nevertheless felt a connection to their culture and community that combined modern patriotism, religious piety, and belief in science – and they expressed it by continuing to perform their rites and even dying for them.

The question of the origin of religion comes down to how these cultures evolved into the clearly-defined religions of the modern day.

I think a big part of this is ossification and separation from context. The Jewish law perfectly preserves what any right-thinking Israelite in 1000 BC would have considered obvious, natural, and not-even-needing-justification (much as any right-thinking American today considers not eating insects obvious). By the time the Bible was being written this was no longer true – foreign customs and inevitable social change were making the old law seem less and less relevant, and I think modern scholarship thinks the Bible was written by a conservative faction of priests making their case for adherence to the old ways. The act of writing it down in a book, declaring this book the sort of thing that people *might* doubt but shouldn't, and then passing that book to their children – that made it a modern religion, in the sense of something potentially separable from culture that required justification. I think that emphasizing the role of God and the gods provided that justification.

The Hebrew Bible never says other gods don't exist; indeed, it often says the opposite. It constantly praises God as stronger and better than other gods. God proves his superiority over the gods of the Egyptians when the serpent he sends Moses eats the serpents the Egyptian gods send Pharaoh's sorcerers. The Israelites are constantly warned against worshipping other gods, not because those gods don't exist but because God is better and also jealous. This is not the worldview of somebody who has very strong ideas

12

about the nature of reality and how supernatural beings fit into that nature. It's the worldview of people who want to say "Our culture is better than your culture". The Bible uses "worshipping foreign gods" as synonymous with "turning to foreign ways". But God has a covenant with Israel, therefore both are forbidden.

This seems to match religion in the classical world – I'm especially thinking of Augustus' conception here, but he wasn't drawing it out of a vacuum. Performing the proper rites to the Roman gods was how you showed you were on board with Roman culture was how you showed you were loyal to Rome. The Roman view of religion seems pretty ridiculous to us – constant influx of new gods and mystery cults that were believed kind of indiscriminately, plus occasional deification of leading political figures followed by their undeification once they fell from power. But throughout it all, this idea that following the rites as Romulus prescribed them showed loyalty, but doing otherwise would result in decadence and defeat, stuck around.

More modern religions like Christianity, Islam, and Buddhism are a bit different. Obviously their respective founders play a huge role, but I still think part of what makes them religions rather than just philosophies or spiritual teachings is that they underwent this ossification process. Just as modern Judaism preserves many features of 10th-century-BC Israel that got encoded into holy writ, so modern Christianity preserves many features of 1st century Judeo-Hellenist syncretism. In fact, it preserves a lot of features of 13th-century scholasticism, since that was when they really became serious about formalizing and recognizing their theology. At the time scholasticism wasn't particularly religious; it was just the best understanding the 13th century academic community had about the world around them. Since the Church recognized it, everyone else drifted away.

I think it's also possible that the first few followers of these religions ended up as a subculture, with as much arbitrary sub-cultural development as any other tribe. My personal experience with subcultures tells me they can get *very* different customs from the surrounding society *very* fast, with or without any connection to real feature of their rallying flag. Those unusual subcultural values then became the values of the religion that developed later.

The important thing about a religion is that it has a rallying flag that encourages it to preserve a certain culture, plus walls against the outside world. Crucially, despite everything I'm saying about ossification the culture changes a lot: King Solomon would probably recognize modern rabbinic Judaism, but only barely. But it changes in a way different from the way the outside secular society changes, and in ways bound by the ossified text, so there's still an element of having this ancient culture preserved in amber and maintained up to the modern day.

At some point, however, religion became a competition. Those entertaining the idea of starting a new faith realized that it had to be something different – sometimes starkly different. The more they tried to be creative, the more insanity entered the world of churches. And religion wasn't like all other things. There were no controls or supervision because a Constitution permitted total freedom, even to the point of lunacy. If you have a church, no inspector will come around to make sure you're doing things right as happens to those owning restaurants. No official will drop by to determine if you are following the tenets of the Bible correctly as happens to those owning private schools needing to follow regulated curriculums. Hell, you don't even need to be certified or with a license. All you need to do is "have a calling."

The result is written across the face of America – and indeed the world – as fantastic lies become church history and charlatans become their founders and martyrs. Once believed, all the falsehoods become indelible upon the human soul, constructed upon the iron and steel of faith. It is not important how many intelligent, thinking people analyze and refute the new, revolutionary religion, it grows and is sustained by belief alone with each criticism serving only to solidify their resolve.

The defiant refusal to accept fact is a characteristic of a cult member. Concerted efforts at influence and control lie at the core of cultic groups, programs, and relationships. Many members, former members, and supporters of cults are not fully aware of the extent to which members may have been manipulated, exploited, even abused. Often times a narrow line exists between religion and a cult and followers fail to realize it. Here are some characteristics of cults that can be easily related to many religious groups.

- The group displays excessively zealous and unquestioning commitment to its leader and (whether he is alive or dead) regards his belief system, ideology, and practices as the Truth, as law.
- Questioning, doubt, and dissent are discouraged or even punished.
- Mind-altering practices (such as meditation, chanting, speaking in tongues, denunciation sessions, and debilitating

14

work routines) are used in excess and serve to suppress doubts about the group and its leader(s).

- The leadership dictates, sometimes in great detail, how members should think, act, and feel (for example, members must get permission to date, change jobs, marry — or leaders prescribe what types of clothes to wear, where to live, whether or not to have children, how to discipline children, and so forth).

- The group is elitist, claiming a special, exalted status for itself, its leader(s), and its members (for example, the leader is considered the Messiah, a special being, an avatar—or the group and/or the leader is on a special mission to save humanity).

- The group has a polarized us-versus-them mentality, which may cause conflict with the wider society.

- The leader is not accountable to any authorities (unlike, for example, teachers, military commanders or ministers, priests, monks, and rabbis of mainstream religious denominations).

- The group teaches or implies that its supposedly exalted ends justify whatever means it deems necessary. This may result in members' participating in behaviors or activities they would have considered reprehensible or unethical before they joined the group (for example, lying to family or friends, or collecting money for bogus charities).

- The leadership induces feelings of shame and/or guilt in order to influence and/or control members. Often, this is done through peer pressure and subtle forms of persuasion.

- Subservience to the leader or group requires members to cut ties with family and friends, and to radically alter the personal goals and activities they had before they joined the group.

- The group is preoccupied with bringing in new members.

- The group is preoccupied with making money.

- Members are expected to devote inordinate amounts of time to the group and group-related activities.

- Members are encouraged or required to live and/or socialize only with other group members.

- The most loyal members (the "true believers") feel there can be no life outside the context of the group. They believe there is no other way to be and often fear reprisals to

15

themselves or others if they leave (or even consider leaving) the group.

Some of all of these characteristics existed in the cults of James Jones, David Koresh and Marshal Applewhite but also exist in well-known "religious" groups such as scientology, Jehovah Witnesses and Mormons. So, what is the appeal of cults? Imagine being part of a group in which you will find instant friendship, a caring family, respect for your contributions, an identity, safety, security, simplicity, and an organized daily agenda. You will learn new skills, have a respected position, gain personal insight, improve your personality and intelligence. There is no crime or violence and your healthy lifestyle means there is no illness.

Your leader may promise not only to heal any sickness and foretell the future, but give you the gift of immortality, if you are a true believer. In addition, your group's ideology represents a unique spiritual/religious agenda (in other cults it is political, social or personal enhancement) that if followed, will enhance the Human Condition somewhere in the world or cosmos.

Who would fall for such appeals? Most of us, if they were made by someone we trusted, in a setting that was familiar, and especially if we had unfulfilled needs.

Much cult recruitment is done by family, friends, neighbors, co-workers, teachers and highly trained professional recruiters. They recruit not on the streets or airports, but in contexts that are "home bases" for the potential recruit; at schools, in the home, coffee houses, on the job, at sports events, lectures, churches, or drop-in dinners and free personal assessment workshops. The Heaven's Gate group made us aware that recruiting is now also active over the Internet and across the World Wide Web.

A 1980 study surveyed and interviewed more than 1,000 randomly selected high school students in the greater San Francisco Bay Area, 54 percent reported they had at least one active recruiting attempt by someone they identified with a cult, and 40 percent said they had experienced three to five such contacts. And that was long before electronic cult recruiting could be a new allure for a generation of youngsters growing up as web surfers.

What makes any of us especially vulnerable to cult appeals? Someone is in a transitional phase in life: moved to a new city or country, lost a job, dropped out of school, parents divorced, romantic relationship broken, gave up traditional religion as personally irrelevant. Add to the recipe, all those who find their work tedious and trivial, education abstractly meaningless, social life absent or inconsistent, family remote or dysfunctional, friends too busy to find time for you and trust in government eroded.

Cults promise to fulfill most of those personal individual's needs and also to compensate for a litany of societal failures: to make their slice of the world safe, healthy, caring, predictable and controllable. They will eliminate the increasing feelings of isolation and alienation being created by mobility, technology, competition, meritocracy, incivility, and dehumanized living and working conditions in our society.

In general, cult leaders offer simple solutions to the increaseingly complex world problems we all face daily. They offer the simple path to happiness, to success, to salvation by following their simple rules, simple group regimentation and simple total lifestyle. Ultimately, each new member contributes to the power of the leader by trading his or her freedom for the illusion of security and reflected glory that group membership holds out.

It seems like a "win-win" trade for those whose freedom is without power to make a difference in their lives. This may be especially so for the shy among us. Shyness among adults is now escalating to epidemic proportions, according to recent research by Dr. B. Carducci in Indiana and a research team in California. More than 50 percent of college-aged adults report being chronically shy (lacking social skills, low self-esteem, awkward in many social encounters). As with the rise in cult membership, a public health model is essential for understanding how societal pathology is implicated in contributing to the rise in shyness among adults and children in America.

Our society is in a curious transitional phase; as science and technology make remarkable advances, antiscientific values and beliefs in the paranormal and occult abound, family values are stridently promoted in Congress and pulpits, yet divorce is rising along with spouse and child abuse, fear of nuclear annihilation in superpower wars is replaced by fears of crime in our streets and drugs in our schools, and the economic gap grows exponentially between the rich and powerful and our legions of poor and powerless.

Such change and confusion create intellectual chaos that makes it difficult for many citizens to believe in anything, to trust anyone, to stand for anything substantial.

On such shifting sands of time and resolve, the cult leader stands firm with simple directions for what to think and feel, and how to act. "Follow me, I know the path to sanity, security and

17

salvation," proclaims Marshall Applewhite, with other cult leaders chanting the same lyric in that celestial chorus. And many will follow.

What makes cults dangerous? It depends in part on the kind of cult since they come in many sizes, purposes and disguises. Some cults are in the business of power and money. They need members to give money, work for free, beg and recruit new members. They won't go the deathly route of the Heaven's Gaters; their danger lies in deception, mindless devotion, and failure to deliver on the recruiting promises.

Danger also comes in the form of insisting on contributions of exorbitant amounts of money (tithing, signing over life insurance, social security or property, and fees for personal testing and training).

Add exhausting labor as another danger (spending all one's waking time begging for money, recruiting new members, or doing menial service for little or no remuneration). Most cult groups demand that members sever ties with former family and friends which creates total dependence on the group for self identity, recognition, social reinforcement. Unquestioning obedience to the leader and following arbitrary rules and regulations eliminates independent, critical thinking, and the exercise of free will. Such cerebral straight jacketing is a terrible danger that can lead in turn to the ultimate twin dangers of committing suicide upon command or destroying the cult's enemies.

Potential for the worst abuse is found in "total situations" where the group is physically and socially isolated from the outside community. The accompanying total milieu and informational control permits idiosyncratic and paranoid thinking to flourish and be shared without limits. The madness of any leader then becomes normalized as members embrace it, and the folly of one becomes the identity of all, and finally, with three or more adherents, it becomes a constitutionally protected belief system that is an ideology defended to the death.

A remarkable thing about cult mind control is that it's so ordinary in the tactics and strategies of social influence employed. They are variants of well-known social psychological principles of compliance, conformity, persuasion, dissonance, reactance, framing, emotional manipulation, and others that are used on all of us daily to entice us: to buy, to try, to donate, to vote, to join, to change, to believe, to love, to hate the enemy.

18

Cult mind control is not different in kind from these everyday varieties, but in its greater intensity, persistence, duration, and scope. One difference is in its greater efforts to block quitting the group, by imposing high exit costs, replete with induced phobias of harm, failure, and personal isolation.

What's the solution?

Heaven's Gate mass suicides have made cults front page news. While their number and ritually methodical formula are unusual, cults are not. They exist as part of the frayed edges of our society and have vital messages for us to reflect upon if we want to prevent such tragedies or our children and neighbors from joining such destructive groups that are on the near horizon.

The solution? Simple. All we have to do is to create an alternative, "perfect cult." We need to work together to find ways to make our society actually deliver on many of those cult promises, to co-opt their appeal, without their deception, distortion and potential for destruction.

No man or woman is an island unto itself, nor a space traveller without an earthly control center. Finding that center, spreading that continent of connections, enriching that core of common humanity should be our first priority as we learn and share a vital lesson from the tragedies of Waco, Guyana and Heaven's Gate.

THE ROCK-IN-THE-HAT TRICK

In the search for the most gullible of all believers, we must stop at the doorstep of the Mormon Temple. Across the world, more than 15.5 million people – including an ex-presidential candidate – believe that in 1820 God and Jesus both appeared to Joseph Smith in a grove of trees near his home in New York. They told him that all Christians on the face of the earth were corrupt and that he had been chosen to restore the true Church. He was a teenager, uneducated, illiterate and cunning and maybe God and Jesus appreciated those characteristics because of all the people on earth, they appeared to Joseph Smith – so he often said later in his life.

Then, in 1823 an angel named Moroni visited 17-year-old Smith and told him to go to a hill nearby his home and dig. Obeying the divine visitor, he went to the hill and dug as commanded and found plates made of gold with a strange writing upon them. He wasn't permitted to take the plates until 1827 when he finally brought them to his home. No one could see the plates except Smith because the holy angel Moroni had ordered that only Smith had that privilege. Some were permitted to lift the box containing the plates, but never to actually witness them. Or so an early version of the story went.

As if the story needed additional drama, Smith's mother was to later recount that after he received the golden plates, he, "wrapping them in his linen frock, placed them under his arm and started for home." After "traveling some distance," he "came to a large windfall, (a term used in the 19th century for a tree that has fallen because of strong winds) and as he was jumping over a log, a man sprang up from behind it and gave him a heavy blow with a gun. Joseph turned around and knocked him down, then ran at the top of his speed." She said her son was attacked twice more, but with super hero powers, he outran them for the three miles to his home. He did all this, incidentally, with a slight limp that he had from a surgery in his childhood.

Now, gold is a pretty heavy metal. Smith claimed the record he received from the angel was "six inches wide and eight inches long, and not quite so thick as common tin." He also said the "volume was something near six inches in thickness, a part of which was sealed." Given these dimensions, we can conclude that the plates were one-sixth of a cubic foot. Since gold weighs 1,204 pounds per cubic foot, we can divide that by six and see that our super hero was hefting 200 pounds as he rain "at top of his speed" for a distance of three miles! Even a stauch LDS defender, Apostle John Widtsoe admitted,

"If the gold were pure, [the plates] would weigh two hundred pounds, which would be a heavy weight for a man to carry, even though he were of the athletic type of Joseph Smith."

Realizing that the story, as told, is quite impossible, many Mormons resort to assuming that God gave Smith supernatural strength to carry the plates. Mormons who offer this explanation at least seem to recognize that the story needs a bit of revision to be believable. However, such an explanation is nothing more than an attempt to cover a tale that should be embarrassing to any believer. Smith never said he needed God's help to carry (or run with) the plates, and he certainly never gave God credit for enabling him to do so.

The writing on the plates was in a language unknown that Smith called "reformed Egyptian." Exactly how he knew the name of the strange tongue remains unknown but the only source for such knowledge would have been the good angel, Moroni, so we must assume that Smith looked at the plates and asked, "Tell me, Moroni, what is this strange language?" To which the good angel needed to reply, "Why, it's reformed Egyptian, Joe." If this didn't happen, how would Smith have related the tongue to any Egyptian root? The alternative, of course, is that Smith invented the name of the language just as he invented the tale about the angel and the plates.

It is a moot point to any of the believers that none of the symbols Smith later noted as having appeared on the plates have any relationship to a known language. Not one linguist – from the best to the ama-teur – has ever heard of a tongue called "reformed Egyptian." Wikipedia tells us, "Scholarly reference works on languages do not, however, acknowledge the existence of either a 'reformed Egyptian' language or 'reformed Egyptian' script as it has been described in Mormon belief. No archaeological, linguistic, or other evidence of the use of Egyptian writing in ancient America has been discovered." And one must wonder why the Egyptian language that has been around since around 2700 BC, should ever have had the need to be "reformed?" And "reformation" implies that something is being returned to its earlier, original form. This is not the case with the scribblings of Smith or true Hieroglyphics.

Okay, so let's get the picture. Here we have a teenaged kid who has 200 pounds of golden tablets containing an unknown language. The angel Moroni instructed Joe to translate the plates into English. That would be a good trick for a kid who couldn't even write

21

English but Joe had a secret power that we learn about from the writings of the Mormon Church.

"The other instrument, which Joseph Smith discovered in the ground years before he retrieved the gold plates, was a small oval stone, or 'seer stone.'[1] As a young man during the 1820s, Joseph Smith, like others in his day, used a seer stone to look for lost objects and buried treasure.[1] As Joseph grew to understand his prophetic calling, he learned that he could use this stone for the higher purpose of translating scripture."

So now we're in the really good part. Joseph Smith could translate the golden plates because he had a seer stone – a magic rock that gave him special perceptional powers. You should be giggling about now, but believe it or not, there's more. Smith could put the stone in his hat, then press the hat over his face and the writing on the tablets would marvelously appear on the stone in English!

If you visit Salt Lake City you can see Smith's magic translating see-stone rock. They've kept it as a religious relic of sorts – like the Shroud of Turin or Buddha's tooth.

It's just a random though but the Mormon bosses should loan the rock to international linguists so they can finally translate Linear-A for the Greeks, the writings of the Olmecs of Mexico, Rongorongo for the historians of Easter Island or the Proto Elamite tongue that has confounded experts at Oxford for decades. But, of course, the magic rock probably only worked for Joseph Smith and would be useless in other hands. Modern experts wouldn't have access to Moroni and to think about it, you would probably also need the original hat.

As I mentioned earlier, Smith was illiterate, at least in the sense that while he could read a little, he could not write. A scribe was therefore necessary to take his rock-inspired dictation. This scribe was at first his wife Emma and then, Smith conned his poor neigh-bor, Martin Harria, into helping with the task.

One can almost admire Smith's skills as a con man. When considering the events taking place at that time, we must conclude that Harris was about as bright as Joe's rock because within a short time, he had mortgaged his farm to help finance the translations and actually moved into the Smith home.

One would think that Harris would have thought it strange that the "translation" was conducted while he sat on one side of a blanket hung across the kitchen, and Smith sat on the other with his translation stones, dictating through the blanket. To add to the drama and the comedy, Harris was warned that if he tried to glimpse the plates, or look at the prophet, he would be struck dead.

Meanwhile, Mrs. Harris was having none of this, and certainly didn't appreciate the idea that her homestead was mortgaged on the insane stories being told by Smith. On one occasion she stole the first hundred and sixteen pages of the translation and challenged Smith to reproduce them. Endowed with the powers from Moroni and his magic rock, certainly it would be a rather easy task. A few tense weeks passed until Joe announced that he had another revelation. He couldn't duplicate the original translation because "it might be in the devil's hands by now" and there would be the risk of satanic verses being inserted into the text.

And so it was that the divine, behind-the-blanket translation continued.

Followers of this insanity divorce from themselves any hint of critical thought that would permit them to realize that he Church of Jesus Christ of Latter-day Saints—hereafter known as the Mormons—was, as the late genius, Christopher Hitchens stated, ". . . founded by a gifted opportunist. It is a simple if tedious task to discover that twenty-five thousand words of the Book of Mormon are taken directly from the Old Testament. These words can mainly be found in the chapters of Isaiah available in Ethan Smith's *View of the Hebrews: The Ten Tribes of Israel in America*. This then popular work by a pious loony, claiming that the American Indians originated in the Middle East, seems to have started the other Smith on his gold-digging in the first place. A further two thousand words of the Book of Mormon are taken from the New Testament. Of the three hundred and fifty "names" in the book, more than one hundred come straight from the Bible and a hundred more are as near stolen as makes no difference. The words "and it came to pass" can be found at least two thousand times, which does admittedly have a soporific effect. Quite recent scholarship has exposed every single other Mormon 'document' as at best a scrawny compromise and at worst a pitiful fake."

Certainly, the ultimate evidence to prove all of Smith's fantasies would be to produce the gold plates for everyone to see. But again we are met with a sad circumstance that cleverly protects Smith's lies. He later wrote (or dictated):

"When, according to arrangements, the messenger called for them, I delivered them up to him; and he has them in his charge until this day, being the second day of May, one thousand eight hundred and thirty-eight."

So aren't we surprised? Joe didn't have the plates to show anyone. He had returned them to Moroni and all that was left to support his incredible story was a hat, a rock, a book and his word. For thinking people, none were that convincing.

Smith could produce divine revelations at short notice and often simply to suit himself (especially when he wanted a new girl and wished to take her as another wife). As a result, he overreached himself and came to a violent end, having meanwhile excommunicated almost all the poor men who had been his first disciples and who had been browbeaten into taking his dictation. Still, this story raises some very absorbing questions, concerning what happens when a plain racket turns into a serious religion before our eyes.

It must be said for the "Latter-day Saints" (these conceited words were added to Smith's original "Church of Jesus Christ" in 1833) that they have squarely faced one of the great difficulties of revealed religion. This is the problem of what to do about those who were born before the exclusive "revelation," or who died without ever having the opportunity to share in its wonders. Christians used to resolve this problem by saying that Jesus descended into hell after his crucifixion, where it is thought that he saved or converted the dead. There is indeed a fine passage in Dante's *Inferno* where he comes to rescue the spirits of great men like Aristotle, who had presumably been boiling away for centuries until he got around to them. (In another less ecumenical scene from the same book, the Prophet Muhammad is found being disemboweled in revolting detail.) The Mormons have improved on this rather backdated solution with something very literal-minded. They have assembled a gigantic genealogical database at a huge repository in Utah, and are busy filling it with the names of all people whose births, marriages, and deaths have been tabulated since records began. This is very useful if you want to look up your own family tree, and as long as you do not object to having your ancestors becoming Mormons.

Every week, at special ceremonies in Mormon temples, the congregations meet and are given a certain quota of names of the departed to "pray in" to their church. This retrospective baptism of the dead seems harmless enough to me, but the American Jewish Committee became incensed when it was discovered that the Mormons had acquired the records of the Nazi "final solution," and were industriously baptizing what for once could truly be called a "lost tribe": the murdered Jews of Europe.

The lunacy of Smith's original story had passed through the decades into the hands of the heads of the church who perpetuated it with programs owning such a poverty of intelligence that they become humorous. Mormon men were marrying Cleopatra with the stern belief that she would be waiting for him when he entered paradise. People across the world live their lives and attend the church of their choice, unknowing that they had been baptized at the Mormon Temple. Missionaries around the world were collecting vital data to forward to the computer base in Utah where people became Mormons without their knowledge or permission.

By the age of 20, Smith was already known as "Joseph the glass-looker" and was arrested for being "a disorderly person and impos-ter." He was to face the same charges again in 1830. He would finally be arrested 42 times and while many of his followers claimed it was persecution against him, some of the charges were never heard in court because he fled out of their jurisdiction.

But there remains the question of the golden plates, right? They could prove everything! The visit of the angel, the magic-rock translation, everything! But wait –Moroni ordered him to return the plates to the good angel's divine hands so they're not available as evidence. All we really have is Joseph Smith's word and, of course, that should be enough. Maybe Moroni buried them on another hill – maybe somewhere in Kentucky or Louisiana this time. Maybe Moroni's looking for some other guy who cons people with a magic rock in his hat – but they're hard to find these days.

I will repeat, across the world, more than 15.5 million people – including an ex-presidential candidate – believe this story without ever it activating their bullshit alarm. In an age when you can read the morning newspaper, check and manage your bank account, com-municate with a friend in Tokyo and see your favorite movie all on your cell phone, there are people swearing that the rock-in-the-hat tale is the gospel truth. Mormon propaganda states, "God gave Joseph Smith a special stone called the seer stone as well as two other special stones called the Urim and Thummim. These stones would shine with light, showing the words of the Book of Mormon in English. Urim and Thummim mean 'light and truth' in Hebrew, a perfect name for stones that shine words of light and truth." Of course, we know that Smith had the magic stone earlier and was using it in his con jobs but then that's just another story.

So Joe translated the golden tablets with his hat and magic rock and created the Book of Mormon. Critics of Mormonism have shown convincing proof that the Book of Mormon is a synthesis of earlier works (written by other men), and what some Catholic scholars have called, "the vivid imaginings of Joseph Smith," and of simple plagiarisms of the King James Bible.

The only Bible that Joseph Smith relied on was the King James Version. This translation was based on a good but imperfect set of Greek and Hebrew manuscripts of the Bible.

Scholars now know the *Textus Receptus* contains errors, which means the King James Version contains errors. The problem for Mormons is that these exact same errors show up in the *Book of Mormon*.

It seems reasonable to assume that since Smith was a prophet of God and was translating the *Book of Mormon* under divine inspiration, he would have known about the errors found in the King James Version and would have corrected them for when passages from the King James Version appeared in the *Book of Mormon*. But the errors went in.

When Catholic authorities speak of "the vivid imaginings of Joseph Smith," they were certainly right because Joe went so far as to claim that Jesus came to America and taught his message to the Indians. Mormon apologists often try to take from ancient Indian legends references that they can connect to this wild claim. Mormon apologists have submitted a long list of ancient legends of white visitors and relating it to their imagined visit by Jesus. They have gone so far as to suggest that Quetzalcoatl, described as being white with a beard, was Jesus. LDS Church President John Taylor wrote:

"The story of the life of the Mexican divinity, Quetzalcoatl, closely resembles that of the Savior; so closely, indeed, that we can come to no other conclusion than that Quetzalcoatl and Christ are the same being."

Wait a minute! "The story of the life of the Mexican divinity, Quetzalcoatl?" Where in the hell did Taylor find a biography of this Aztec/Mayan divinity? Maybe he used the stone and a hat.

No effort is made to explain the feathered serpent relation to Jesus Christ or Quetzalcoatl's promise to return in 52 years or in one period of 52 years in the future. Jesus promised a return, but didn't put a date on it like did Quetzalcoatl. None of that sounds very Jesus-like. By that line of thinking, we must also assume that the white visitors to the northern islands of Japan, who "fell from the sky" were also, Jesus Christ.

The *Book of Mormon* describes a vast pre-Columbian culture that supposedly existed for centuries in North and South America. It goes into amazingly specific detail describing the civilizations erected by the "Nephites" and "Lamanites," who were Jews that fled

Palestine in three installments, built massive cities in the New World, farmed the land, produced works of art, and fought large-scale wars which culminated in the utter destruction of the Nephites in A.D. 421.

The awkward part for the Mormon church is the total lack of historical and archaeological evidence to support the *Book of Mormon*. For example, after the cataclysmic last battle fought between the Nephites and Lamanites, there was no one left to clean up the mess. Hundreds of thousands of men and beasts allegedly perished in that battle, and the ground was strewn with weapons and armor.

Keep in mind that A.D. 421 is just yesterday in archaeological terms. It should be easy to locate and retrieve copious evidence of such a battle, and there hasn't been enough time for the weapons and armor to turn to dust. The Bible tells of similar battles that have been documented by archaeology, battles which took place long before A.D. 421. Pharaoh Shishak's conquest of Judah in the fifth year of the reign of King Rehoboam, the brainless son of Solomon, and how Solomon's temple in Jerusalem was robbed of its treasures on that occasion is commemorated in hieroglyphic wall carvings on the Temple of Amon at Thebes.

Second Kings 3 reports that Mesha, the king of Moab, rebelled against the king of Israel following the death of Ahab. A three-foot stone slab, also called the Mesha Stele, confirms the revolt by claiming triumph over Ahab's family, c. 850 BC, and that Israel had "perished forever."

Scientists have demonstrated that honey bees were first brought to the New World by Spanish explorers in the fifteenth century, but the *Book of Mormon*, in Ether 2:3, claims they were introduced around 2000 B.C.

The problem was that Joseph Smith wasn't a naturalist; he didn't know anything about bees and where and when they might be found. He saw bees in America and threw them in the *Book of Mormon* as a little local color. He didn't realize he'd get stung by them.

The embarrassing truth — embarrassing for Mormons, that is —that no scientist, Mormon or otherwise, has been able to find anything to substantiate that such a great battle took place. There's no evidence of the golden plates. There's no evidence or witness of the personal visit by God. No one has found a single trace of the marvelous civilizations founded in the Americas or their great cities.

27

Unlike archaeological finds supporting Old Testament accounts, the Book of Mormon finds no support in any realm of science. It remains what it was from the beginning – the ramblings of a 19th century con man taking advantage of his time and place. After all, he was operating in the same hectically pious district that gave us the Shakers and several other self-proclaimed American prophets. So notorious did this local tendency become that the region became known as the "Burned-Over District," in honor of the way in which it had surrendered to one religious craze after another. Second, he was operating in an area which, unlike large tracts of the newly opening North America, did possess the signs of an ancient history.

A vanished and vanquished Indian civilization had bequeathed a considerable number of burial mounds, which when randomly and amateurishly desecrated were found to contain not merely bones but also quite advanced artifacts of stone, copper, and beaten silver. There were eight of these sites within twelve miles of the underperforming farm which the Smith family called home. There were two equally stupid schools or factions who took a fascinated interest in such matters: the first were the gold-diggers and treasure-diviners who brought their magic sticks and crystals and stuffed toads to bear in the search for lucre, and the second those who hoped to find the resting place of a lost tribe of Israel. Smith's cleverness was to be a member of both groups, and to unite cupidity with half-baked anthropology.

Everything about Smith's life, including his alleged "revelation" ordering him to practice plural marriage, is fiercely justified by some of the most radical believers on earth. A thinking person would realize that Smith was not the kind of guy you want to date your daughter. Their "faith" apparently prohibits any real investigation into Smith's life and conduct and if they did their research, perhaps even truth would be denied. If they would read the studies of historian Richard Van Wagoner, they would discover:

"In the early 1830s another group of "Saints" emerged from the social upheaval in New York. Disciples of revivalist preachers Erasmus Stone, Hiram Sheldon, and Jarvis Rider claimed they were perfect and could no longer sin. They became known as "Perfectionists." As part of their doctrine. "all arrangements for a life in heaven may be made on earth. spiritual friendships may be formed, and spiritual bonds contracted, valid for eternity." .

"Another practitioner of spiritual wifery was Robert Matthews, alias "Mathias the Prophet." Matthews announced that "all marriages not made by himself, and according to his doctrine, were of the devil, and that he had come to establish a community of property, and of wives." In 1833 Matthews convinced two of his followers that, as sinners, they were not properly united in wedlock. He claimed power to dissolve the marriage, married the woman himself, prophesied that she was to 'become the mother of a spiritual generation,' and promised to father her first 'spiritual child' himself. After a brief prison sentence, Matthews turned up on Joseph Smith's doorstep in Kirtland as 'Joshua, the Jewish Minister.'"

The thinking person easily perceives from where Smith received his "revelation" because in the two years that followed, he made proposals of marriage to at least thirty-three women who accepted his offer, apart from those who refused. Of those accepting the role to be one of his concubine, eleven were girls aged 14 to 19. Several were house maids and eleven of them were over the age of 19. Another eleven were married women leaving their spouses to be one of the "prophet's" wives.

Former Smith apostle William McLellin on August 28, 1847 recorded that: "Mrs. Joseph Smith, the widow of the Prophet, told me in 1847 that she knew her husband - the Prophet – practiced both adultery and polygamy."

After his final arrest on the charge of ordering one of his followers to commit arson, he was placed in the jail at Carthage, Illinois and during the late afternoon, a mob of frenzied entered and shot Smith and his brother, Hiram, to death.

The legacy of this recorded con man spinning his absurd tale to an endless flock of robotic followers, is the empire of the Mormon Church.

After Smith's death, leadership passed into the hands of Brigham Young who followed suit by having 55 wives. It was Young who led his Mormon followers westward to finally settle in what is now Utah. They formed their community and when a territorial government was established in 1850, Young, the second head of the Church of Latter-day Saints, became the territory's first governor. The principle of "separation of church and state" carried little weight in the new territory. The laws of the territory reflected the views of Young. In a speech before Congress, federal judge and outspoken Mormon critic John Cradlebaught said, "The mind of one man permeates the whole mass of the people, and subjects to its unrelenting tyranny the souls and bodies of all. It reigns supreme in Church and State, in morals, and even in the minutest domestic and social arrangements. Brigham's house is at once tabernacle, capital, and harem; and Brigham himself is king, priest, lawgiver, and chief polygamist."

Young violently opposed federal authority, and on one occasion announced angrily, "Any President of the United States who lifts his finger against these people shall die an untimely death and go to hell!"

In 1857, Parley Pratt, a well-respected Mormon apostle and great-great grandfather of 2008 Republican presidential candidate Mitt Romney, was murdered in western Arkansas. With no knowledge of the event, a group comprised of various families left Arkansas to head toward California. Meanwhile, news of the Pratt murder, commit-ted by a non-Mormon angered over Pratt taking his wife from him, soon reached Utah and citizens were furious and turned their anger against all non-Mormons. Once the wagon train entered southwest Utah, Mormon leaders started to seek vengeance. They attempted to incite the Paiute chiefs against the emigrants, enticing them with the promise that the tribe could have all the cattle moving with the train. Soon after, the wagon train was attacked.

The emigrants were well armed and what had been anticipated as a brief battle turned into a siege. Before long, the Indians lost interest in what was obviously a white man's problem and left. The remaing attackers – some dressed and painted to appear as Indians – started to seek solutions to end the standoff. At last, two of the Mormon military leaders approached the wagons under white flags and told the emigrants that if they would surrender all their arms, they would be given safe conduct for the next 35 miles to back to Cedar City. After much debate, it was finally decided to trust the attackers since no other solution could be found.

Samuel McMurdy, a member of the Mormon force, took the reigns of one of the wagons into which were loaded some of the youngest children. A woman and a few seriously injured emigrant men were loaded into a second wagon. John Lee positioned himself between the two wagons as they pulled out. Following the two wagons, the women and the older children of the party walked behind. After the wagons had moved on, Higbee ordered the emigrant men to begin walking in single file. An armed Mormon "guard" escorted each emigrant man.

When the escorted men had fallen a quarter mile or so behind the women and children, who had just crested a small hill, Higbee yelled, "Halt! Do your duty!" Each of the Mormon men shot and killed the emigrant at his side. Meanwhile, on the other side of the

30

hill, Nelphi Johnson shouted the order to begin the slaughter of the women and older children. Men rushed at the defenseless emigrants from both sides, and the killing went on amidst "hideous, demon-like yells." Nancy Huff, four years old at the time of the massacre, later remembered the horror: "I saw my mother shot in the forehead and fall dead. The women and children screamed and clung together. Some of the young women begged the assassins after they run out on us not to kill them, but they had no mercy on them, clubbing their guns and beating out their brains." It was over in just a few minutes. 120 members of the emigrant party were dead. The youngest children, seventeen or eighteen in all, were gathered up, to later be placed in Mormon homes. None of the survivors was over seven years old.

The first published reports of the massacre began appearing in California newspapers in October. One came from John Aiken, who with mail carrier John Hunt, passed by Mountain Meadows in late September with a pass signed by William Dame. Aiken wrote, "I saw about twenty wolves feasting upon the carcasses of the murdered. Mr. Hunt shot at a wolf, and they ran a few yards and halted. I noticed that the women and children were more generally eaten by the wild beasts than were the men." The *Los Angeles Star* called it the "foulest massacre ever perpetrated," and added that respon-sibility for the attack "will not be known until the Government makes a full investigation of the affair." The *San Francisco Bulletin* was far less restrained, calling for "a crusade against Utah which will crush out this beast of heresy forever." Public outrage grew. Americans from California to Washington, D. C. begin calling for military action against those responsible for the crime.

Aware of the sensitivity of the events at Mountain Meadows, Mormon officials from Young on down worked to shift the blame for the massacre either to Indians or the emigrants themselves. By November, John Lee completed a fictionalized account of the massacre, attributing all the killing to Indians, and sent the report on to Young. Young, as Superintendent of Indians in addition to his other titles, prepared a report blaming the massacre on the mistreatment of Indians by non-Mormons, and sent it on to the Indian Commissioner. "Capt. Fancher (leader of the emigrant train) & Co. fell victim to the Indians' wrath near Mountain Meadows," Young wrote. "Lamentable as the case truly is, it is only the natural consequences of that fatal policy which treats Indians like wolves, or other ferocious beasts."

None of the Mormon-drafted reports, however, prevented Congress from debating the massacre. On March 18, 1858, Congress ordered an official inquiry into the cause of the tragedy of September 11. The next month, one fourth of the United States army reached Fort Bridger, in present-day Wyoming. Rather than fight the Nauvoo Legion forces guarding the canyons leading to Salt Lake, General Albert Alston decided to overwinter at the Fort. President Buchanan expressed his determination to put down the "rebellion" in Utah, with force if necessary: "Humanity itself requires that we should put it down in a manner that it shall be the last."

In this dark moment of Mormon history, Brigham Young had the good fortune in April 1858 of being replaced as Governor of Utah by Alfred Cumming, a gullible man who believed Young's promise to get to the bottom of the Mountain Meadows matter, and who established, as his principal goal, preserving peace in the Utah territory. Governor Cumming planned a trip south to Mountain Meadows almost as soon as he took office to investigate "that damned atrocity," as he put it. Young, in a visit to Cumming's office, succeeded in convincing the governor of his genuine desire to identify the perpetrators. Cummings decided to put "the whole matter" in Young's hands, trusting him "to put the finger upon the miscreants." He also recognized, as he later told Young, "I can do nothing here without your influence." Pushing to open again free emigration on the south route, Cummings took pleasure in announcing on May 11, "the Road is now open." Over time, Cummings became convinced that the threats to the territory's peace of an aggressive inquiry into the Mountain Meadows massacre, in his mind, outweighed the benefits. He also lacked the will to challenge Young and was, in the words of one observer, "mere putty" in the Mormon leader's hands.

In the latter half of 1858, the federal government began to reassert some measure of federal control in the Utah territory. On June 26, federal troops marched through Salt Lake City, on their way to a fort forty miles from the city under the terms of a deal brokered with Young. (The deal included a pardon for those acts considered part of "the rebellion.") In November, U. S. District Judge John Cradlebaugh arrived in Utah and, unlike the governor, saw no reason not to aggressively pursue justice for the victims of the Mountain Meadows massacre. After several months of investigation, Judge Cradlebaugh issued arrest warrants for John Lee, Isaac Haight, and John Higbee for the murders. Angered by his discovery that the massacre was committed "by order of council," the judge wrote a letter to President Buchanan seeking his commitment to secure convictions for the guilty. Cradlebaugh's efforts, however, were frustrated when the federal case is essentially dropped after the U. S. marshal declared his unwillingness to execute arrest warrants without federal troops to protect him from local citizens--and that help was not provided.

By 1860, with the Union ready to split apart, interest in prosecuting the Mountain Meadows case waned. Governor Cumming saw little reason to press for prosecution, especially in a territory where the law put jury selection entirely in the hands of Mormon officials. "God Almighty couldn't convict the butchers unless Brigham Young was willing," Cumming said.

Within months, arrest warrants for nine men: Lee, Higbee, Haight, Dame, Klingensmith, Stewart, Wilden, and Jukes. Federal authorities arrested John Lee, long considered Mormon officials' most likely candidate for scapegoat for the massacre, after finding him hiding in a chicken coop near Panguitch, Utah, on November 7, 1874. Shortly thereafter, Dame was also arrested. The best prospects for conviction seemed to rest with Lee, so the decision was made to proceed first with his trial.

During this time, a new federal law limited Mormon-held courts and opened jury selections to non-Mormons. Lee's trial began and finally began and the prosecution, in Brigham's Young's Utah with a jury that included eight Mormons, never expected a guilty verdict--and they didn't get one. The jury hung, with the eight Mor-mons and the one former Mormon voting to acquit Lee, and the three non-Mormons voting to convict. A newspaper in Idaho presented a typically cynical view of the trial's outcome: "It would be as unreasonable to expect a jury of highwaymen to convict a stage robber as it would be to get Mormons to find one of their own peculiar faith guilty of a crime."

The second trial of John D. Lee bore almost no resemblance to the first. Mormon witnesses against Lee suddenly materialized in the second trial, many with enhanced memories that put Lee in the middle of the killing. The prosecutors, in a rejection of the strategy in the first case which placed shared blame well up the Mormon command chain, suddenly seemed only too willing to present Lee as the driving force behind the massacre.

What happened, apparently, is that a deal--or at least an under-standing--was reached. In April 1876 Sumner Howard replaced William Carey as the U. S. Attorney for Utah. Under pressure from Washington and the public to convict *someone* for the massacre, Howard pondered how a unanimous jury verdict could ever be achieved in the case without Brigham Young giving the prosecution his blessing. It couldn't, he concluded. An agreement with Young had to be struck. Howard and Young met in Salt Lake. Young was anxious to put the Mountain Meadows matter behind and accepted that someone had to be sacrificed. The excommunicated Lee was the obvious candidate. The terms of the agreement between Howard and Young were never disclosed, but former U. S. attorney Robert Baskin outlined his speculation as to the key understandings. Baskin believed that Howard agreed to impanel an all-Mormon jury, place Brigham Young's 1875 affidavit in evidence, present testimony that would tend to exonerate higher Mormon officials, and--after trying Lee--promised to prosecute no one else for what happened at Mountain Meadows. In return, Young would help round up witnesses who would incriminate Lee and see to it that the jury returned a conviction. (Not everyone is willing, however, to accept Baskin's speculation as truth. Howard denied that a deal had been struck in a letter he sent to Attorney General Taft. Howard instead suggested that Lee's attorney manufactured the deal theory in a last-ditch attempt to gain sympathy for his client. Critics of the deal theory also note that the government made some efforts--although rather half-hearted--to pursue other massacre perpetrators until 1888, when the case was finally dropped.)

The second trial began on September 14, 1876, soon after the prosecution dropped all charges against William Dame. Jury selection went quickly, as a report sent to Brigham Young noted: "Howard made no effort to get Gentiles on the Jury – In fact the word Mormon was scarcely mentioned in court all day." The surprising turn of events – the Church aiding the prosecution – left Lee's defense attorney, William Bishop, angry and confused. Before the trial began, Bishop assumed that the Mormon leadership would protect his client. Writing a few months after trial, Bishop's anger poured out: "I claim that Brigham Young is the real criminal, and that John D. Lee was an instrument in his hands. That Brigham Young used John Lee, as the assassin uses the dagger to strike down his unsuspecting victim; as as the assassin throws away the dagger, to avoid the bloody blade leading to his detection, so Brigham Young used John Lee to do his horrid work; and when the discovery becomes unavoidable, he hurls Lee from him and casts him far out into the whirlpool of destruction."

34

From its opening statement on, the prosecution made clear that its goal was to convict John Lee, not try the entire Mormon hierarchy. The prosecution case made Lee to appear even more guilty than he was. Lee incited the Indians to attack the wagon train. Through deception, Lee lured other Mormons into the battle. Lee hatched the plan that led to the massacre. Lee himself killed a number of emigrants, then helped divide the plunder. Out of the Utah woodwork came a whole host of loyal Mormons ready to testify as to Lee's bad deeds. Samuel Knight testified that he watched Lee club a woman to death. Samuel McMurdy said he saw Lee shoot a woman, as well as two or three of the wounded emigrants. Jacob Hamblin told the court he witnessed Lee throw down a girl "and cut her throat." Nelphi Johnson testified that Lee and Klingensmith seemed to be "engineering the whole thing."

Lee could do little against the onslaught but complain. Pacing his cell floor during a break in the trial, Lee bitterly complained that witnesses were charging him with "awful deeds that they did with their own wicked hands." Everyone could see the game plan: the buck stops with Lee. The memories of witnesses memories suddenly faded when asked to name other Mormons present at the battle see. No one could remember who else might have participated in the killing.

Resigned to his fate, Lee asked his attorneys to present no defense after the prosecution closed its case. With little evidence from which to draw, William Bishop in his summation could only note the obvious: "The Mormon Church had resolved to sacrifice Lee, discarding him as of no further use." On September 20, 1876, at 3:30 in the afternoon in Beaver, the all-Mormon jury returned its verdict. John Lee was guilty of murder in the first degree.

When asked by Judge Boreman if he wished to say anything prior to sentencing, Lee remained silent. Boreman sentenced Lee to be executed in three weeks. Lee told the judge, "I prefer to be shot." Under some circumstances, condemned prisoners in Utah can ask for the firing squad still today.

Appeals delayed Lee's scheduled execution over five months. Lee used much of the time to write his autobiography. On a March afternoon in 1877 in Beaver, Utah, U. S. Marshal William Nelson led John Lee to a closed carriage that would take him south over the emigrant trail to Mountain Meadows. On March 23, Lee, dressed in a red flannel shirt, enjoyed breakfast and a cup of coffee near the site of the 1857 massacre. A minister walked the condemned man to his own coffin. Lee sat down on the coffin while the Marshal read his death warrant. When the reading ended, he rose to address the federal officers, firing squad, and seventy or so spectators.

"I feel as calm as the summer morn," Lee told the gathering, "and I have done nothing intentionally wrong. My conscience is clear before God and man....Not a particle of mercy have I asked of the court, the world, or officials to spare my life. I do not fear death, I shall never go to a worse place that I am now in...I am a true believer in the gospel of Jesus Christ. I do not believe everything that is now being taught and practiced by Brigham Young. I do not care who hears it. It is my last word--it is so. I believe he is leading the people astray, downward to destruct-tion. But I believe in the gospel that was taught in its purity by Joseph Smith. I have been sacrificed in a cowardly, dastardly manner. Having said this, I feel resigned. I ask the Lord, my God, if my labors are done, to receive my spirit."

Lee shook hands with those around them and resumed his seat on his coffin. He shouted to the firing squad, hidden in three wagons forming a semi-circle around him: "Center my heart, boys! Don't mangle my body!" When the shots came, he fell back without a cry.

Sometimes called the darkest page in Mormon history, the spirit of justice was never known to the massacre; Mormons pro-tected Mormons with no consideration of right and wrong or even a social conscience. Little was to change until well into the 20th cen-tury when the manipulations of Joseph Smith and a sense of self-survival were resurrected within the church.

Joseph Smith, perhaps in his zeal to increase membership in his church, accepted negroes as active Mormons. With his demise and the authority passed into the hands of Brigham Young, the policy was changed and blacks were not permitted membership. He described black people as cursed with dark skin as punishment for Cain's murder of his brother. "Any man having one drop of the seed of Cane in him cannot hold the priesthood," he declared in 1852. Young deemed black-white intermarriage so sinful that he suggested that a man could atone for it only by having "his head cut off" and spilling "his blood upon the ground." Other Mormon leaders con-vinced themselves that the pre-existent spirits of black people had sinned in heaven by supporting Lucifer in his rebellion against God. It was not until 1978, under heavy pressure from the public and organizations, the LDS church changed its policy. They had little choice, the protests were mounting from all sides. 13

members of the University of Wyoming football team boycotted a game against Brigham Young University (owned and operated by the LDS Church) and Stanford University ended all athletic relations with BYU.

Wherever you go in the world, you will find a Mormon missionary with his white shirt and black name tage. Missionaries generally begin serving when they are from 18 to 19 years old. Missionaries serve from 18 months to 2 years, and are not paid for their service. Usually, they are better received in foreign lands than they are in their own since only about two percent of Americans are Mormons. But there is are places where Mormons are always welcome – the government crime agencies. In agencies like the Department of Homeland Security, the FBI and the CIA, Mormons are seen as particularly desirable recruits and have a reputation for hiring a disproportionate number of people who belong to the LDS church. Mormons end up in these agencies for perfectly logical reasons. The disproportionate number of Mormons is usually chalked up to three factors: Mormon people often have strong foreign language skills, from missions overseas; a relatively easy time getting security clearances, given their abstention from drugs and alcohol; and a willingness to serve. They also give evidence that they will believe and accept anything – however absurd – so there's no problem convincing them that secret torture centers, spying on innocent citizens or overthrowing foreign governments are part of the everyday business of an efficient government.

Mormon defenders ask how it would be possible for an 18-year-old, uneducated man compose a 500-600 page book. Hugh Nibley, Mormon apologist, stated:

"Since Joseph Smith was younger than most of you and not nearly so experienced or well-educated as any of you at the time he copyrighted the Book of Mormon, it should not be too much to ask you to hand in by the end of the semester (which will give you more time than he had) a paper of, say, five to six hundred pages in length. Call it a sacred book if you will, and give it the form of a history. Tell of a community of wandering Jews in ancient times; have all sorts of characters in your story, and involve them in all sorts of public and private vicissitudes; give them names--hundreds of them--pretending that they are real Hebrew and Egyptian names of circa 600 b.c.; be lavish with cultural and technical details--manners and customs, arts and industries, political and religious institutions, rites, and traditions, include long and complicated military and economic histories; have your narrative cover a thousand years without any large gaps; keep a number of interrelated local histories going at once; feel free to introduce religious controversy and philosophical discussion, but always in a plausible setting; observe the appropriate literary conventions and explain the derivation and transmission of your varied historical materials.

"Above all, do not ever contradict yourself! For now we come to the really hard part of this little assignment. You and I know that you are making this all up--we have our little joke--but just the same you are going to be required to have your paper published when you finish it, not as fiction or romance, but as a true history! After you have handed it in you may make no changes in it (in this class we always use the first edition of the Book of Mormon); what is more, you are to invite any and all scholars to read and criticize your work freely, explaining to them that it is a sacred book on a par with the Bible. If they seem over-skeptical, you might tell them that you translated the book from original records by the aid of the Urim and Thummim--they will love that! Further to allay their misgivings, you might tell them that the original manuscript was on golden plates, and that you got the plates from an angel. Now go to work and good luck!"

Sounds convincing, doesn't it? But religions are always formed by those most able to convince. Personally, I don't look at 18-year-old Joseph Smith as just another young man. I see him as an extraordinary young con man. He was already practicing the con crafts as evidenced by the court actions against him. He was already playing with the idea of making himself appear almost divinely endowed with powers to find hidden treasures and locations of mineral deposits. So in answer to the lengthy question of whether or not Joseph Smith could have written (or even translated) the Book of Mormon, I answer a resounding "no."

According to Joseph Smith's own father-in-law, Isaac Hale, Joseph translated the Book of Mormon by the same means that he used to search for buried treasures: "I first became acquainted with Joseph Smith, Jr. in November, 1825. He was at that time in the employ of a set of men who were called 'money -diggers;' and his occupation was that of seeing, or pretending to see by means of a stone placed in his hat, and his hat closed over his face. The manner in which he pretended to read and interpret, was the same as when he looked for the money-diggers, with the stone in his hat, and his hat over his face, while the Book of Plates were at the same time hid in the woods!"

Printed as an opening statement in the front part of the Book of Mormon is:

"BE IT KNOWN unto all nations, kindreds, tongues, and people, unto whom this work shall come: That we, through the grace of God the Father, and our Lord Jesus Christ, have seen the plates which contain this record, which is a record of the people of Nephi, and also of the Lamanites, their brethren, and also of the people of Jared, who came from the tower of which hath been spoken. And we also know that they have been translated by the gift and power of God, for his voice hath declared it unto us; wherefore we know of a surety that the work is true. And we also testify that we have seen the engravings which are upon the plates; and they have been shown unto us by the power of God, and not of man. And we declare with words of soberness, that an angel of God came down from heaven, and he brought and laid before our eyes, *that we beheld and saw the plates, and the engravings thereon*; and we know that it is by the grace of God the Father, and our Lord Jesus Christ, that we beheld and bear record that these things are true. And it is marvelous in our eyes. Nevertheless, the voice of the Lord commanded us that we should bear record of it; wherefore, to be obedient unto the commandments of God, we bear testimony of these things. And we know that if we are faithful in Christ, we shall rid our garments of the blood of all men, and be found spotless before the judgment-seat of Christ, and shall dwell with him eternally in the heavens.. And the honor be to the Father, & to the Son, & to the Holy Ghost, which is One God. Amen.'
Signed: Oliver Cowdery & David Whitmer & Martin Harris

In the years that followed, all the three witnesses had left the church and denounced much of its teachings. David Whitmer said in 1887: "If you believe my testimony to the Book of Mormon; if you believe that God spake to us three witnesses by his own voice, then I tell you that in June, 1838, God spake to me again by his own voice from the heavens, and told me to 'separate myself from among the Latter-day Saints."

An early Mormon convert, Stephen Burnett sent a letter in which he explains why he decided to leave the Church:

"...but when I came to hear Martin Harris state in public that he never saw the plates with his natural eyes only in vision and imagination, neither Oliver nor David and also that the eight witnesses never saw them and hesitated to sign that instrument for that reason, but were persuaded to do it, the last pedestal gave away. I therefore three weeks since in the Stone Chapel, the reasons why I took the course which I was resolved to do, and renounced the Book of Mormon."

Joseph Smith himself question the integrity of at least four of the eleven witnesses Such characters as McLellin, John Whitmer, David Whitmer, Oliver Cowdery and Martin Harris, "are too mean to mention; and we had liked to have forgotten them." Eventually almost all of these men are accused of lying, stealing, no integrity, apostasy, and dishonest business activities.

But Apostle John A. Widtsoe does not agrees with their founder. Despite clear instability on these witnesses and certainly fertile imaginations, Apostle John A. Widtsoe states The Book of Mormon plates were seen and handled, at different times, by "eleven competent men, of independent minds and spotless reputations, who published a formal statement of their experience."

What about The Testimony Of Eight Witnesses

"BE IT KNOWN unto all nations, kindreds, tongues, and people, unto whom this work shall come: That Joseph Smith, the translator of this work, has shown unto us the plates of which hath been spoken, which have the appearance of gold; and as many of the leaves as the said Smith has translated we did handle with our hands; and we also saw the engravings thereon, all of which has the appearance of ancient work, and of curious workmanship. And this we bear record with words of soberness, that the said Smith has shown unto us, for we have seen and hefted, and know of a surety that the said Smith has got the plates of which we have spoken. And we give our names unto the world, to witness unto the world that which we have seen. And we lie not, God bearing witness of it."

Signed: Christian Whitmer & Hiram Page & Jacob Whitmer & Joseph Smith, Sen. Peter Whitmer, Jun. & Hyrum Smith & John Whitmer & Samuel H. Smith

While the most perfect book states only three witnesses, eight more men are able to give their testimony in the Book of Mormon, found directly under the "Testimony of Three Witnesses."

"And in addition to your testimony (Joseph), *the testimony of three of my servants*, whom I shall call and ordain, unto whom I will show these things.... And *unto none else will I grant this power*, to receive this same testimony among this generation. And the testimony of three witnesses will I send forth of my word." Smith must have felt it necessary to prove this by an additional eight since he may have seen some doubt in the first three.

Martin Harris was asked, "Did you see the plates with your natural eyes, just as you see this pencil case in my hand? Now say yes or no." He answered, "Why I did not see them as I do that pencil case, I saw them *with the eye of faith.* I saw them just as distinctly as I see anything around me - though at the time they were covered over with a cloth."

When Joseph showed plates to the eight witnesses he had them sign a testimonial. Apparently, showing the plates to his father and brothers did not require the power of God, but supernatural power was needed for showing them to the three witnesses. What makes this interesting is that All of the witnesses (except Martin Harris) were related to Joseph Smith or David Whitmer?

By 1847 not a single one of the surviving eleven witnesses were part of the Mormon church. Five of these witnesses joined The Church of Christ started by William McLellin, and Oliver Cowdery indicated he was supportive of this group, though he never joined.

Yet Joseph Smith in May 1844 proclaimed this: "I have more to boast of than any man ever had. I am the only man that has ever been able to keep a church together since the days of Adam. Neither Paul, John, Peter, nor Jesus ever did it. I boast that no man ever did such a work as I."

No amount of apologetics can avoid the facts surrounding Smith and his rock-in-the-hat book. Think about it, not only has there been no archeological proof of anything in their book, the original plates are gone, the earliest manuscript has been altered and all the ones that the book mentions as witnesses departed.

The authorship of the Book of Mormon should not be assigned to faith alone. Considering the recantations of the "witnesses" to its translation and their abandonment of the church, we are entitled to doubt the entire story. The book could have easily fallen into Smith's hands, written by another person and the fabrication of the golden tablets, divine visits, the translation and his magic stone all part of his fertile imagination.

Parallels between Bunyan's The Pilgrim's Progress (1678) and the Book of Mormon have not gone entirely unnoticed. As early as 1831, Eber Howe, in his anti-Mormon book Mormonism Unvailed, noted the use of names — "Desolation" and "Bountiful" from Pilgrim's Progress reappear in the Book of Mormon — but most observations have been similarly limited in scope or suffered from lack of a systematic methodology. Bunyan wrote upwards of 60 books, tracts, and pamphlets, including Grace Abounding, A Few Sighs from Hell, Holy War and The Life and Death of Mr. Badman, and these texts provide extensive narrative parallels to the Book of

Mormon, often containing unique characteristics shared only by Bunyan and Smith.

When Bunyan composed his stories in the late seventeenth century, he did so by cobbling together narrative elements, concepts and ideas from multiple biblical and literary sources (along with his vivid imagination and events from his own life). His characteristic patchwork of old and new story elements resulted in recognizable narrative patterns that act as "fingerprints" in the text, identifying Bunyan's unique alterations to the scriptural and secular tales he recombined.

Several of Bunyan's distinctive narrative patterns repeatedly appear in the Book of Mormon. One of the most prominent examples is the template that forms the narrative foundation for both the story of Faithful, a Christian martyr in Pilgrim's Progress, and the story of the Prophet Abinadi in the Book of Mormon.

James Adair wrote *A History of the American Indians* in 1775. It attempted to prove that the natives had descended from the ancient Israelites. This theme is also found in the Book of Mormon. On pages 377 and 378 of Adair's book there is a series of phrases describing Indian fortifications. These phrases are identical to the phrases which describe the construction of defensive forts in Chapters 48-50 of the Book of Alma in the Book of Mormon.

It is also worth noting that *"View of the Hebrews or the tribes of Israel in America"* by Ethan Smith was published in 1823 and was very popular in New York. A copy of the second edition of this book is available online which you can compare to the original version of the book of Mormon.

Now for thinking people, this is the most likely scenario of how Joseph Smith got credit for composing The Book of Mormon. Wayne Cowdrey, one of the authors of *"Who Really Wrote the Book of Mormon? The Spalding Enigma,"* tells us:

"The Book of Mormon is really a clever adaptation of an obscure, unpublished historical novel written during the War of 1812 in Conneaut, Ohio and Pittsburgh, Pennsylvnia by a down-and-out ex-preacher named Solomon Spalding, a Revolutionary War veteran and bankrupt land speculator who died at Amity, Washington County, PA in 1816 and lies buried in the churchyard there. Prior to his death, Spalding had complained to friends and relatives that a draft of his novel, *A Manuscript Found*, had been stolen from the shelves of Pittsburgh publisher R.& J. Patterson, by one Sidney Rigdon. This same Rigdon later became one of the three principal founders of the Mormon religious movement along with co-conspirators Joseph Smith, Jr., and Smith's cousin Oliver Cowdery, an itinerant book peddler and sometimes printer."

Spalding's book was inspired by the excavation of a nearby Indian mound, and was about the migration of a group of Israelites to the new world. The manuscript was read to Spalding's friends, relatives, neighbors, and parishioners between 1812 and 1815.

Spalding later submitted his manuscript to the publisher. J.H. Lambdin was the printer for the firm and was often seen by towns-folk in the company of Sidney Rigdon.

Before his death, Spalding told a minister friend named Joseph Miller that "Rigdon had taken it, or was suspected of taking it." Spalding's widow also stated as early as 1820 that she believed Sidney Rigdon had copied the manuscript (remember, this was years before the Book of Mormon was published).

Oliver Cowdery's law partner (Cowdery was one of the original three witnesses to the Book of Mormon) in Tiffin Ohio, Judge W. Lang, stated, "Rigdon got the original (*Manuscript Found*) at the job printing office in Pittsburgh."

The authors make it clear that the entire process from the theft of the manuscript to the invention of the visit from God and Jesus to the entire rock-in-the-hat translation story was a scheme on part of them all to simply form a new religion and reap the benefits. In a 1829 letter, Joseph Smith referred to his "Gold Bible business."

"At the time of the conspiracy, Smith and Cowdery lived in western New York. Rigdon resided in the Pittsburgh area until 1818, and then spent the next dozen years in various locations around western Pennsylvania and eastern Ohio. According to evidence presented by the authors, it was Oliver Cowdery, who eventually brought Rigdon and Smith together, and who later served as Smith's personal scribe during the process of creating *The Book of Mormon* from Spalding's manuscript."

According to this theory, someone else (either Sidney Rigdon or some other close friend of Smith) wrote the book and allowed Smith to take credit for it. Some consider this theory more probable than the view that Smith wrote the book himself. Both Sidney Rigdon and Oliver Cowdery had more formal education and could have helped Smith author the book. According to one theory, after dictating the primary text, Smith and his scribes would spend the evenings poring over the text, editing and making adjustments. In this case, the *Book of Mormon* would be considered a collaboration between Smith and his scribes, primarily Oliver Cowdery.

One can see that there are many alternatives to the rock-in-the-hat fantasy and each of them is far more logical and believable. The account of the manuscript theft bears far more evidences than the testimonies of eleven people who later rejected the church they helped found. Crowdery's expose also tells us that:

1. A Dr. J. Winter testified that he saw Rigdon *with the manuscript,* and Rigdon told him that a Presbyterian minister had brought "this" to the printers to see if it would pay to publish it. Mrs. Amos Dunlap was the niece of Rigdon's wife. She stated that as a child she visited the Rigdon family (around 1826-27). "During my visit Mr. Rigdon went to his bedroom and took from a trunk which he kept locked a certain manuscript. He came out into the other room and seated himself by the fireplace and commenced reading it. His wife at that moment came into the room and exclaimed, "What! you're studying that thing again? Or something to that effect. She then added, "I mean to burn that paper." He said, "No, indeed, you will not. This will be a great thing someday."

2. Martin Harris, one of the three witnesses to the Book of Mormon, was snowbound in a hotel in Mentor Ohio, with a man named R.W. Alderman. Alderman states that he learned from Harris then that "Rigdon had stolen a manuscript from a printing office in Pittsburgh, Pa., which Spalding had left to be printed. Jo (Smith) and Rigdon did (print it), as the Book of Mormon."

3. Sidney Rigdon, during the 4-year period between 1823 and 1827, was a minister, who kept an official itinerary record, and in it were many gaps. He apparently made numerous trips from his home in Bainbridge, Ohio, to Palmyra NY (250 miles) where Joseph Smith lived, being gone for weeks at a time.

4. Although Rigdon denied having known Smith before the Book of Mormon was introduced (around 1829) he was seen at Joseph Smith's home and reported to be with Smith by all of the following according to their testimony:

5. Able Chase, an acquaintance, a teenager at the time - "I saw a stranger there who they said was Mr. Rigdon. He was at Smith's several times, and it was in the year of 1827 when I first saw him there, as near as I can recollect."

6. Mr. Gilbert, proofreader for the Book of Mormon - he states that in a conversation with a Mr. Lorenzo Saunders, who

knew the Smiths well, Saunders said "he knows that Rigdon was hanging around Smith's for eighteen months prior to the publishing of the Mormon Bible."

7. Mrs. S.F. Anderick, a neighbor stated "Several times while I was visiting Sophronia Smith at old Jo's house, she told me that a stranger who I saw there several times in warm weather and several months apart, was Mr. Rigdon."

8. Daniel Hendrix, acquaintance of Joseph Smith and Rigdon: he related hearing Joseph Smith tell people in 1828 about the "bonanza he had found – golden tablets". "For the first month or two at least Joe Smith did not say himself that the plates were any new revelation or that they had any religious significance, but simply said that he had found a valuable treasure in the shape of a record of some ancient people. He (Rigdon) and Joseph Smith fell in with each other and were cronies for several months. It was after Rigdon and Smith were so intimate that the divine part of the finding of the golden plates began to be spread abroad. Smith and Rigdon had hard work to get funds together for the new Bible."

9. Mr. Pearne, former neighbor of Smiths told others he saw Smith and Rigdon together before the Book of Mormon was published.

10. Mrs. Eaton, interviewed Smith's neighbors regarding Rigdon, and concluded that a stranger came to the Smith's home in the summer of 1827, whose name was Sidney Rigdon.

11. Rigdon was a Campbellite Minister in 1827-29, who had been excommunicated from being a Baptist minister because of teaching heretical beliefs. During this time period before the Book of Mormon came out, his congregation heard him often preach about a coming new revelation that would make the Bible outmoded, and he even seemed to know it would speak of America's ancient inhabitants, solve the mystery of the mounds, there would be the return of miracles, and a new system of sharing all things in common, and more. Some state this information was given as early as 1827, and was detailed enough that they concluded that he must have known all about the Book of Mormon when he preached these things.

12. Rigdon himself told a man named James Jeffries the following information, according to Jeffries: "He and Joe

Smith used to look over the M.S. and read it on Sundays. Rigdon said Smith took the MS. and said, "I'll print it," and went off to Palmyra, New York."

13. An acquaintance of both Rigdon and Smith named Dr. J.C. Bennett stated the following in 1842: "I will remark here that the Book of Mormon was originally written by the Rev. Solomon Spaulding, A.M., as a romance, and entitled the *"Manuscript Found,"* and placed by him in the printing-office of Patterson and Lambdin, in the city of Pittsburgh, from whence it was taken by a conspicuous Mormon divine, and re-modeled, by adding the religious portion, placed by him in Smith's possession, and then published to the world as the testimony exemplifies. *This I have from the Confed-eration,* and of its perfect correctness there is not a shadow of doubt." (the Confederation refers to the inner circle of Smith's friends).

14. Sarah Pratt, the wife of an early Mormon leader, read this view of Dr. Bennett's in a book he wrote, and said the following: "This certifies that I was well acquainted with the Mormon Leaders and Church in general, and know that the principle statements of John C. Bennett's book on Mormonism are true."

15. (While the above could be referred to as a hostile witness, consider the following:) Isaac Butts who knew Rigdon from 1820 on, stated that when he came back to Ohio after Mormonism had made converts there, people he had known earlier in New York who were converts to the church told him that they had seen Sidney Rigdon much with Joseph Smith before they were converted. (Rigdon supposedly was converted about the same time as they were).

16. David Whitmer, the 3rd witness to the Book of Mormon did not believe the "Spalding theory", but stated in his booklet, *"An Address to All Believers in Christ"*, that the story had been printed in the Encyclopedia Britannica and the American Cyclopaedia.

    He believed Rigdon and Smith first met in the winter of 1830. But he also states that Rigdon and Smith immediately became intimate, and Rigdon was given the position of first councilor and vice president of the church by the end of 1830. (The Bible prohibits putting a novice into leadership so quickly.)

Whitmer states that the whole idea of the Priesthood was not a part of the original church nor in the original revelations (compare early sections of the 1830 Book of Mormon with their counterparts in the Book of Commandments to see this is true), but it "*all originated in the mind of Sidney Rigdon.*"

Whitmer outlines other doctrinal problems in his booklet, and states "If you believe my testimony to the Book of Mormon;...then I tell you that in June, 1838, God spake to me again by his own voice from the heavens, and told me to "separate myself from among the Latter Day Saints.""

Perhaps the most interesting detail and the final nail in the Joe Smith mythology is that the manuscript of "*Manuscript Found*" was found in Hawaii in 1884, and is now at Oberlin College in Oberlin, Ohio. The manuscript body is handwritten by Spaulding, and is 116 pages long (does that number ring a bell?). The Book of Mormon is about 538 pages long. (There would have been over two years of time that Rigdon and Smith had to collaborate on and expand the manuscript, according to the above-mentioned records and testimony).

There are many parallels between the two documents: Both have the same content or story line. The Book of Mormon has much more religious or doctrinal content. Both documents purport to give a *condensed history of the extinct inhabitants of ancient America.*

Both manuscripts describe in similar terms how the author came by the ancient records upon which the story is based. Spaulding says the records are found in an artificial cave on the top of a mound near his home. A lever is used to lift the heavy stone which covers the entrance to the cave. The Book of Mormon says the records were in a stone box buried in the ground near the top of a hill not far from his home. He, too, uses a lever to lift a large stone that serves as a cover to the box.

Both tell that the author encounters supernatural difficulties in removing the records from their hiding place. Both relate that the author made a "translation of the Old World language used in the records and that this translation is a condensation of earlier civil and sacred records.

Both state that the condensed version thus produced will be reburied along with the original so that it will remain preserved to come forth in the future when the Gentiles (Europeans) inhabit America.

Both describe a sea voyage with a great storm which causes them to pray for deliverance; both describe light and dark-skinned people, the same arts and sciences being known to the ancient people, a God-person who is white, the use of seer stones, a war to the death between two nations who were once brothers, and a final battle fought on a hill.

Even in some details we see resemblance: Both Spalding and Smith have the group of travelers of *about the same number*; both find America teeming with wild beasts; both groups appoint judges, have all things in common, and urge each other not to intermarry with the natives. In both accounts, the native Americans wear animal skins about their loins, *shave their heads and paint them red*, and carry slings, bows and arrows as weapons.

Both writers make the same mistake of stating that the planets revolve about the sun, long before such knowledge would have been known by humans. Both stories describe modern horses, domesticated mammoths or elephants, the use of steel, and the cultivation of wheat in ancient America, even though there is no archaeological evidence of any of this.

Theological concepts that are similar are presented in the same order.

The first quarter of Spalding's manuscript is written in the first person, and the rest in the third person. The Book of Mormon follows that pattern, and the change occurs *at the same place in both stories*.

To quote Vernal Holley, who wrote *Book of Mormon Authorship: A Closer Look*:

"Identical or similar word combinations, redundant sentences, parallelisms, contradictory thoughts in sentence structure, indecision in the use of words, poor sentence composition, the use of lengthy runs, biblical-like meta-phors, and the use of King James Bible English by both Spaulding and the Book of Mormon author are all further arguments that Spaulding may have been the author of the Book of Mormon."

In 1839, Spaulding's widow, Matilda Spaulding Davison, made this statement:

"After the 'Book of Mormon' came out, a copy of it was taken to New Salem, the place of Mr. Spaulding's former residence, and the very place where the "*Manuscript Found*" was written. A Mormon preacher appointed a meeting there and in the meeting read and repeated copious extracts from the "Book of Mormon" The historical part was immediately recognized by all the older inhabitants, as the identical work of Mr. Spaulding in which they had been so deeply interested years before."

Many of Smith's neighbors, in their testimony about him, also stated that he was lazy, was a liar, and in the mid 1820's often engaged in digging at nighttime for buried treasures, using a seer stone or peep-stone. Court records show he was convicted of being a "glass-looker" (he was charging for fortune-telling about treasures that did not materialize when dug for) in 1826. It is also a fact that as soon as he had a good number of converts, he led them to sell their homes and farms and *give the money to the church (him)* and go to Ohio.

There should be a drum roll at this point and all Mormon's should shake their heads in shame for their gullibility. Those who yet refuse to accept the account of how Smith stole his holy Book of Mormon should hang their heads in shame for their ignorance. But most of all, the lesson should be learned of how leaders of religions manipulate, control and create their own, holy propaganda to mislead, misinform and mistreat. Most of the faithful are more victims than they are devout. They chose to believe more than think and in that process they accepted the fantasies of faith, no matter how far they strayed from normal thought, the recognition of reality or the limits that belief can be strained.

It is true that we treat religion as an inheritance. Mothers take their children by the hand and lead them into the church attended by her father and grandfather and teach them the same message they learned as children. But at some point in life, we must evaluate what we were taught to believe and question if we can truly believe what we were taught.

The premises of the Mormon belief rate along with the hollow earth and the medicine man at Wounded Knee teaching that if they did the Ghost Dance, the white man's bullets couldn't harm them. That more than fifteen million people list themselves as believers says nothing about the quality of the religion but speaks volumes about the everlasting ignorance of man.

THE YOUNG EARTHERS

Not long ago, I encountered tourists while having a stay at my home in Italy. I soon learned that it was a group comprised of two families from Tennessee. They were dining at a long table in the restaurant of a local hotel when I entered for my usual Sunday morning breakfast. I suppose my skin tone and face betrayed the fact that I wasn't Italian and the group soon struck up a conversation with me. Learning that I wasn't Italian but I was a resident of the area, they were soon asking about things to see in the region. The village where I lived was only about 100 miles from Milan and I started recommend museums within the city. When I mentioned the Natural History Museum, I could see their expressions grow somber and grim smiles touching their lips.

"We're not much for seeing old rocks, fossils and things," the eldest of the group informed me. "We really don't believe in all that stuff."

I found the comment almost humorous but being of an inquisitive sort, I decided to probe a bit.

"You don't believe in geology or archaeology; anthropology or paleontology?"

"Big names for little minds," the man laughed with a frown of scorn. "Do you really believe the earth is billions of years old?"

I paused to give the waiter my order and sipped of my coffee before nodding, "Yes, as a matter of fact, I do. How else can I explain fossils that are millions of years old? I've found a few plant fossils myself in Yorkshire, England."

Suddenly, the entire group wore the faces of Dominicans at the Inquisition. "Satan put them there to confuse humanity, sir," offered a young woman with freckles scattered over her nose. She was very pretty to be so ignorant.

It was at this point that it occurred to me and I blurted, "You believe that Bishop Ussher stuff?"

The man was stone serious as he replied, "Brother Ussher only recognized the truth, my friend, and gave it to the world for those who are wise enough to accept it."

Well, I guess that put me in my place and I was grateful when the waiter, at that moment, brought me the morning newspaper that I rudely opened and furtively watched the group return to their breakfast.

The experience forced me to remember the old movie and stage play, *Inherit the Wind* and how Spencer Tracy playing the famous attorney Clarence Darrow made Fredrick March (William Jennings Bryan) sweat on the witness stand. But believers in a young earth were not new and in the time of the famous monkey trial there were many believers that the earth was only about 6,000 years old.

The idea is based primarily on a chronology of Biblical events prepared by a seventeenth-century Irish bishop, James Ussher. American fundamentalists in 1925 found — and generally accepted as accurate — Ussher's careful calculation of dates, going all the way back to Creation, in the margins of their family Bibles. (In fact, until the 1970s, the Bibles placed in nearly every hotel room by the Gideon Society carried his chronology.) The King James Version of the Bible introduced into evidence by the prosecution in the famous Monkey Trial that challenged evolution being taught in schools, contained Ussher's famous chronology, and Bryan was more than once forced to resort to the bishop's dates as he tried to respond to Darrow's questions.

The chronology first appeared in *The Annals of the Old Testament*, a monumental work first published in London in the summer of 1650. In 1654, Ussher added a part two which took his history through Rome's destruction of the Temple in Jerusalem in 70 A.D. The project, which produced 2,000 pages in Latin, occupied twenty years of Ussher's life.

The date forever tied to Bishop Ussher appears in the first paragraph of the first page of *The Annals*. Ussher wrote: "In the beginning, God created heaven and earth, which beginning of time, according to this chronology, occurred at the beginning of the night which preceded the 23rd of October in the year 710 of the Julian period." In the right margin of the page, Ussher computes the date in "Christian" time as 4004 B.C.

Although Ussher brought stunning precision to his chronology, Christians for centuries had assumed a history roughly corresponding to his. The Bible itself provides all the information necessary to conclude that Creation occurred less than 5,000 years before the birth of Christ. Shakespeare, in *As You Like It*, has his character Rosalind say, "The poor world is almost six thousand years old." Martin Luther, the great reformer, favored (liking the round number) 4000 B.C. as a date for creation. Astronomer Johannes Kepler concluded that 3992 B.C. was the probable date.

As paleontologist Stephen Jay Gould points out in an essay on Ussher, the bishop's calculation of the date of Creation fueled much ridicule from scientists who pointed to him as "a symbol of ancient and benighted authoritarianism." Few geology textbook writers resisted taking a satirical swing at Ussher in their introductions. How foolish, the authors suggested, to believe that the earth's geologic and fossil history could be crammed into 6,000 years. Gould, while not defending the bishop's chronology, notes that judged by the research traditions and assumptions of his time, "Ussher deserves not criticism, but praise for his meticulousness. The questionable premise underlying Ussher's work, of course, is that the Bible is inerrant."

Ussher began his calculation by adding the ages of the twenty-one generations of people of the Hebrew-derived Old Testament, beginning with Adam and Eve. If the Bible is to be believed, they were an exceptionally long-lived lot. Genesis, for example, tells us that "Adam lived 930 years and he died." Adam's great-great-great-great-great-grandson, Methuselah, claimed the longevity record, coming in at 969 years. Healthier living conditions contributed, or so it was believed, to the long life spans of the early generations of the Bible. Josephus, a Jewish theologian writing in the first century, explained it this way: "Their food was fitter for the prolongation of life – and besides, God afforded them a longer lifespan on account of their virtue."

To calculate the length of time since Creation, knowledge of more than the ages of death of the twenty-one generations was required; one also needed to know the ages of people of each generation at the time the next generation began. Fortunately, the Bible provided that information as well. For example, Genesis says that at the time Adam gave birth to his first son, Seth, he had "lived 130 years." Augustine (as might a lot of people) wondered how a 130-year-old man could sire a child. He concluded that "the earth then produced mightier men" and that they reached puberty much later than did people of his own generation.

The Old Testament's genealogy took Ussher up to the first destruction of the Temple in Jerusalem during the reign of Persian king Nebuchadnezzar. Ussher's key to precisely dating Creation came from pinning down, by references in non-Christian sources, the precise dates of Nebuchadnezzar's reign. He finally found the answer in a list of Babylonian kings produced by the Greek astronomer Ptolemy in the second century. By connecting Greek events to Roman history, Ussher tied the date of Nebuchanezzar's death (562

B.C.) to the modern Julian calendar. Once the date of 562 B.C. was calculated, there remained only the simple matter of adding 562 years to the 3,442 years represented by the generations of the Old Testament up to that time: 4004.

Ussher next turned his attention to identifying the precise date of Creation. Like many of his contemporary scholars, he assumed that God would choose to create the world on a date that corresponded with the sun being at one of its four cardinal points — either the winter or summer solstice or the vernal or autumnal equinox. This view sprang from the belief that God had a special interest in mathematical and astronomical harmony. The deciding factor for Ussher came from Genesis. When Adam and Eve found themselves in the Garden of Eden, the fruit was invitingly ripe. Ussher reasoned, therefore, that it must have been harvest time, which corresponded with the autumnal equinox: "I have observed that the Sunday, which in the year (4004 B.C.) aforesaid, came nearest the Autumnal Aequinox, by Astronomical Tables, happened upon the 23 day of the Julian October."

A London bookseller named Thomas Guy in 1675 began printing Bibles with Ussher's dates printed in the margin of the work. Guy's Bible's became very popular — though their success might be as much attributed to the engravings of bare-breasted biblical women as to the inclusion of Ussher's chronology. In 1701, the Church of England adopted Ussher's dates for use in its official Bible. For the next two centuries, Ussher's dates so commonly appeared in Bibles that his dates "practically acquired the authority of the word of God."

Gallup Polls has a lot of fun with the question of earth age and has, since the 1980s conducted polls with the question:

> "Which of the following statements comes closest to your views on the origin and development of human beings: human beings have evolved over millions of years from other forms of life and God guided this process, human beings have evolved over millions of years from other forms of life, but God had no part in this process, or God created human beings in their present form at one time within the last 10,000 years."

In 2009, a survey that clarified how many people really think the earth is only 10,000 years old was published by *Reports of NCSE*. Surprisingly, 18% agreed that "the earth is less than 10,000 years old." But he also found that 39% agreed "God created the universe, the earth, the sun, moon, stars, plants, animals, and the first two people within the past 10,000 years." One has to wonder how a 21% difference can occur to what was basically the same question. But we should not be surprised. Maybe the answer is found in the dumbing-down of America. After all, a poll conducted by the National Science Foundation revealed that one in every four Americans believe the sun moves around the earth. To the question "Does the Earth go around the Sun, or does the Sun go around the Earth," 26 percent of those surveyed answered incorrectly. In the same survey, just 39 percent answered "true" that "The universe began with a huge explosion" and only 48 percent said "Human beings, as we know them today, developed from earlier species of animals."

The leader of the American 6,000-year-old-earth movement is Ken Ham, a self-described president and CEO of "Answers in Genesis, a Christian apologetics ministry who is also a Biblical literalist – which of course means that he believes a donkey and a snake talked, the sun stood still for Joshua to kill more people and Lot's wife turned into a pillar of salt. He built the Creation Museum in Ohio with a website proclaiming, "Adam and Eve live in the Garden of Eden. Children play and dinosaurs roam near Eden's Rivers. The serpent coils cunningly in the Tree of the Knowledge of Good and Evil." At the same time, in Kentucky, Ham is reconstructing the biblical ark in precise detail.

Personally, I have to wonder how constructing a replica of Noah's Ark with modern technology contributes to the argument for a supposed truth of Young Earth Creationism? The Ark Encounter's official website shows that close to $19.5 million has so far been collected out of a goal of $29.5 million for the project's completion. Now that raises some questions, too. Ham needs almost $30 million to do the same thing that a 600-year-old goat herder reportedly did by himself?

Ham tries to counter these points in his website with:

> "... we don't have an evolutionary view of history. Many think Noah was a very primitive person with no technology. But prior to the Flood men were making musical instruments and forging instruments of bronze and iron: 'His brother's name was Jubal; he was the father of all those who play the lyre and pipe. Zillah also bore Tubal-cain he was the forger of all instruments of bronze and iron' (Genesis 4:21–22). By the time of Noah, who knows what advanced technology they had?"

54

Loonies like Ham point to the Seven Wonders of the World to suggest that a high degree of technology existed in those days but the idea is like most of his others – fantasy. First of all, the ark is ordered to be made of gopher wood and a blueprint is provided – well okay, a plan -- that the ark is to be 300 cubits long, 50 cubits wide and 30 cubits tall or, 450X75X45 feet. It needs to be three stories high with a large door on its side and a one-cubi-square window on the top. Each floor needed to be divided into rooms and all the walls, inside and out, are to be sealed with pitch.

The reason for all this is that the ark was constructed to hold animals and plants, particularly two of "every living thing of all flesh – to keep them alive with thee" (Genesis 6:19), it will have to be constructed accordingly.

People like Ham accept each word of this without question. After all, he's a fundamentalist – a person believing that every word of the Bible is an absolute truth. In *The Ark on Ararat,* authors LaHaye and Morris note, "It is hard to believe that intelligent people see a problem here" as if thinking people are to be scorned for seeking logic within ancient myths. What's really hard to believe is that intelligent people would suggest that there existed a high level of technology in the time of Noah, much less trying to use the Seven Wonders as examples. Only the Great Pyramid of Cheops comes within 2,000 years of the time the ark was being constructed. As Desmond Stewart tells us in *The Pyramids and Sphinx:*

> "But the Great Pyramid did not spring *de novo* from the desert sands; rather, it was the culmination of over a century of architectural evolution, beginning when the "experimenting genius," Imhotep, inspired by the ziggurats of Babylon, built the Step Pyramid around 2680 BC, passing through some intermediate step pyramids to the Bent Pyramid of Snofru, then the first true pyramid, and finally the masterpiece at Cheop.

> "On the other hand, in an era when hollowed-out logs and reed rafts were the extent of marine transport, a vessel so massive appeared that the likes of it would not be seen again until the mid-nineteenth century AD. Before he could even contemplate such a project, Noah would have needed a thorough education in naval architecture and in fields that would not arise for thousands of years such as physics, calculus, mechanics, and structural analysis. There was no shipbuilding tradition behind him, no experienced craftspeople to

offer advice. Where did he learn the framing procedure for such a Brobdingnagian structure? How could he anticipate the effects of roll, pitch, yaw, and slamming in a rough sea? How did he solve the differential equations for bending moment, torque, and shear stress?"

In his *The Impossible Voyage of Noah's Ark,* Robert A. Moore summarizes the problems of determining what creatures were on the ark:

"Creationists realize that the ark had a limited amount of room and they are aware of the large number of species in the animal kingdom. Therefore, they have employed various tactics to reduce the population needed on board. Probably the most important tactic is to restrict the command to "kinds" rather than species and to argue that the former are much fewer in number than the latter.

"A kind (or "baramin" in creationist jargon) is the unit of life originally made by God. Within each kind is an enormous potential for variation, resulting, during the past six thousand years or so, in a large number of similar animals that scientists classify into species. Meyer contends that "He created into the reproductive apparatus of genes and chromosomes the possibility of endless hereditary combinations producing the possibility of endless variety within each `kind'." By juggling the number of kinds, LaHaye and Morris reduce the total population aboard the ark to 50,000, Whitcomb and Morris reduce it to 35,000, while Dr. Arthur Jones squeezes it down to a bare bones total of 1,544."

Of course, we must – in order to be "intelligent people" and not see a problem with all this, imagine a waterlogged Stegosaurus splashing about for 371 days waiting for the water to subside. And we have to ask about animals that needed to migrate for their survival and those who needed to hibernate. And what about animals from different climatic zones now crowded into a space with a constant temperature. What about parasites and diseases brought by some animals and threatening to spread to others?

And who had the job of checking the sex of the animals as they entered the ark? And if just one of the teeming hoard of animals turned out to be sterile, that species would become extinct. Could Noah verify everyone's fertility? For that matter, could he even verify that the couple on the gangplank were male and female? A great many animals, including 30 percent of the birds and even some mammals, are sexually monomorphic and cannot be distinguished without modern veterinary techniques or even hormonal analysis? Most fish are indeterminant as juveniles and will only become male or female when mature, while some female worms will change into males when starved.

Creationists insist on a strictly literal interpretation of Genesis; so when those animals which reproduce by asexual budding, or the over one thousand thelytokous (all-female) species from insects to lizards, converged toward the ark, another special miracle would have been called for to fulfill the explicit command to take both male and female aboard. By the time Noah encountered the sea star, *Asterina gibbosa,* which begins life as a male and eventually becomes female, he must have been ready to decide not to enter the ark himself.

And what about the incredibly diverse dietary needs of the creatures? where did Noah get the huge quantities of fresh meat required for carnivorous animals? The creationist response is that God (miraculously) altered them so that they could thrive on a vegetarian diet during the voyage. Some claim that the eating of meat never occurred anywhere until after the flood. Thus these animals were originally vegetarian, then became meat-eaters after the Fall, vegetarians again for the year of the flood, finally returning to their carnivorous ways afterwards. Three times the Lord magically changed the physiology and anatomy of a substantial proportion of the animal kingdom. And if this is true of carnivorous mammals, it must also be so for insect-eating birds, amphibians, reptiles, for the multitudes that live on fresh fish and other aquatic creatures, and for arthropods which eat other invertebrates. Were the slender, sticky tongues of tamanduas, pangolins, and other anteaters, so difficult to feed in zoos, altered to eat hay? Were vampire bats and mosquitos able to substitute tomato juice for fresh blood? Did the whales adapt to kelp instead of krill? And what of our ever-troublesome parasites? Were tapeworms and leeches content to spend a year sucking on an old log?

Even if everyone ate only plants, there were still enormous obstacles. Many animals have highly specialized diets: koalas eat only certain types of Eucalyptus leaves; the giant panda eats bamboo shoots; three-toed sloths so prefer Cecropia leaves that they are almost impossible to keep in captivity. Primates need fresh fruit; many birds develop cramps and spasms if they don't get sufficient calcium; desert rodents are poisoned by excessive protein; and the list goes on. How did Noah know what foods to get, how much and where to get them?

How were the stores kept from rotting during the lengthy voyage? Even hay rapidly becomes moldy and unusable. Apologist E. Young in his *The General Care and Nutrition of Wild Mammals in Captivity* insists that feeding troughs be cleaned daily and uneaten food removed to prevent decay. Giraffes and moose must have their troughs high or they can't reach them, while animals with large antlers can't get their mouths into a basket placed against a wall. Carnivores deprived of bones to chew develop peridontal disease; rodents, too, need to gnaw or their teeth will overgrow. The tearing beak of eagles, the seed-cracking beak of parrots, the bill strainer of flamingos also overgrow if unused. Many animals, from fish to snakes, penguins to bats, will only eat living food because they must see it move to seize it. Even praying mantises eat only live food and will eat each other if nothing else is available. And considering that Ham shows dinosaurs in the Garden of Eden in his Creation Museum, we must assume that there was room for the Steppe Mammoth, Amphicoealias and all the other prehistoric monsters and their gigantic appetites. When one reporter suggested that Tyrannosauruses would have eaten the sheep, Ham replied, "Many dinosaurs were smaller than chickens." The fact that most were much, much, much larger than chickens was not permitted into the discussion.

But we have Ken Ham collecting millions to recreate the boat that finds its true origin in the myths of Mesopotamia reaching far back in antiquity and not in Genesis and the protagonist was not named Noah, rather was known as Utnapishtim. To get an idea of how old the myth is, it is also found in the Epic of Gilgamesh that is considered one of the oldest writings known and yet Gilgamesh is a first millennium Assyrian copy of the older tale. Centuries later it entered the Old Testament that Ham probably believes was written from the first day of creation onward. But none of that is important to Ham because if words appear in Genesis, they must be the words of God simply because they're there. That mindset might not be understood by intellectuals but Ham isn't after the intellectuals, he's after the sheep, the followers, the robotic masses willing to accept his claims either from ignorance or the fear of the hellish consequences. His Creation Museum is a working symbol of modern technology – the same science he frequently denies in his talks that resemble rampages.

"Why shouldn't we as Christians use the best technology we can?" asks Ham who is not only a creationist but an oppositionist. He knows that his ministry, *Answers in Genesis*, draws the scorn of sophisticates, and so he takes special delight in portraying himself as a rational Daniel in the lions' den of militant secularism, the lions being the media and the scientific establishment and the ghost of Clarence Darrow and millions of liberal and even not so liberal Christians and pretty much anyone who disagrees with Ken Ham.

In Ham's museum, one exhibit presents with blunt force the case against godlessness, depicting the lives of modern families that have made the tragic error of rejecting the literal truth of God's word. "In this 7 minute video," one introductory placard reads, "the boy in the background is 'on a killing spree' on his video game. His older brother is looking at internet pornography and has a bag of drugs." The Creation Museum is not a museum so much as it is a 3-D hellfire sermon with a food court.

At the same time, Ham is iron-clad adamant in his beliefs and rejects findings that represent the true progress of man over the past few decades. Contrary to the repeated insistence of Ham, every single shred of relevant scientific data indicates the Earth is about 4.5 billion years old. Ham and his AiG crew will insist that there is evidence of a young Earth – that the Grand Canyon was cut by the Genesis flood draining away – that fossils were created in a flash by the whoosh of water – that light travelling from distant stars somehow went faster than it does today – that the ocean would be a solid salt block if the Earth were billions of years old – that the atmosphere would be unbreathable – that the moon would have left orbit by now – and all kinds of other nonsense that a quick bit of research would show to be scientifically absurd.

Richard Dawkins publicly stated that he refused to debate creationists because:

"When the debate is with someone like a Young Earth creationist, as the late Stephen Gould pointed out – they've won the moment you agree to have a debate at all. Because what they want is the oxygen of respectability.

"They want to be seen on a platform with a real scientist, because that conveys the idea that here is a genuine argument between scientists. They may not win the argument – in fact, they will not win the argument, but it makes it look like there really is an argument to be had. Just as I wouldn't expect a gynecologist to have a debate with somebody who believes in the Stork-theory of reproduction, I won't do debates with Young Earth creationists."

What Ham and those like him fail to realize is that in their refusal to recognize science as the authority of issues like age dating, they join the anti-science ranks of the Dominicans at the Inquisition, those who burned Bruno at the stake and the ultimate stupidity of the witch hunts. To assert that the Bible is inerrant is to ignore the 14,800 differences existing within the texts of the world's oldest copies of the Bible and those found in modern homes today. Ham does not represent a doctrinal position, rather pitiful ignorance that he administers to other as if it was a blessing.

And now his propagandist museum and phony ark that has iron supports within it are not enough. He wants to expand into the world of Disney. It is described in one publication as:

> Ark Encounter is a Christian fundamentalist project based on discredited science and a literal interpretation of Genesis. The $172 million biblical-themed amusement park is designed to be an exercise in Christian propaganda: a deplorable attempt to deceive children and others by denying the scientific reality of biological evolution and promoting Christian mythology as scientific fact.
>
> The planned Christian theme park is dedicated to indoctrinating children with ridiculous and discredited claims from the dubious field of 'creation science,' claims such as the earth is only 6,000-years-old, that human beings and dinosaurs lived on the earth at the same time, and that the story of Noah's Ark is true."

Watching the video at the site of the ark depicting the partial construction of the Ark, with all the attending modern technology, equipment, and know-how necessary to build the replica, should be evidence enough to convince any reasonable person that the Biblical account of Noah's Ark is a fiction, and that to claim otherwise is folly. Anthony Blair stated, "Ken Ham needs more than $100 million, modern machinery, a huge team of labor, roads, lumber mills, and tax breaks and never once thinks 'You know, I don't think a 500 year old man could pull this off with tools from the Bronze Age.'

Ham does what most dictators do – he dominates conversations and attempts to humiliate those disagreeing with him. But if he would shut up long enough and permit recent science to have a voice, he would discover what was revealed on major wire services in October of 2015:

"Researchers have found evidence in Western Australia that Earth may be 300 million years older than we thought.

"That is the conclusion from a team of geochemists at UCLA and Stanford University who found evidence that life likely existed on Earth at least 4.1 billion years ago and may have begun shortly after the planet formed 4.54 billion years ago.

"Twenty years ago, this would have been heretical; finding evidence of life 3.8 billion years ago was shocking," said Mark Harrison, professor of geochemistry at UCLA and the co-author of the research published this week in the journal Proceedings of the National Academy of Sciences.

"Life on Earth may have started almost instantaneously," he said in a statement. "With the right ingredients, life seems to form very quickly."

"Because Earth's rock record only extends to 4 billion years, earlier periods of history are accessible only through mineral grains deposited in sediments, the researchers wrote.

"In this case, researchers led by UCLA's Elizabeth Bell studied more than 10,000 zircons originally formed from molten rocks, or magmas, from Western Australia. The scientists then identified 656 zircons containing dark specks that could be revealing and closely analyzed 79 of them with Raman spectroscopy, a technique that shows the molecular and chemical structure of ancient microorganisms in three dimensions.

"They were searching for carbon, the key component for life. One of the 79 zircons contained graphite - pure carbon - in two locations. The carbon contained in the zircon also has a characteristic signature - a specific ratio of carbon-12 to carbon-13 - that indicates the presence of photosynthetic life.

"From that, the researchers concluded that life existed prior to the massive bombardment of the inner solar system that formed the moon's large craters 3.9 billion years ago.

"If all life on Earth died during this bombardment, which some scientists have argued, then life must have restarted quickly," said Patrick Boehnke, a co-author of the research and a graduate student in Harrison's laboratory.

"The researchers know the zircon is 4.1 billion years old, based on its ratio of uranium to lead. They can't say how much older the graphite is."

Scientific fact, however, rolls over the fundies who have Teflon beliefs that never yield to valid information or logic. It is not always that their faith is so strong, rather that their intellect is so weak.

One of the most challenging tasks for the modern day creationist to is reconcile the belief in a 6,000 year old Earth with the ever-growing mountain of scientific evidence pointing to a vastly different conclusion — namely a universe that's 13.5 billion years old and an Earth that formed 4.5 billion years ago. So, given these astoundingly dramatic discrepancies, biblical literalists and 'young Earth creationists' have had no choice but to get pretty darned imaginative when brushing science aside in favor of bullshit.

Quite obviously, creationists aren't able to gloss over the fact that dinosaurs existed. They are clearly a part of the fossil record. But in accordance with the Bible, creationists insist that they lived contemporaneously with humans. And in fact, they say this explains why dragons play a prominent role in our mythological record. Moreover, creationists claim that human footprints have been found alongside dinosaur tracks at Paluxy, that a petrified hammer was found in Cretaceous rocks, and that some sandal footprints have been found alongside trilobites. Other theories suggest that the Great Flood shook up and redeposited the fossil record so that it *appears* that dinosaurs lived millions of years before humans arrived. Real evidence and *proper* interpretation of the fossil record, however, supports the idea that humans first emerged about 200,000 years ago — long after the demise of dinosaurs who went extinct 65 million years ago.

When we look up at the sky at night, we're actually looking back in time. Given the vastness of the universe, it can take upwards of millions and even billions of years for the light from the most distant celestial objects to reach us. Creationists have a rather convenient explanation for this problem: The universal constants, including the speed of light, are not *constant* at all. It's quite possible, they surmise, that the speed of light was *significantly* faster in the past, allowing it to reach the Earth in time for Adam to see it. Others speculate that the Big Bang theory is simply wrong, and that a new 'creationist cosmology' is required to reconcile the apparent anomaly in our observations. As the *Creation Answers Handbook* claims:

> "The basic biblical framework, because it comes from the Creator, is nonnegotiable, as opposed to the changing views and models of fallible people seeking to understand the data within that framework."

Failing this, creationists can always default to the most convenient of explanations: God simply created the light 'on its way,' so that observers on Earth could see the stars immediately without having to wait. God becomes the scapegoat for every excuse creationists have for what they cannot legitimately explain. They are that special breed placing belief above knowledge and giving unsupported credence to ancient writings by anonymous authors about acts and events that cannot be found in any historic reference. To those like Ham, belief is everything and it is held up like a trophy of achievement instead of a dunce's cap.

A belief is a lever that, once pulled, moves almost everything else in a person's life. Your beliefs define your vision of the world; they dictate your behavior; they determine your emotional responses to other human beings. If you doubt this, consider how your experience would suddenly change if you came to believe one of the following propositions:

1. You have only two weeks to live.
2. A secret organization will take over and govern the world in six months.
3. Aliens have implanted a receiver in your skull and are manipulating your thoughts.

These are mere words—until you believe them. Once believed, they become part of the very apparatus of your mind, determining your desires, fears, expectations, and subsequent behavior. There seems, however, to be a problem with some of our most cherished beliefs about the world: they are leading us, inexorably, to kill one another. A glance at history, or at the pages of any newspaper, reveals that ideas which divide one group of human beings from another, only to unite them in slaughter, generally have their roots in religion. It seems that if our species ever eradicates itself through war, it will not be because it was written in the stars but because it was written in our books; it is what we do with words like "God" and "paradise" and "sin" in the present that will determine our future.

Our situation is this: most of the people in this world believe that the Creator of the universe has written a book, each making an exclusive claim as to its infallibility. People tend to organize themselves into factions according to which of these incompatible claims they accept — rather than on the basis of language, skin color, location of birth, or any other criterion of tribalism. Each of these texts urges its readers to adopt a variety of beliefs and practices, some of which are benign, many of which are not. But once a person believes — *really* believes — that certain ideas can lead to eternal happiness, or to its antithesis, he cannot tolerate the possibility that the people he loves might be led astray by the blandishments of unbelievers. Certainty about the next life is simply incompatible with tolerance in this one.

A few minutes spent wandering the graveyard of bad ideas suggests that the idea that only one belief system can be absolute and true will one day fade into the back pages of history. Consider the case of alchemy: it fascinated human beings for over a thousand years, and yet anyone who seriously claims to be a practicing alchemist today will have disqualified himself for most positions of responsibility in our society. Faith-based religion must suffer the same slide into obsolescence. What is the alternative to religion as we know it? As it turns out, this is the wrong question to ask. Chemistry was not an "alternative" to alchemy; it was a wholesale exchange of ignorance at its most rococo for genuine knowledge. We will find that, as with alchemy, to speak of "alternatives" to religious faith is to miss the point.

To hold the idea, as does Ken Ham, that any one of our religions represents the infallible word of the One True God requires an encyclopedic ignorance of history, mythology, and art even to be entertained — as the beliefs, rituals, and iconography of each of our religions attest to centuries of cross-pollination among them. Whatever their imagined source, the doctrines of modern religions are no more tenable than those which, for lack of adherents, were cast upon the scrap heap of mythology millennia ago; for there is no more evidence to justify a belief in the literal existence of Yahweh and Satan than there was to keep Zeus perched upon his mountain throne or Poseidon churning the seas.

According to Gallup, 35 percent of Americans believe that the Bible is the literal and inerrant word of the Creator of the universe. Another 48 percent believe that it is the "inspired" word of the same—still inerrant, though certain of its passages must be interpreted symbolically before their truth can be brought to light. Only 17 percent of us remain to doubt that a personal God, in his infinite wisdom, is likely to have authored this text — or, for that

64

matter, to have created the earth with its 250,000 species of beetles. Some 46 percent of Americans take a literalist view of creation (40 percent believe that God has guided creation over the course of millions of years). This means that 120 million of us place the big bang 2,500 years *after* the Babylonians and Sumerians learned to brew beer and produce glue. If our polls are to be trusted, nearly 230 million Americans believe that a book showing neither unity of style nor internal consistency was authored by an omniscient, omnipotent, and omnipresent deity. A survey of Hindus, Muslims, and Jews around the world would surely yield similar results, revealing that we, as a species, have grown almost perfectly intoxicated by our myths. How is it that, in this one area of our lives, we have convinced ourselves that our beliefs about the world can float entirely free of reason and evidence?

The first thing to observe about the moderate's retreat from scriptural literalism is that it draws its inspiration not from scripture but from cultural developments that have rendered many of God's utterances difficult to accept as written. In America, religious moderation is further enforced by the fact that most Christians and Jews do not read the Bible in its entirety and consequently have no idea just how vigorously the God of Abraham wants heresy expunged. One look at the book of Deuteronomy reveals that he has something very specific in mind should your son or daughter return from yoga class advocating the worship of Krishna:

> If your brother, the son of your father or of your mother, or your son or daughter, or the spouse whom you embrace, or your most intimate friend, tries to secretly seduce you, saying, "Let us go and serve other gods," unknown to you or your ancestors before you, gods of the peoples surrounding you, whether near you or far away, anywhere throughout the world, you must not consent, you must not listen to him; you must show him no pity, you must not spare him or conceal his guilt. No, you must kill him, your hand must strike the first blow in putting him to death and the hands of the rest of the people following. You must stone him to death, since he has tried to divert you from Yahweh your God. . . .(Deuteronomy 13:7-11)

While the stoning of children for heresy has fallen out of fashion in your country, you will not hear a moderate Christian or Jew arguing for a "symbolic" reading of passages of this sort. (In fact, one seems to be explicitly blocked by God himself in Deuteronomy 13:1—"Whatever I am now commanding you, you must keep and observe, adding nothing to it, taking nothing away.") The above passage is as canonical as any in the Bible, and it is only by ignoring such barbarisms that the Good Book can be reconciled with life in the modern world. This is a problem for "moderation" in religion: it has nothing underwriting it other than the unacknow-ledged neglect of the letter of the divine law. To truly believe and abide by scripture as ken Ham claims to do, leads one to ask how many homosexuals he has killed in obedience to Old Testament law.

Ours is a society established upon the need for evidence. Court procedures require "beyond a doubt" based upon the evidence pres-ented. Even most fundamentalists live by the lights of reason in this regard; it is just that their minds seem to have been partitioned to accommodate the profligate truth claims of their faith. Tell a devout Christian that his wife is cheating on him, or that frozen yogurt can make a man invisible, and he is likely to require as much evidence as anyone else, and to be persuaded only to the extent that you give it. Tell him that the book he keeps by his bed was written by an invisible deity who will punish him with fire for eternity if he fails to accept its every incredible claim about the universe, and he seems to require no evidence whatsoever.

Religious moderation springs from the fact that even the least educated person among us simply *knows* more about certain matters than anyone did two thousand years ago — and much of this knowledge is incompatible with scripture. Having heard something about the medical discoveries of the last hundred years, most of us no longer equate disease processes with sin or demonic possession. Having learned about the known distances between objects in our universe, most of us (about half of us, actually) find the idea that the whole works was created six thousand years ago (with light from distant stars already in transit toward the earth) impossible to take seriously. Such concessions to modernity do not in the least suggest that faith is compatible with reason, or that our religious traditions are in principle open to new learning: it is just that the utility of ignoring (or "reinterpreting") certain articles of faith is now overwhelming. Anyone being flown to a distant city for heart-bypass surgery has conceded, tacitly at least, that we have learned a few things about physics, geography, engineering, and medicine since the time of Moses.

While moderation in religion may seem a reasonable position to stake out, in light of all that we have (and have not) learned

66

about the universe, it offers no bulwark against religious extremism and religious violence. From the perspective of those seeking to live by the letter of the texts, the religious moderate is nothing more than a failed fundamentalist. He is, in all likelihood, going to wind up in hell with the rest of the unbelievers. The problem that religious moderation poses for all of us is that it does not permit anything very critical to be said about religious literalism.

Moderates do not want to kill anyone in the name of God, but they want us to keep using the word "God" as though we knew what we were talking about. And they do not want anything too critical said about people who really believe in the God of their fathers, because tolerance, perhaps above all else, is sacred. To speak plainly and truthfully about the state of our world — to say, for instance, that the Bible and the Koran both contain mountains of life-destroying gibberish — is antithetical to tolerance as moderates currently conceive it. But we can no longer afford the luxury of such political correctness. We must finally recognize the price we are paying to maintain the iconography of our ignorance.

And so it is I have dealt kindly with the creationists and their belief in a young earth. It is not true of course, and I remain bewildered how people can believe it is, but the fact remains that like real spiritual experiences that have created religious concepts, ignorance has done the same. And perhaps that is the final word on the topic. We can surmise that Catholics are historians and traditionalists since they attend churches representing the very root of all Christianity. All the denominations of Protestants are the inquirers, thinkers and movers of religion, trying to find truth in the maze of Christian thought. And then there are those who need to feel instead of think. They need to be inspired from a pulpit since they find no inspiration within themselves. They are the ones speaking in tongues and dancing with poisonous snakes. They are the ones who lost their lives in Guyana under the spell of Jim Jones. They are the ones who bought new tennis shoes and wore black clothing so they could commit suicide as taught by Marshal Applewhite and go into the heavens to live in a distant kingdom. They were the victims of Waco.

There can be no doubt that the founders of early history of Christianity were intelligent and often brilliant. For more than 400 years the Bible remained exclusively in their care and they edited, inserted, deleted as necessary to compliment an evolving doctrine and history. To believe that it is inerrant today is an insult to their efforts. But just as some religions were born of genius, so are others designed for the ignorant, by the ignorant. They are the ones discarding knowledge in favor of belief – no matter how unsubstantiated that belief may be. They will embrace the idea that their earth, littered with valid evidences attesting to its true age, is only 6,000 years old. They will reject every scientific method for establishing ages as inadequate or conducted by those dedicated to error. They are the ones echoing the absurdities of their leader, Ken Ham, who challenges scientists concerning the Big Bang with the juvenile question, "Were you there?" It doesn't matter that Ham wasn't in the Garden of Eden and yet reproduces it from his imagination in his museum. He wasn't there with the building of the Ark and yet promises that his reproduction of the Ark is a "faithful replica." He wasn't there in any of the scenarios the rants about and yet exercises the ultimate stupidity with his spurious questions. He is the first to argue against evolution and yet represents clear proof that he is not so far from the ape after all. So how do so many believe the ridiculous teachings of this character?

God works in mysterious ways.

THE DOOR KNOCKERS

Of all the victims of religion in the world, perhaps none are as pathetic as the Jehovah's Witnesses. Yet another womanizer, fraud and con man founded the movement that now claims to have no less than eight million people knocking on doors across the world. They are so misled and openly brainwashed that they are firmly convinced that because they are members of the sect, only they will entered the Kingdom of Heaven.

They find much of their beliefs in a secular rag, *Watchtower,* that has produced more prophetic errors over the years than all the phony TV evangelists put together. Their religion, unlike Mormonism, isn't an esoteric one with secret doctrines known only to an initiated few. When Mormons come to your door, they don't tell you that they believe in many gods, that Jesus and Lucifer were "spirit brothers," and that dark skin (in the case of blacks, Indians, and Hispanics) is supposedly a curse from God in punishment for wickedness. If they told you such things up front, you'd close the door immediately. Such teachings are saved for initiates. Thus, Mormonism is an esoteric religion (Webster: "esoteric: designed for or understood by the specially initiated alone").

The religion of the Jehovah's Witnesses, on the other hand, is exoteric (Webster: "suitable to be imparted to the public"). They're happy to tell you up front exactly what they believe, and they tell you not just when at your door, but in their publications. In their booklet entitled *Jehovah's Witnesses in the Twentieth Century,* for example, may be found a chart titled "What Jehovah's Witnesses Believe;" this chart list beliefs and the supposed scriptural authority for them. Maybe the beliefs are a bit off the normal intelligence chart, but to them they are moral mandates coming down from higher sources. What they don't know is that those higher sources are not from heaven, rather some mahogany paneled offices in New York.

It all began with a guy named Charles Taze Russell who was born on February 16, 1852 in Allegheny, Pennsylvania, the second of five children born to Joseph and Ann Russell. Charles grew up in a devout home and his parents were respected members of the Presbyterian church. When he was young, his family moved to Pittsburgh, where his father came to own a number of haberdashery stores. In his early teens Charles became a partner in this business and soon owned several of the locations.

As a boy Charles had a great deal of religious enthusiasm, and while still only a teenager left his Presbyterian congregation to attend a Congregational church. As a form of evangelism he would often go to public locations and use chalk to write out Bible verses related to sin and damnation. But then, at the age of sixteen, he engaged in a debate with a friend that led him to question the reliability of the Bible and the validity of the Christian faith. He embarked on a period of religious searching and dabbled in many Eastern religions before determining that they, too, were empty and unsatisfying.

When Charles was eighteen he encountered Adventist preaching and began to regularly attend a Bible study. It was not long before he determined that he could not reconcile an eternal hell with a merciful God. Over the next two years he came to question many other historic Christian doctrines and became convinced that the historic creeds betrayed true Christianity. At the same time he adopted Adventist teachings: that the end times had begun in 1799, that Christ had returned invisibly in 1874 and been crowned King of Heaven four years later, that all Christians who had already died would be resurrected before the end of 1878, and that 1914 would mark the end of a harvest period and usher in Armageddon. He sold his five clothing stores, an act that generated a substantial amount of money (today's equivalent of several million dollars), and committed his life to writing, publishing, and funding the propagation of the message of Christ's imminent return. He did this at first through a partnership with Nelson H. Barbour and his Adventist periodical *Herald of the Morning*.

When 1878 came and went without any of the predicted events, he was forced to re-examine his beliefs and to distance himself from some of his Adventist peers, including Barbour. He founded his own periodical which he titled *Zion's Watch Tower and Herald of Christ's Presence*. At this time he also married Maria Frances Ackley in an apparently celibate union that would last until 1897 before ending in an acrimonious divorce.

In 1881 Russell founded the Watch Tower Bible and Tract Society which grew to a substantial publishing venture, and there were soon some 16 million of his books and booklets in print. His ministry and his opportunities to preach grew exponentially and Pastor Russell, as he became known, soon had followers all over the Northern and Eastern states. He preached and wrote constantly, his sermons were printed in several thousand newspapers around the globe, and he became one of the most famous preachers in the world. He eventually moved the headquarters of the Watch Tower Society to Brooklyn, New York, where they remain today.

Russell died of cystitis on October 31, 1916, near Pampa, TX, as he attempted to return to his home in Brooklyn. By the time of his death, his writings had become among the most widely-distributed works in the world. Some estimate that when he died, only the Bible and the Chinese almanac were in greater circulation than his myriad books and pamphlets.

Unlike so many other false teachers before and after him, Russell did not rely upon visions or other extra-biblical revelation. Rather, he simply interpreted, and misinterpreted, the Bible. While claiming to be a Christian and, in fact, a Christian who was restoring the faith of the New Testament, he denied many key Christian doctrines including eternal punishment, the Trinity, the deity of Christ, and the existence of the Trinity.

Russell, as with most Adventists, denied the existence of hell as a place where the wicked face God's wrath. He also held that the soul simply ceases to exist after death.

As with Arius centuries before, he held that Jesus was a created being, and was actually Michael the Archangel in human form. While he taught that this Jesus died on behalf of humanity, he also taught that Jesus rose only spiritually rather than physically. While he denied the *divinity* of Jesus, he denied the *existence* of the Holy Spirit, teaching that the Spirit is not a person, but simply a name given to express a specific manifestation of God's power. In denying the divinity of Jesus and the existence of the Holy Spirit, he necessarily denied the Trinity.

Those who followed Russell during his lifetime referred to themselves as Bible Students. In the years following his death, Joseph Franklin Rutherford succeeded him as president of the Watch Tower Society. Despite many people withdrawing from the Bible Study movement, and despite those who remained splitting many times over, Rutherford's followers maintained control of the Watch Tower Society and officially renamed themselves Jehovah's witnesses in July 1931.

The Watch Tower Society remains the official religious body of the Jehovah's Witnesses. Though both their beliefs and their structure have evolved in the past century, they continue to state that there is one God in one person, that there is no Trinity, that Jesus was God's first created being, that the Holy Spirit is an impersonal force, and that there is no hell. While Russell is honored among Jehovah's Witnesses, they do not refer to him as their founder. Rather, they hold that Jesus is their founder while Russell was simply a man used by God to restore beliefs that had been lost.

Although there is no unified historical record concerning the founding of the Witnesses, according to a WatchTower Yearbook, "a few Christian persons met together in a little house in Pennsylvania to discuss the Scriptures relative to the coming of Christ and His Kingdom." This Bible study group bestowed upon Russell the title "Pastor". In court. Russell was asked, "Now; you never were ordained by a bishop, clergyman, presbytery, council, or any body of men, living?" Russell answered, "I never was."

According to the Witnesses, Armageddon or the "Holy War" between Christ and His disciples and Satan and his followers during which the world as we know it will be destroyed, is always "just around the corner." Many times the WatchTower and Bible Society has given dates for the end of the world. For example, in July of 1917, the year 1925 was established as a "significant date" - that is, the year of Armageddon. Similarly, 1975 was established as a "significant date" in June 1966. Of course, both times thousands of Witnesses left the organization because Christ did not come. These dates alone, which are the product of faulty - indeed fatuous - Biblical exegesis, render the claim of the Governing Body of the WatchTower Society that they are "God's representatives on Earth" blatantly absurd.

Again, many thousands came to this conclusion when his wife, Maria Ackley (1906), sued Russell for divorce. They reasoned, correctly, that being a prophet of God precluded getting a divorce. Her grounds were four-fold:

"That his conceit, egotism and domination were such as to make life intolerable to any sensitive woman; that his conduct in relation to other women was improper; that on one occasion he was silent to his wife for four weeks and only communicated with her by letters of a reproachful character, and that he sought by most despicable means to isolate his wife from society, and designed to get her pronounced insane in order to put her away."

Mrs. Russell won the suit, and her alimony payment was $6,036. Moreover, she received back alimony payments from officials of the WatchTower Bible and Tract Society:

"Mr. Rutherford testified to the fact that he and four other prominent Witnesses grouped together in 1909 to raise $10,000 which they paid to Mrs. Russell for back alimony. From 1909 until the time of the death of Mr. Russell; these men paid Mrs. Russell $100 a month out of their own funds" *WatchTower, Feb. 1917*

Mr. Russell died on October 31, 1916. Why would these five officials have to pay Mrs. Russell what is due her? After all, her husband owned 990 of the 1000 shares of the Watchtower Bible and Tract Society. Walter Martin observes, "Thus Russell apparently controlled the entire financial power of the Society and was not accountable to anyone." So any money sent to the Society belonged to Russell. Although he refused to relinquish alimony, he spent very liberally on himself and his cronies. His wife explains at the trial, "His life was one continuous round of expensive touring, at tremendous cost to many of his deceived followers. At a convention he and his special favorites were settled in palatial quarters apart from the main company. There he held daily receptions, to which live hundred each day were admitted by ticket, all being treated to refreshments, free boat ride, and carfare from the convention grounds to his quarters."

Russell toured the world in 1912 to promote his new religion. But he was dishonest while doing so. The Brooklyn Eagle, a newspaper in New York hat ran an expose of Russell, elaborates: "All during this time the 'Pastor's' sermons were being printed in newspapers throughout the world. [He] caused accounts to be published in his advertised sermons telling of enthusiastic greetings at various places he visited. It was shown in many cases that the sermons were never delivered in the places that were claimed."

Not only did Russell lie while touring the world, he lied under oath. A Protestant minister, J.J. Ross, published a pamphlet calling Russell's religion "the destructive doctrines of one man who is neither a scholar nor a theologian" and who "never attended the higher schools of learning; knows comparatively nothing of philosophy, systematic or historical theology, and is totally ignorant of the dead languages."

Russell sued for "defamatory libel", claiming that Ross' charges were untrue and exposed him to public ridicule and contempt, thereby irrevocably injuring his reputation. In court, however, all of Ross' charges were proven to be true. For example, when asked if he knew the Greek alphabet Russell answered: "Oh, yes." Then when he was asked to identify some letters, he rejoined, "I don't know that I would be able to." Finally, he was asked, "Are you familiar with the Greek language?" He replied, "No." The case, Dr.

Walter Martin rightly concludes; "established him beyond a doubt as a premeditated perjurer."

To make more money - as if he did not have enough - Russell lied once again: the Society advertised wheat seed for sale at $1 a pound. It was called "Miracle Wheat" because - are you ready for this? - it supposedly grew five times as much wheat as any other brand. The Brooklyn Daily Eagle noticed the scam and published an incriminating cartoon. Once again Russell sued for libel - and once again, he lost the case.

Knowing full well that Russell was a habitual liar, how can anyone trust what he asserted in his writings? On page after page this pompous man proffers misinformation and propaganda in order to deceive the most naive and gullible people. The following is a typical example taken from his *Studies in the Scriptures*: "Few realize that from the time creed-making began, A.D. 325, there was practically no Bible study for 1260 years."

To affirm that there was no Bible Study from 325 to 1585 is absolutely ludicrous. Shortly after the Council of Nicaea, Pope Damasus ordered Saint Jerome to produce a Latin version of the Scriptures from the original languages. Known as the "Vulgate," it is recognized by the Catholic Church as an authentic and authorized version. Moreover, Russell is an intellectual and moral pigmy compared to the giants of Catholicism: Saint Jerome, Saint Augustine, Origen, Saint Bonaventure, Saint Thomas Aquinas - the list is virtually endless. The writings of just these intellectuals are libraries in themselves. More importantly, they were renowned for holiness during their lifetimes and eventually became great saints. Russell; on the other hand, proclaimed:

> "The testimony of the so-called Early Fathers," has been omitted." And we know why - the Faith of the early Fathers is Catholicism. The New Testament writers passed on the Catholic Faith - this is a historical fact. This is why the Catholic Church proclaims that what the Fathers unanimously teach to be of faith, is of faith, and what they unanimously reject as heretical, is heretical."

Although Russell praised Protestantism in general, he voiced the following criticism: "But since their day Protestants have made little progress, because, instead of walking in the light, they have halted around their favorite leaders, willing to see as much as they saw but nothing more." This applies even more to Russell and his followers: they slavishly echo his doctrine and his ideas; blind sheep being led to the slaughter by a deranged wolf.

Despite having only a seventh grade education, Russell boasted that he was the incarnation of truth, for he referred to his Studies in the Scriptures as "not mere comments on the Bible, but they are practically the Bible itself." *The WatchTower, Sept. 15; 1910* He insisted that the Bible was not studied for over 1200 years and that only he was competent to interpret it - completely ignoring the Church Fathers. No wonder Mrs. Russell lambasted her husband for his "egotism and conceit."

Like all persons who establish their own religion; Russell set himself up as "the pillar and mainstay of the truth." In reality, however, he was an uneducated liar who managed to portray himself as a reformer, thus bilking many people out of millions of dollars. He charged that organized religion is a "racket", and his religion shows that in his case it is true.

Long after Russell's death, the phony doctrines of the witnesses continued. By the mid-20th century, it was decided that they should have their own Bible. A new "translation" was made- producing the New World Bible. Once completed, there were questions about the credentials of the translators and The Watchtower's Bible subject index handbook, *Reasoning from the Scripture,* states:

"When presenting as a gift the publishing rights to their translation, the *New World Bible Translation Committee* requested that its members remain anonymous. *The Watch Tower Bible and Tract Society of Pennsylvania* has honored their request."

The reason cited is because the "translators were not seeking prominence for themselves." However, the fact is that the men who comprised this committee had no adequate schooling or background to function as skilled critical Bible translators.

The translation committee was headed by (then vice -president of the Jehovah's Witnesses), Frederick W.Franz. Other members included Nathan H. Knorr (then president of the Jehovah's Witnesses), Albert D. Schroeder, Ceorge D. Gangas and Milton Henschel.

Raymond Franz wrote in his *Crisis of Conscience,* "Fred Franz was the only one with any knowledge of the Bible languages to attempt translation of this kind. He had studied Greek for two years in the University of Cincinnati but was only self-taught in Hebrew."

Later investigations proved Franz's writing to be true. In fact, four out of the five men on the committee had no Hebrew or Greek training at all, and only a high school education. Franz studied

Greek for two years at the University of Cincinnati, but dropped out after his sophomore year. When asked in a Scotland courtroom if he could translate Genesis 2:4 into Hebrew, Franz replied that he could not. The truth is that Franz was unable to translate Hebrew or Greek. And yet these were the men translating the official Bible for Jehovah's Witnesses to use. What's more, the translation process has not ended as part of the opening of the New World Bible states:

"However, the English language has changed during the past half century. Such change prompted current members of the New World Bible Translation Committee to initiate this comprehensive revision. Our goal has been to produce a translation that is not only faithful to the original texts but also clear and easy to read."

Original texts? What original texts? There are no original texts of the Bible, only copies of copies going back to the fourth century. But the learned group forming the translation committee probably didn't know that just as Fred Franz didn't know that he was going to commit perjury in a Scottish court.

During a court trial held in Scotland in 1954 (during the same period that the New World Translation was being made) Franz was asked if he had made himself familiar with Hebrew. His reply was "Yes." He also acknowledged under oath that he could read and follow the Bible in Hebrew, Greek, Latin, Spanish, Portuguese, German and French. The following day, during the same court trial, his linguistic abilities were put to the test.

He was asked to translate Genesis 2:4 into Hebrew. He failed the test as he was unable to do so. In fact he did not even try, but rather stated "No, I wouldn't attempt to do that."

To the question of the translator's credentials, the Watchtower has led its followers to believe that although the backgrounds of its translators are not made known, the translation will stand on its own. It does not.

The 1985 edition of the *Kingdom Interlinear Translation of the Greek Scriptures* states for its readers the guidelines and goals endorsed by the translation committee. The Society claims that, "We offer no paraphrase of Scripture. Our endeavor throughout has been to as literal a translation as possible where the modern English idiom allows for it or where the thought content is not hidden due to awkwardness in the literal rendition" and that "To each major word we have assigned one meaning and have held to that meaning as far as context permitted"

However, based on these claims for its translation of the Bible, the committee failed miserably.

The Watchtower Society leads its followers to believe that its translation is also superior on the basis that it has restored the divine name Jehovah (Yahweh) to the pages of the Bible. The Watchtower's publication, "The Divine Name That Will Endure Forever" announces that it was a "apostate" Christian church that removed the divine name and has substituted "Lord" in its place.

One of the Jewish names for God was YHWH, referred to as the Tetragrammaton. The Old Testament contains YHWH over 6,000 times, yet the Tetragrammaton *never* appears in the New Testament. It has not been found in a single ancient Greek New Testament manuscript.

Inclusion of the word Jehovah in the New Testament of the *New World Translation of the Holy Scriptures* (NWT) is one of the most important errors in Watchtower theology, as it:

- Changes the meaning of key Bible passages
- Undermines the integrity of the Bible
- Leads Jehovah's Witnesses to believe than any person not using the word Jehovah cannot have a personal relationship with God

When examining the corruptions within the translations contained in the New World Bible we are faced with the decision of whether or not the Watchtower movers are misinformed or simply liars. The latter seems the most logical choice. The Watchtower tells its readers that Jehovah was originally in the New Testament, but was removed, disappearing without a trace. Not only does the claim undermine the integrity of the entire Bible, but suggests that if one very important word was deleted, what other corruptions occurred to the testament?

One Watchtower publication *Proclaimers* blatantly stated:

"The conventioners were thrilled to learn that this new translation [NWT] **restored** the divine name Jehovah 237 times in the main text from Matthew to Revelation!"

The New Testament is one of the most attested ancient works in existence. The *Journal of Biblical Literature Vol. 87* has listed 5,255 known New Testament Greek fragments. The Tetragrammaton does not appear in the New Testament either as YHWH or as the Greek transliterations PIPI, YAW and Iabe in a single one of these ancient New Testament manuscripts. (The Tetragraminaton is four Hebrew letters (Yod, He, Waw and He). The four characters are the four Hebrew letters that correspond to YHWH and are transliterated IAUE or Yahweh, sometimes pronounced as Jehovah)

This is despite "some papyrus fragments of the Christian Greek Scriptures that go back to the middle of the second century."

When attempting to build faith in the Bible the Watchtower asserts the New Testament is complete without omissions – silent in regards to their belief that the most important word has disappeared without trace.

"No striking or fundamental variation is shown either in the Old or the New Testament. There are *no important omissions* or additions of passages, and no variations which affect vital facts or doctrines."

In the publication *All Scripture is Inspired of God and Beneficial,* we find the false claim:

"Not only are there thousands of manuscripts to compare but discoveries of older Bible manuscripts during the past few decades take the Greek text back as far as about the year 125 C.E., just a couple of decades short of the death of the apostle John about 100 C.E. These manuscript evidences provide strong assurance that we now have a *dependable Greek text* in refined form."

The story changes when explaining why the Watchtower Society added the word Jehovah into the New Testament, alleging the removal of YHWH from the New Testament during the second century.

"Sometime during the second or third century C.E. the scribes removed the Tetragrammaton from both the Septuagint and the Christian Greek Scriptures and replaced it with Ky´ri·os, "Lord" or The·os´, "God."" *New World Translation of the Holy Scriptures – With References.*

There is no proof whatsoever to support this claim. Several available manuscripts date back to this period. P47 dates prior to 300 A.D. and contains four uses of Kyrios from Revelation that the NWT translates as Jehovah. P66 dates from around 200 A.D. from John (written in 98 A.D) and contains five occurrences of Lord that appear in the NWT as Jehovah. Some manuscripts go back to within 25 years of John's writings, yet none contains YHWH.

Numerous scholars with true credentials in the Biblical languages have condemned the Watchtower's New World version. In fact, just about everything about the JWs has been condemned by thinking people across the world. Why? Because it is obviously so blatantly false that one is challenged to imagine how so many could be so completely brainwashed.

Jehovah's Witnesses are the Stepford Wives of all missionary movements and the most strict practicing Christians in today's society. They believe themselves to be the "true" Christians and reject many popular ideas in other versions of Christianity. They do not believe in hellfire, or the inherent immortality of the soul. They believe that when you die, you are in a state of nonexistence — both physical and spiritual.

They believe an Armageddon will occur when satan attacks Jehovah's Witnesses and god is forced to step in and destroy all governments and those people that do not follow him. Witnesses believe that Armageddon will be triggered by the United Nations (you can't make this stuff up) which is represented by the scarlet-colored wild beast of the book of Revelation chapter 17 in the scriptures. After Armageddon, god will choose 144,000 of his most loyal, trusting Witnesses to help him lead the Earth which he will transform into a paradise similar to the Garden of Eden and they will serve on his council of government. Those that have died before the Armageddon took place will gradually be resurrected and judged based on their current actions (rather than their past deeds) for a thousand years. After that thousand years has passed, Satan will be sent to Earth one last time to test those left and "the end result will be a fully tested, glorified human race. Christ will then hand all authority back to God."

Which leads us to the next big difference between Witnesses and most other forms of Christianity: Witnesses do not believe in the trinity. They believe that God (or "Jehovah" derived from the biblical name given to God in the Tetragrammaton JHVH or YHWH) is the creator of all things, the "one true God", and is therefore the only thing worthy of worship. Jesus, or Christ, is God's only direct creation and the holy spirit is God's power in the world. They also believe Satan to be a fallen angel, once perfect in the kingdom of God who now comes to Earth to mislead people and create evil and human suffering.

Witnesses do not celebrate birthdays, Christmas, Easter or any other "typical" holiday as they believe them to be derived from Pagan rituals and, therefore, not properly representative of their Christian faith. I like to say that they don't celebrate Halloween because they don't like strange people knocking on their door. They also refuse to pledge allegiance to any country, take part in any nationalistic celebration or song and vehemently refuse to serve in the military. They do this because they feel that Christianity has no nationality and one's allegiance should only ever be to God and nothing or no one else. "They consider secular society to be morally corrupt and under the influence of Satan, and most limit their social interaction with non-Witnesses." This places them in a state of segregation from everyone else (including fellow Christians who are not Witnesses) by choice, until they are called upon to evangelize. All members are required to evangelize and each must submit a monthly log of their activity. If you do not, you can be considered inactive and eventually be "disfellowshipped" and shunned by the community — an act highly dreaded by those that faithfully follow.

Worship involves frequent church meetings on the local level as well as national/international meetings that are more like conventions . They are taught how to read the scriptures by a governing body composed of all men (surprise, surprise) called, The Watch Tower Society. These men create publications that are to be given as much weight as the Bible itself and are not, under any circumstances, to be re-interpreted or challenged in any way (to do so would result in their being immediately disfellowshipped). If one publication comes out as being in disagreement with a previous publication, it is said that God is gradually revealing his will to the Watch Tower Society and they can, therefore, only publish what they know, when they know it.

The wild claims reach the point of heresy as found in the Watchtower of April 15, 2010:

"Consider, too, the fact that *Jehovah's organization alone*, in all the earth, is *directed by God's holy spirit or active force*." And in 1939, "1939 "It should be expected that the Lord would have a means of communicating to his people on the earth, and he has clearly shown that the magazine called The Watchtower is used for that purpose.

There is zero tolerance for sex outside of marriage, homosexuality, drunkenness, gambling, illegal drugs and tobacco. Witnesses must dress modestly and follow a strict patriarchal home-life in which divorce in only permitted in the case of adultery (per the Bible). Any divorce not a result of adultery (a scriptural divorce) or a legal separation due to excessive abuse or disdain for the union ("absolute endangerment of spirituality") is considered illegal and any re-marriage considered adultery. "Marrying a non-believer, or endorsing such a union, is strongly discouraged and carries religious sanctions."

This leads me to the reason I believe the Jehovah's Witness style of Christianity is most harmful to society: segregation. They segregate themselves and their children from the outside world and all others that are different from them. Their children are never given the opportunity to learn about the world and make decisions about it on their own which causes a great deal of intolerance and un-acceptance. I believe we become better, more fulfilled people when we are surrounded by people who are different from ourselves. I believe that is the only way we can truly learn and grow. Strip that away and we are nothing but the product of our parents and a slave to their ideals.

Believing you are living the "one and only" truth and being completely un-accepting of other beliefs is never a good thing. It's arrogant and ignorant and when both of those traits come together it almost always spells disaster.

As I write these words, the news reports that a Jehovah Witness woman died refusing a blood transfusion and that other witnesses applauded her death as if it was to be celebrated. Arguing the semantics of this confusing teaching is one thing, but when friends and other JWs applaud a woman's decision to sacrifice her own life and leaving her child without a mother because a *bodily fluid* is more important, that is an obscenity. Rather than taking this opportunity to really examine the issue of blood transfusions and see if Jehovah's Witnesses have a belief supported by the bible and questioning this ever-changing doctrine, they instead applaud the loss of a life. Not that any life is more or less valuable than another, but they also applaud a new mother who only got to hold her baby for a brief time before leaving her behind.

Sacrificing a life for a worthy cause I might understand, but sacrificing your life for a faulty doctrine determined by a group of strangers who have proven time and again that they have no special knowledge, wisdom, or guidance from god is unacceptable. Applauding this needless sacrifice is disgusting. Jehovah's Witnesses are a Jonestown in slow motion, and while they may claim that they don't believe in faith healing, throwing away a life based on faith in ignorant men is really no different. The men who dole out these beliefs without really understanding them or listening to a critical opinion are also no different than those who handed out the Kool-Aid at Jonestown. But more than anything, the incident reveals to what extent the door knockers have been brainwashed.

Perhaps the most ironic thing about the entire Jehovah Witness movement is that it is based upon an ancient fraud. It is now agreed by almost all theologians that the Book of Mark is the oldest of the gospels. Matthew obviously copied Mark and Luke did the same. That means any error contained in Mark was repeated in the two following gospels. In the earliests New Testament manuscripts available – the Codex Sinaiticus or Codex Vaticanus and others – the Gospel According to Mark ends in chapter 16, verse 9. It tells of Mary Magdalene going to the tomb with friends, being told by a young man in the tomb that Jesus is gone and she leaves very afraid. There is nothing more – only that.

What this means is that, "He said to them, "Go into all the world and preach the gospel to all creation," the very essence of the JW mission, *is a later insertion by some zealous early church father*. It has no scriptural validity and all the door knocking in the world will never change that truth. This is an agreed fact known to theologians across the world – but apparently not the the Jehovah's Witnesses who apparently don't have anyone of theologian caliber.

Jehovah's Witnesses in Russia are struggling to keep their movement alive but at times their propaganda went beyond the legal limits. A news release from Orel read:

"One of the largest and most active destructive religious sects operating on the territory of the province is the Orel Jehovah's Witnesses religious organization. This organization is a member of the structure of the centralized religious organization the Administrative Center of Jehovah's Witnesses in Russia.

"On the basis of materials from personnel of law enforcement agencies regarding the chairman of this organization and other active members in 2015 and the current period of 2016, agencies of the prosecutor's office issued 9 warnings about the impermissibility of conducting extremist activity.

"On 14 June 2016, the Orel provincial court issued a decision granting the administrative petition of the Directorate of the Ministry of Justice of the Russian Federation for Orel province for finding the local religious organization of Jehovah's Witnesses of Orel to be extremist and for its liquidation and removal from the Uniform State Register of Legal Entities.

"The basis for issuing the judicial decision was the conclusion of the prosecutor's office that participated in the case regarding the frequent distribution by the religious organization of extremist literature that is forbidden in the Russian federation, which the leadership of the organization admittedly knew about."

Anti-JW sentiments have been growing in Russia for years and appear to have reached their boiling point. In some places citizens put signs on their homes telling Witnesses not to bother them with their missionary nonsense but the door knockers refused to heed the announcement and annoyed almost everyone they contacted. At the same time, some of the materials being passed out by the door knockers was deemed totally unsuitable under Russian law. An apologist article read:

"On 19 February 2016 a Serov district court of Sverdlovsk province banned two publications of Jehovah's Witnesses. These were a brochure, "Listen to God,' and an issue of the magazine *Awake* for January 2015 with a lead article "How did life appear?".

"'Listen to God' is a small book with colorful illustrations whose entire text consists of brief quotations from the Bible in the New World Translation, that is, the Russian translation of the Jehovah's Witnesses. The forbidden issue of the magazine *Awake* covers the question of the appearance of life from the point of view of the Jehovah's Witnesses and it also describes the unique shape of a honey comb, gives advice on restraining anger and answers to questions about the implication of God in the sufferings of people, and publishes brief news about Costa Rica and an interview with a sick girl. The reasons for banning the publication are unknown to us, but we note that in both there is a reference to the website of the Jehovah's Witnesses, which was prohibited in Russia.

"We consider the ban of these two publications for extremism to be illegal. We consider in general finding publications of Jehovah's Witnesses and prosecution of believers for their distribution to be religious discrimination.

"Previously, in the autumn of 2015, a former founder of the local religious organization in Serov was fined for possession of extremist materials for the purpose of mass distribution. A warning about the impermissibility of extremist activity was issued to the congregation and the Jehovah's Witnesses did not succeed in appealing its legality in court."

It doesn't seem to soak in to these robotic followers of the JW sham that Russia is simply fed up with them and is seeking whatever means necessary to give citizens some rest from their incessant door knocking.

No matter how much public opinion exists against the Witnesses, it will be seen as a persecution against the purity of their beliefs. God wants them to be opposed, ridiculed and attacked because He is there with them as they knock on door and if they are rejected, it was a blessing because they continued in divine service.

In short, they are brainwashed to a point that would make North Korea jealous. Their world is black and white. They are the good ones and all others are bad. It's them against the world. There are no half-measures. Either you are 100% Jehovah Witness or there is a distinct possibility of being labeled "bad association" or losing privileges in the congregation. This is mirrored in the shunning policy: If you don't believe in every little word the Governing body publishes, you are an apostate. All or nothing.

The leadership of Jehovah's Witnesses maintains a policy of over generalizing everything. A single successful preaching day means that they truly have Jehovah's blessing. An earthquake or military conflict somewhere means that they are indeed living in the last days. The experience of some Jehovah's Witnesses being saved from a harmful situation showed how Jehovah's spirit works.

The problem: When they overgeneralize, they tend to forget everything that might negate their pattern. They block out that practically all other preaching days were rubbish. They didn't want to realize that there have always been earthquakes and conflicts but they are hearing more about them due to better and faster news delivery. And while being in awe of Jehovah's alleged spirit in action with these lucky Brothers and Sisters, they totally forget about all the other times Jehovah's Witnesses were killed or hurt badly.

Despite Armageddon being late, Jehovah's Witnesses are still going strong on that "last days" shtick. It's amazing mankind has survived so far, considering we've been living in the alleged worst part of human history. That is because of Jehovah's Witnesses' confirmation bias leads them to think that the world situation is worse than it is.

Take any Watchtower publication and flick through it to any page. Read a paragraph. There's a good chance you will stumble upon a sentence along the lines of "How happy we are to be part of God's people," "How thrilling it is to know God will destroy the wicked" or something like that. This is very manipulative. One ex-Jehovah Witness later testified, "I remember thinking, 'Actually, I don't feel *that* happy. Something must be wrong with *me.*' Or, 'Everybody else is happy, so I must be happy to.' As Jehovah's Witnesses one gives more weight to emotive thoughts than to reason.

Fortune telling is a vital part of the JW doctrine. There are different ways this pattern applies to Jehovah's Witnesses. The most obvious are the failed predictions, of course. Funny how nobody seems to care among Jehovah's Witnesses. This is due, in part, to the Governing Body claiming affiliation with prophets of ancient time who seemingly had the gift of foretelling future events. So, if it worked out for them, it will have to work out for the Governing Body in the long run, right? JWs just *have* to believe. Plus: It says so in the Bible. On a smaller scale, they are all prone to fortune-telling. Why? Because they were made to believe that if something goes wrong it is always their fault or our lacking of faith. If things go well: Thank you, Jehovah!

JWs are brainwashed into thinking that whatever they do, it is never enough. They are driven to attend talks where they hear about that disabled sister who spent 300 hours in field ministry every month? Or they tell about the African brothers selling their vegetables so that a Kingdom Hall can be built? Every single so-called encouraging talk is basically about showing the rank and file that it still isn't enough, no matter how much time and energy they are already investing.

Unlike the Mormons who built a government and society around their pseudo-religion, Jehovah Witnesses are recruited through sly and deceptive messengers of false hope and doctrine. Their education comes through publications like Watchtower and Awake and they believe their content as if the computer keys had been punched by God Himself. After all, that's what the shysters in New York tell them. The misguided little people are the ones pound-ing on doors in the blistering sun, torrential rains or bitter cold while the top rank deceivers live the good life with their only responsibility being what lie they will offer their sheep next.

The Watchtower Society was reported as being one of the top 40 NYC corporations with an Annual revenue of 951 million dollars. Where does all of that money go?

If you don't believe the information below, please check with your local elder. Please remember, you have to sound as if you are curious. Asking in a rude manner, or arguing with an elder will get you in trouble.

This is how the old system worked....

Every Kingdom Hall is built on a loan from the Watchtower Bible and Tract Society. That loan was given out of donated money! That loan has to be paid back with interest by each individual congregations. If that loan is not paid in a month, the body of elders of each congregation have to use their own money and pay out of their own pocket, or somehow raise money to pay for the loan.

In 2014 however, there has been a new letter to the Body of Elders sent out to the society. The letter states that all congergations have been forgiven their debts. But, they are to permanently send in donations to the society in an amount that's either equal to, or greater than their previous mortgage payments. It's like a never ending debt. It's a compulsory "donation" that each congreagation has to send to the society.

The letter says that there are 13000 Kingdom Hall PROJECTS and 35 assembly hall PROJECTS in progress worldwide. Total Congregations Worldwide: 113,823.

If on a monthly basis, each congregation gives one hundred dollars, the Watchtower Bible and Tract Society gets $11,382,300! That's over eleven million dollars a month and close to one hundred and forty million dollars a year! And one hundred dollars is close to the minimum received from most congregations.

The WTBTS has hit the ultimate jackpot!!! Raking in millions of dollars from the congregations worldwide, making them believe that this is what "Jehovah" wants. In reality, about over 80 percent of witnesses accept everything without question from the society.

This reminds me of the November Watchtower Study edition, where the society tells the rank and file members, "at that time the life-saving message that they receive must be obeyed, even if it seems unpractical from a human standpoint."

An additional thing that the letter mentions is that there is a need for 13,000 Kingdom Hall projects, and 35 Assembly halls. Most witnesses automatically figure that 13,000 Kingdom Halls are needed. In reality, If you built 13,000 Kingdom Halls, each with just one congregation and 50 members in total, you would need 650,000 new members!!! But the growth the society has, is not equivalent to 650,000 Members per year. Let's take a look at the real growth:

This information is based on the 2014, and 2013 yearbook provided on wol.jw.org

In 2012, the Jehovah Witnesses listed a total membership of 7,538,994 and in 2013, it had grown to 7,689,377. That's an increase of 159,383. If you divide the increase of the total members of 159,383 by 50 members per congregation, per Kingdom Hall, you would have 3,188.

I used the number 50 to show an extremely low number of members per congregation. However, if you increase that number to 100, the number of Kingdom Halls decrease even further, not counting the fact that most Kingdom Halls are shared by at least 2 congregations. At that rate, you would have to divide by 200. For example, if you divide the total nembers of 159,383 by 100 members for 2 congregations, per Kingdom Hall, you would have 797 Kingdom Halls that would be required to be built. If you divide the total members of 183,608 by 100 members for 2 congregations, per Kingdom Hall, you would have 918 Kingdom Halls that would be required to be built.

If I confused you, I apologize. The point of the above was to show that 13,000 Kingdom Halls is just a ridiculously high number for witnesses to think that they are growing that much.

In fact, now with this new arrangement, I doubt that the society is going to be investing that much money into building new Kingdom Halls, unless of course, with the intent to get more monthly income from them.They will also most likely stop doing Kingdom Hall renovations – because renovating a kingdom hall will now directly cost them money out of their own pockets.

So the only part that costs WTBTS money is when it comes to the printing of books and magazines. The rest is done by volunteers for free. In addition, all those volunteers worldwide, presently at at almost 8 million people donate money to their local WTBTS branches, and also to the headquarters.

How much money do they need? Selling buildings has been the specialty of the WTBTS. They buy a building, renovate it with free labor, then resell the building for double or triple the value. And then they keep asking for more money from their rank and file members.

The purpose of the 1st circuit overseer visit in 2013 was to beg for money. Now you can donate online with a credit card. Where does all of that money go? There's no real accountability. Local congregations show accountability. Where is the accounts report from the WTBTS headquarters?

In 2015, there was an even newer arrangement of building Kingdom Halls that are commercially designed. This was showed in a video-conference to all of the elders in the US. Most likely the rank and file Jehovah's Witnesses do not know about this new plan. However, all those new Kingdom Halls are going to be built using their donations. Why would a religious organization build a commercially styled place of worship? So that it can be readily sold to new bidders who are willing to pay money. The new Kingdom halls can be readily converted into a bank, a restaurant, or any other business. Was Solomon's temple built with a commercial-applications plan? Did Solomon ever plan to sell his temple?

Most witnesses never realize that they are victims of a century old sham. Their dealings are with their local elders who are usually the most radical of their group. To investigate the organization would be an act of extreme offense with dire consequences. This is how complete the brainwashing has been done. They would cover their ears to hear it said, but theologically, Jehovah's Witnesses are a cult of Christianity. The oppressive organization does not represent historical, Biblical Christianity in any way. Sociologically, it is a destructive cult whose false teachings frequently result in spiritual and psychological abuse, as well as needless deaths.

The witnesses are taught to smile and greet people kindly and if there is a spark of interest, to cherry pick verses that appear to support the JW message. While that message may be tainted by the translation created by inept amateurs, in their mind it remains the true word of their God. They are innocents, manipulated into believing that by serving their gods in Brooklyn, New York, they will automatically be entered into heaven. All St. Peter needs to see is the Watchtower in their hand and the pearly gates will swing wide. It's a juvenile belief, indeed. Thinking people don't accept the follies printed in the Watchtower and Awake, but the New York bosses don't seek out the intelligent, the educated – they concentrate on humble or the academically educated person who received a form of child abuse by being taught to be a witness of Jehovah.

Children of JW families need to pray that they never become gravely ill, in need of a transfusion. They need to pray that they never have an accident where blood is needed to save their lives. They need to pray that they will not be sacrificed to the insane beliefs of their prents. The intelligent ones will pray that one day they will escape from the restrictive life of their parents and the JW belief system; that they can dance, drink a Coca Cola, enjoy the marvels of Christmas and essentially be normal.

The bewildering thing that brings a tinge of saeness is that the teaching of this lunacy brings millions of dollars into the accounts of the organization in New York – and it is tax free. The hard working member of society bears the burden of making up for the millions in taxes evaded by organizations like this.

Perhaps the most pathetic part of the doctrine of this sect – and it's something the typical witness never thinks about – is that its followers and believers want this world to end. They want the end of the world so that they can be taken up to heaven and if millions of others suffer in the calamity, it's then no concern of theirs. They knocked on the disbeliever's door, so the condemned had a chance and rejected it. It is these things they believe as they yearn for everything humanity has ever known or achieved to be utterly destroyed – and they hope it comes soon. If that isn't lunacy, then we need to liberate every asylum in the world.

To imagine that nearly eight million people are dedicated of this dribble is discouraging to the idea that humanity has progressed and reached a higher level of awareness and ability. One must wonder where could be found eight million people so gullible and void of reasoning powers. How could so many put critical thinking in the trash can? But they will continue knocking on doors and believing that 144,000 of their number will go to heaven and the rest will never die and prefer to live on earth. Of course, the earth will be their sole domain since all those who turned them away are roasting in hell.

Certainly thee's something to be enjoyed in this scenario. The JWs – as sole residents of the earth – can take their clothes from the finest stores and cook food left in the best of restaurants. The can drive cars off the showroom floors and empty the jewelry stores at will. But will God keep running the generators producing electricity for them? Will God produce oil and gasoline as they need it? Will the water system continue to function without any sinners to operate it? Or will they alowly decline into a primitive world to match their thinking? Will they learn to make candles and will they hunt the forests for meat? Or will the great calamity ending the earth as it was known also kill animal life and leave them with little resources for sustenance?

In this imagined paradise, will no one get sick or injured? JWs are told they will never die while living in the paradise of the new world but little is said about injury or illness. Imagine having an accident and going blind or losing a leg – forever. JW artists portray the new paradise in JW publications and show a child resting against a tiger or people gazing in awe over vast expanses of green fields. The imagery is impressive, but the logic is anemic.

I'm sure some will call me cynical and abrasive to the religious beliefs of others but it is difficult to be sensitive to ignorance. I hope, of course, that some Jehovah Witnesses do make it to heaven, but if they do, I am convinced God will hide behind the door and pretend that He's not home.

THE GREATEST SHOW ON EARTH

Census, a Greek writer at the time of the early church, wrote of the Christian teachings, "They are forever repeating: Do not examine. Only believe, and thy faith will make thee blessed. Wisdom is a bad thing in life, foolishness is to be preferred." He also lamented that ignorant men were allowed to preach, and says that "weavers, tailors, fullers, and the most illiterate and rustic fellows set up to teach strange paradoxes. They openly declared that none but the ignorant were fit disciples for the God they worshipped and one of their rules was, let no man that is learned come among them."

The rules haven't changed much when it comes to the wacky world of evangelists. Everything about their spectaculars depends on faith. If logic ever came into the picture, you'd probably see them at a McDonalds window asking if you want fries. But these are the miracle workers who with a wave of their hand have idiots falling from their chairs in the balcony. I don't know if they are shills or just stupid, but it happens.

Miracles have always been an integral part of all religions. And if people believe in miracles, some shyster will come along to give them a few. We can turn the pages of history back to almost any point where there were believers and find a miracle worker. Bochia of the Persians performed miracles and the places where he performed them were consecrated and crowds went to visit them. Ilorus, the Egyptian savior, performed great miracles, including raising the dead to life. Zoroaster, the founder of the religion of the Persians, was persecuted and escaped by performing miracles. Osiris of Egypt also performed miracles as did the virgin goddess Isis.

Pilgrimages were made by the sick to the temples of Isis in Egypt. Diodorus, the Grecian historian, says that, "Those who go to consult in dreams the goddess Isis recover perfect health. Many whose cure has been despaired of by physicians have by this means been saved, and others who have long been deprived of sight, or of some other part of the body, by taking refuge, so to speak, in the arms of the goddess, have been restored to the enjoyment of their faculties."

The point is that for some people, revivals are God's marketplace and the choir, theatrical lighting and motion, the charismatic phoney and the electrifying zeal of ten thousand morons is exactly what they need to have a spiritual experience.

The invention of television was all the world of evangelists needed to have mega audiences and to spew their brand of religion. It wasn't pretty – in fact it was often grotesque and mindless – but it caught on and soon they had audiences in the millions. That also meant that they could ask for their "donations" to support God's work like buying BMWs, private jets, mansions and amusement parks.

Billy Graham said that he could reach more people in just one night on television than the Apostle Paul in all of his life, and that's no doubt true. Christian television and televangelism in effect are the main, if not the only, religious experience that many people have today. Any wrong teaching, distorted information, false idea, or bad image will be their only reference of this religion. For instance, Benny Hinn's show "This Is Your Day" airs in over 130 countries over several different networks, making it the most widely seen program in the world. And "This Is Your Day" promotes every unbiblical doctrine that is to be advocated. Beyond that, it insults thinking people with Broadway type presentations, one of which actually had the Holy Ghost on the stage with Hinn – and, of course, Hinn was the only one the Holy Ghost would permit to be there with him. As arrogant and obnoxious as it sounds, even more repugnant was that there were thousands of brain-dead believers standing in awe as a line of preachers came to be touched by the divine spirit, each collapsing dramatically as it happened. Not only is this profane, it's so incredibly childish that professional wrestling does a better job than that. But it goes to prove that some people – and "some" includes millions – will believe absolutely anything.

Many of these televangelists claim to have the power of God to heal the sick and perform other miracles; power which can be seen in every show, where large numbers of people supposedly get healed. But if just dozens of people were really miraculously healed, it would be very difficult to keep it from the media, which is constantly searching for news. A large number of miracles and healing would be a great proof that Christianity is the real religion. Nonetheless, no news about healing or any other miracle. Instead, what we see is witnesses and victims denouncing those performers, and documentaries and other reporting exposing them and proving them to be a fraud.

In March of 1992, the news contained the story, "A second widow who received letters promising miracles for her dead husband has sued television evangelist Robert Tilton, setting the stage for what her attorney said could be a class-action lawsuit.

"Dorothy Ries said yesterday that within a month after her husband, Fred, died of throat cancer Jan. 6, Tilton sent him three letters promising healing and miracles.

"It was the second such suit filed against Tilton in two weeks. At a news conference, Ries displayed a letter that her attorney said was a replica of a note Tilton sent to another man whose widow last month sued the preacher. Tilton's ministry is based in Farmers Branch, Texas, near Dallas.

"In the February suit, Beverly Crowley of Wynona, Okla., said she received mail from Tilton promising a miracle for her husband, Tom, five months after he died of kidney failure.

"The letters to both men said God told Tilton that he wanted to restore their health."

In 2002 and again in 2005 Dateline NBC did an expose on Benny Hinn and his ministry. He was asked to provide medical proof of the miracles he and his followers claim to be experiencing, but to date no medical proof of any healing or other definitive evidence has been provided by the ministry. But a number of the people that he and other preachers proclaimed healed have died. Although many could have been saved, if they had gotten adequate medical attention on time.

Dateline NBC also questioned the ministry's financial integrity. Although Benny Hinn's ministry does not release information about its finances to the public, Dateline was able to find many problems in the financial aspect. An investigation showed severe problems with accountability, revealing that Benny Hinn maintains an extravagant lifestyle at the expense of his followers. In 1997 a CNN report also criticized him for lavish spending practices. There are estimates that total ministry revenue exceeds $100 million a year. This has allowed him to accumulate a fortune as a television faith healer and to live in a big, expensive mansion. The personal perks for Hinn, family and his entourage include a $10 million seaside mansion; a private jet with annual operating costs of about $1.5 million; a Mercedes SUV and convertible, each valued at about $80,000.

Televangelism has become a business, where preachers work towards better rating and more donations. It takes the Scriptures out of context to manipulate people to give, often beyond their means. It is estimated to be a several billion dollars business that preys on the elderly (mostly women), the poor, the biblically illiterate, and the desperate; all in the name of God. And it is not just a handful of television preachers, it is most of them. One reason is that there is no accountability for televangelists. If you sent money to any of them, you most likely helped that particular preacher to pay for his jet or his mansion.

England has a law that requires claims of healing and other supernatural phenomena to be verified before being broadcast. The United States should enact a similar law and use the IRS to regulate what they do. The U.S. congress should also enact some laws to protect the public from these professional deceivers. At present, churches are exempted from disclosing their finances, so anything goes with impunity. Most of these televangelists do not release any type of financial information. They do not want anyone to know what they do with the contributions and donations received by the ministry. That tax-exempt status is simply wonderful.

Paul and Jan Crouch are the owners of Trinity Broadcasting Network, the largest faith based broadcaster network in the world. This is a $4 billion operation and yet they are still begging for money, although they live like kings. The Los Angeles Times has reported that their combined salary is nearly $800,000. TBN has posted surpluses averaging nearly $60 million a year since 1997. Its balance sheet for 2002, the most recent available according to the Times investigation, lists net assets of $583 million, including $238 million in Treasury bonds and other government securities and $31 million in cash. TBN collects more than $120 million a year from viewers of its Christian programming — more than any other TV ministry. TBN owns an airplane worth $7 million and two mansions whose combined worth is $10 million, a mountain retreat in Lake Arrowhead, Calif.; a ranch in Texas; and at least 30 other homes. Such figures have prompted questions about why the network continues to plead for contributions. But no mention is ever made of the ministry's flush finances. A central element of their gospel is that no one is too poor or too indebted to donate. Do they really want your money?

In 1998, a former TBN employee, Enoch Lonnie Ford, was paid $425,000 for agreeing not to publicize Mr. Ford's allegations that he and TBN founder Paul Crouch had a homosexual affair years earlier. Questions still remain regarding the source of those funds.

Randy and Paula White are the founders and pastors of Without Walls, a nondenominational church. The newspaper Tampa Tribune reported that Without Walls took in $35 million in tithes and offerings in 2006, according to a recent audit by Lewis, Birch & Ricardo CPAs. How much of the revenue goes to the Whites, the couple won't say. The audit lists more than $5.5 million in salaries for 2006. They travel in a $1.9 million business jet. They own a home they purchased for $2.1 million and a $3.5 million Trump Tower condo in New York. They believe in appearances. Both the Whites have undergone cosmetic surgery, seeming to grow younger over the past five years. "We're on television, and you've got to look the part," Randy said.

In his autobiography, "Without Walls," and on a 2002 Web profile, Randy said he enrolled at the former Lee College in Cleveland, Tenn., and earned a bachelor's degree in ministerial studies and a master's in divinity. He said he was awarded an honorary doctorate in humane letters from Virginia State University in Petersburg, Va. Representatives from both schools said he did not receive degrees there, though Lee confirmed he took two classes. According to documents Randy gave the Tribune in April, he received a doctorate of humane letters from Commonwealth Assistance Foundation Institute of International Studies in Alexandria, Va., in May 1993. An in-depth Internet search found no mention of the school. There is no telephone listing for it.

According to a 2003 series in the St. Louis Post-Dispatch, the ministry of Joyce Meyer spent $4 million from 1999 to 2003 on five homes for the Meyer family. The ministry pays for all utilities, maintenance and landscaping costs. Joyce and Dave live in the largest house, $2 million, 10,000 square-foot property with a large fountain, gazebo, private putting green, pool, poolhouse and an independently cooled garage. Meyer told the Post-Dispatch that with her being on the road most of the time, she doesn't have time to take care of maintenance issues herself.

Mike Murdock Ministry documents show that several individual donors give thousands of dollars. Murdock urges people watching his TV program, Wisdom Keys, to sacrifice by giving money to his ministry even if they cannot afford to do so. He says God will provide. He also asks them to send specific dollar amounts, such as $58. Many do just that. In December 2003, more than 60 checks written for $58 were returned to the ministry because the donors' checking accounts had too little money to cover them. Other months reviewed showed similar returned checks. Is he sacrificing too? Nope, he lives a life of luxury. He wears a $25,000 Rolex, owns a private jet, likes fast cars, expensive jewelry, and lives in a estate with exotic animals, which includes a lion and a camel. According to Randy Foret (ex-general manager for the ministry), after articles by the Fort Worth Star-Telegram came out questioning the spending practices of the Mike Murdock Evangelistic Association, Murdock started a church to avoid public scrutiny of the ministry's finances through the tax exempt status. As a church , its spending is kept secret. Good move Mike! No more uncomfortable questions to answer. He showed wisdom there, although the title of doctor is honorary, given by the International Seminary in Florida. In reality, Murdock dropped out of Southwestern Assemblies of God University in Waxahachie in 1966.

David and Barbara Cerullo bring home more than $1.5 million a year, making him the best-paid leader of any religious charity tracked by watchdog groups. His salary dwarfs those of executives leading far larger religious nonprofits. David and Barbara Cerullo live in a 12,000 square-foot lakefront home in south Charlotte – complete with an elevator and an 1,100-square-foot garage. Their home, in a gated community, is valued at $1.7 million, real estate records show. At a time when Inspiration Networks has been cutting jobs, freezing wages and even adjusting the office thermostat to save money.

In 1988 pictures were taken of Jimmy Swaggart with a prostitute. He issued a lengthy on-air apology for his actions and even cried on television. The best part about that confession is that he never mentioned exactly what the crime was. The photographs had been taken as a result of a rivalry with fellow TV Evangelist Marvin Gorman, who had been defrocked shortly after being accused of immorality by Swaggart. In 1991 again he was stopped by police in a car with another prostitute.

Peter Popoff was a self-proclaimed faith healer. He was ex- posed as a fraud when it was discovered that his healing was part of an elaborately staged setup including planting audience members. Skeptic James Randi visited a show and discovered radio trans- missions of Popoff's wife, Elizabeth, off-stage reading information which she and her aides had gathered from earlier conversation with members of the audience. Popoff would simply listen to these promptings with his in-ear receiver and repeat what he heard to the crowd. After tapes of these transmissions were played on The Tonight Show, Popoff's popularity and viewing audiences declined sharply, and his ministry declared bankruptcy later that year.

In 1991, Diane Sawyer and ABC News conducted an investigation of Robert Tilton (as well as two other Dallas-area televangelists, W.V. Grant and Larry Lea). The investigation, spearheaded by Trinity Foundation president Ole Anthony and broadcast on ABC's Primetime Live on November 21, 1991, found that Tilton's ministry threw away prayer requests without reading them, keeping only any money or valuables sent to them by viewers, garnering his ministry an estimated $80 million a year.

Mark Haville's is an extraordinary story. Converted into the Pentecostal/Charismatic church he quickly came under the spell of the Word-Faith teaching of men like Kenneth Copeland. But things did not stay that way for Mark. Still in his mid-20's, Mark became an itinerant minister travelling the country earning large sums of money through his ability to perform 'signs and wonders'. Remarkably, he has renounced his former life, his beliefs, and his practices as a Word-Faith minister and is now speaking out boldly against the beliefs and practices of the current Signs and Wonders movement.

"Basically, I copied it," he says. "I learned gradually to do what all these speakers like Copeland, Cerullo, Benny Hinn and others do. They manipulate audiences and individuals simply by the power of suggestion. They call the result 'signs and wonders'. They are deluded. Gradually, I too had learned the process of controlling meetings and inducing hypnotic techniques through suggestion in churches. I did many of the so-called signs and wonders.

"First, the people in these meetings are already coming with high expectancy – they want it to be God. Second, you need to create the right atmosphere – hence the long periods of singing certain types of songs to make people feel relaxed and warm.

"It is very important to use songs and words that are focused on the Holy Spirit. This creates a far more mystical atmosphere. Songs full of Christian or Biblical doctrine work against people suspending their critical faculties. The effect is to create a mindlessness that will open your audience up to suggestion. Most people have no idea just how powerful suggestion can be. Let me add that all this is not necessarily done wilfully by leaders. This is something many of them have stumbled upon. It works, so they do it and call it 'the Holy Spirit'. If you do not believe that it is God that is doing these things in the meeting, there is no way you will fall down. But remember, I am the one running the show. Just like any good hypnotist, I will be 'working' the audience. I can tell which ones are the more suggestive by asking certain questions. I can then bring people forward, having gotten them into a very relaxed and accepting state. You have to remember, people who come really want to believe that God is at work. By telling them to stand in a particular place I am strongly influencing their belief that by standing where I have told them – on that exact spot – something is going to happen. By telling them someone will stand behind them, because we wouldn't want them to get hurt if they fall, it is all heightening the sense of anticipation and suggestiveness. The rest is easy.

"I find it very hard knowing how I unconsciously deceived good people into believing that the Holy Spirit was at work when it was common or garden hypnosis. But at the time I suppose I did believe, however incorrectly, that these things were the activity of God. But the reality is, I learned these techniques by watching others, and anybody can do them given enough training. They are psychological techniques – nothing else."

A person identifying themselves as only "Glen" posted in a site called *Endtime Prophesies* told of having attended a Benny Hinn revival in Orlando, Florida and some of his comments should remind us of what Mark Haville said about how he bilked people.

"Much time was taken to sing songs to the Lord in praise and worship and that was great." What did Haville say? "Second, you need to create the right atmosphere – hence the long periods of singing certain types of songs to make people feel relaxed and warm."

But Glen continues, "However some things took place that once Again I can say that were used to make people think that some healings took place there that did not actually take place. And here is what I base this statement on. I myself do have a disability. I came through the entrance where the disabled people entered the stadium. There was a section of the stadium that was set aside for people in wheelchairs and I kept a very close eye on that section when the healings or so called healings were taking place. When Mr Hinn started his healing portion of his ministry his people would try to encourage people to stand up out of their wheelchairs and so on. I noticed that as his people were going around trying to get people to stand up and walk that most of what I saw the people would try but then sit right back down in disappointment and I saw a few even start crying when they were unable to walk. I saw this time and time again. People being encouraged to walk and the people not being healed but sitting right back down in disappointment without a healing. I was careful to watch all that was going on.

"Now suddenly Mr Hinn said, "Now bring up all those empty wheelchairs" and I saw *his people* bring up onto the stage about 15 or so empty wheelchairs and the crowd began to cheer, but the so called *empty wheelchairs* did not come from the section where the people who came off the street into the stadium but rather it appeared that the *empty wheelchairs* were brought from the side of the stage and seemed to be props and not legitimate wheelchairs that real people came in and got out of. This is what I saw and a person I was with saw it as well. The so called *empty wheelchairs* seemed to be props brought from the side of the stage and I did not see anybody who legitimately came in a wheelchair from the street actually stand up and walk. Every time I saw them try to get a person out of their wheelchair, it was not successful. But yet now a bunch of practically brand new *empty wheelchairs* were brought up on stage and It seemed they were props and not legitimate *empty wheelchairs* that legitimate people got out of. At least some deception was used there.

"Also as far as what was allowed to be shown on camera was very carefully orchestrated. Nobody from the audience was allowed on the stage unless they first claimed to have had a healing and I also felt like at least a few people that claimed to be healed did not come from the legitimate audience. Mr Hinn's people brought up a few people and they actually would speak for the person and not let the person speak themselves; it was something like. 'Mr Hinn this is John Doe who has had such and such disease for 7 years and now he has been healed.' They were careful about what was allowed on camera and who was allowed on stage and what they were able to speak in front of the audience. It was very much controlled.

"There was also a lady who came up there and claimed to be healed and it appeared as if it was staged. I did not see this lady in the wheelchair section and her testimony was such a picture perfect type of story and seemed to be very phony almost as if it had been rehearsed. It's possible that it was legitimate but it seemed very suspicious. This lady came from the side of the stage at just the right time and had this very perfect type of healing story and she seemed to know exactly what to say at the right time all in perfect sync with Mr. Hinn's healing message. It is possible it was real but was all very suspicious.

"It also got to the point where Mr. Hinn was talking about how he was 'hot with the annointing' and then he began waving his magic finger at people on stage and people were falling down supposedly slain in the spirit. But the funny thing was is that it was mostly his own people that were doing this. He came on stage with about 20 or so people in the beginning and those seemed to be the people that were falling all over the place. They were very careful who they let on the stage and I know for a fact that a large portion of the people that were on the stage falling down by direction of Mr. Hans magic finger were part of his entourage. Some of his own pastors would start running at Mr. Hinn and Mr. Hinn would wave his magic finger and they would start convulsing and falling down and all of that in a very over dramatic way and they were all the people that I saw him enter the area with."

And it was poor Benny who moaned during one interview, "It hurts when people call you a fake and a fraud." Obviously, he should hurt more often.

If my wife saw a photo of me walking the streets of Rome while holding the hand of a shapely blond, there would be some fast talking to be done and none of it would be believed. But when the same thing happened to Benny, he denied the entire affair – and I do mean *affair.*

The news reports stated, "Television preachers Benny Hinn and Paula White have rejected reports in the press last week suggesting that they are romantically involved."

The two Faith Healers and prosperity teachers were caught by a Papparatzi, and the photo was published in the infamous gossip magazine The National Enquirer. The magazine showed pictures of the televangelists entering and leaving a hotel in Rome holding hands. They deny any wrongdoing during their visit to Italy, saying that they had been there for ministry duties and were never alone.

Paula White responded, "We were never alone and were in the constant company of staff and other associates. My relationship with Pastor Benny is genuine and pure and should not be taken out of context."

In February, 2010, Hinn's wife filed for divorce after 30 years of marriage. White split from her husband Randy in 2007. MSNBC.com reports that both Hinn and White said they were in Italy to meet with Vatican officials, traveling independently for respective ministry duties. The Norwegian Christian Daily Dagen, did not buy Hinn's claim of a Vatican appointment at face value. A journalist called up the Vatican secretariat, to cross check if Hinn had had meet with Vatican officials.

Priest Federico Lombardi is the official spokesman for the Vatican. He denies that Hinn had any official appointments in the Vatican last week. But Lombardi confirms that Hinn was invited to the Vatican in 2008.

Benny Hinn was first visited the Vatican in 1989, when he had a personal meeting with Pope John Paul II. "Some of the visitors wanted to sit on the first row at a Papal audience. Hinn was one of them. They were considering to donate funds to the restoration of a large orgel" explains Lombardi.

So Hinn lied. He did not have an appointment with the Vatican. He *just happened* to fly to Rome in the company of Paula White and they *just happened* to stay at the same hotel. They *just happened* to walk down the street holding hands – thinking, of course, that they were on the other side of the world and no one would know. So they just happened to get caught and made up a lie to cover everything.

Imagine being so safe and cozy in faraway Rome and suddenly out of the catacombs arrives an ill-mannered paparazzi photographer and snapped the two during their Italian tryst shopping for a glove that fit for two, and in that moment the evangelical world stopped on a dime.

Naturally, both "independently determined" that the report was utter poppycock – sure, totally independent although they repeated each others' press release – and the news kept on coming. From blogs to mainstream Christian media, no one believed them and everyone doubted them.

Indubitably, they both took a hit and considering both are in the news more for what they are not doing for the Gospel, I would say this could create a ripple in the financial blessings of both of their worlds. Something had to be done, and wouldn't you know it? Evangelist Benny Hinn recently admitted at a crusade in Oakland, California, to having a "friendship" with fellow minister Paula White while he was still married. Not one to totally come clean, however, Hinn admitted only to making the error of taking her along on the trip to Rome. Sure, like every red blooded man, I would take a woman who was only "a friend" on a trip to Rome with me. Only friends – that's Benny's story.

Brother Benny, what in the world do you call the "friendships" you have with fellow male ministers in the TBN circuit? Holy Ghost encounters? No, you call them friendships, you dolt! You know, like the rest of the world. You may roll with the Holy Ghost a lot more than most of us, but I'm fairly certain that doesn't mean you are smarter than the rest of us.

Here's a news flash – I'm married, and I have "friendships". With women. [Cue scary music]. And guess what, I don't fly them to Rome to buy Gucci, fool. But just in case the Church wasn't on to the rouse Captain Nehru was exhibiting, there's more to this uh, "confession."

"A friendship did develop," Hinn said of White in Oakland on July 30, 2010. "Hear this: No immorality whatsoever. These people out there are making it sound like we had an affair. That's a lie."

Dude, your wife split and Paula left her man while he was sick and bankrupt. A classy catch she does not make, but so what? Whatever floats your coifed ~~hairpiece~~ – excuse me, hairdo.

To wrap up the interview, we have the most real words Hinn echoed: "I don't care how strong you are," Hinn added. "I don't care if the anointing of God is mighty on you. Nobody wants to be alone. I don't care who you are. I am a human being just like you."

Yes, Brother Benny. Yes, you are. You stink like us. You mislead like us. You lie like a dog like us. And you did all of them with this report.

"Birds of a feather flock together" is an old adage for a reason. It's been true for so many years. You know who marries cops? Lots of other cops. Lawyers? That's right, attorneys and the occasional paralegals. So, why is it so hard to believe that national televangelists would not find more than just "common ground" in each other's company? Admit that and you gain respect. Admit to a harrowing "friendship" as if you are some eunuch with a slow pulse and people laugh at you even more. Surely, you must have asked the Holy Ghost that one. Well, then again, maybe not.

But Hinn has always had one foot over the ledge, proposing bizarre feelings and ideas. During a sermon on the "Holy Spirit", Hinn offered the following testimony:

"One of the strangest experiences I had a few years ago was visiting Aimee's tomb in California.

"This Thursday I'm on TBN. Friday I am gonna go and visit Kathryn Kuhlman's tomb. It's close by Aimee's in Forest Lawn Cemetery.

"I've been there once already and every so often I like to go and pay my respects brcause this great woman of God has touched my life. And that grave, uh, where she's buried is closed, they built walls around it. You can't get in without a key and I'm one of the very few people who can get in.

"But I'll never forget when I saw Aimee's tomb. It's incredibly dramatic. She was such a lady that her tomb has seven-foot angels bowing on each side of her tomb with a gold chain around it. As incredible as it is that someone would die with angels bowing on each side of her grave, I felt a terrific anointing when I was there. I actually, I – hear this – I trembled when I visited Aimee's tomb. I was shaking all over. God's power came all over me.

"I believe the anointing has lingered over Aimee's body. I know this may be shocking to you. And I'm going to take David [Palmquist] and Kent [Mattox] and Sheryl [Palmquist] this week.

"They're gonna come with me. You—you—you gonna feel the anointing at Aimee's tomb. It's incredible. And Kathryn's. It's amazing. I've heard of people healed when they visited that tomb. They were totally healed by God's power. You say, 'What a crazy thing.' Brother, there's things we'll never understand. Are you all hearing me?"

Maybe it was while visiting Aimee McPherson's tomb that he got the inspiration to play house with Paula in Rome. After all, Aimee – this "such a lady" was well known for her own escapades. We need to take a short trip back to 1926 to appreciate this early evangelist who was far from being a lady. I have personally visited her old home in Elsinore, California and talked to some who knew her.

On that day in 1926, A Coast Guard cutter patrolled just off-shore as deep-sea divers plunged into the water. Aimee Semple McPherson, evangelist, faith-healer, founder of the Foursquare Gospel Church and builder of the Angelus Temple, was believed to have disappeared during a swim on May 18 of that year. In the hours that followed, rescuers were sparing no effort to find her.

"God wouldn't let her die," one of her believers told a reporter. "She was too noble. Her work was too great. Her mission was not ended. She can't be dead."

Already, one young church member had drowned herself in her grief. Soon after that, a diver died while trying to find McPherson's body. In the coming days, her followers would dynamite the waters of Santa Monica bay, hoping to raise her body from the depths. Yet the blasts surfaced only dead fish, and the passing time merely gave rise to countless rumors. She'd disappeared to have an abortion. Or plastic surgery. Or an affair. As the days turned to weeks, McPherson's body, much to the chagrin of police and the California Fish and Game Commission, remained missing. Soon, witnesses were coming forward to contradict the report, given by McPherson's secretary, Emma Shaeffer, that the evangelist had vanished shortly after entering the water.

There were accounts from a detective in San Francisco that McPherson was spotted at a railway station there. "I know her well by sight," the detective said, "and I know that I am not mistaken." A ransom note delivered to McPherson's mother, Minnie Kennedy, demanded $50,000 for the safe return of her daughter and warned, "Mum's the word—keep police away." Meanwhile, some faithful church members, convinced that the evangelist was dead, clung to the belief that she would be resurrected by supernatural powers.

Newspaper headlines trumpeted alleged McPherson sightings in cities across the United States. Another ransom letter surfaced— this one promising to sell the evangelist into "white slavery" unless a half-million dollars was paid in cash. Convinced her daughter was already dead, Minnie Kennedy threw away the letter. By the summer of 1926, no woman in America commanded more headlines than the vanished "Sister Aimee."

The woman at the center of this media storm was born Aimee Elizabeth Kennedy in 1890 to a religious family on a farm in Ontario, Canada. But unlike her Methodist parents, she questioned her faith at a young age and began to rebel against her "tamborine-thumping Salvation Army" mother by reading novels and attending movies.

Yet when Charles Darwin's theory of evolution made its way into Canadian schools, Aimee rebelled again — this time, against evolution. Before her 18th birthday, she married an Irish Pentecostal missionary named Robert Semple, became pregnant, and set off for Asia on an evangelical tour. But the young couple contracted malaria, and Robert succumbed to the disease in August 1910. Aimee gave birth one month later to Roberta Star Semple and returned to the United States.

In 1912, she married an accountant, Harold Steward McPherson, but after giving birth to a son, Rolf McPherson, and trying to settle into a life as a housewife in Providence, Rhode Island, Aimee felt a sudden calling to preach the Gospel. In 1915, she ran out on her husband, taking the children, and hit the road in a Packard touring car ("Jesus is Coming Soon—Get Ready" painted on the side), preaching in tent revivals and churches across the country.

As a female preacher and something of a Pentecostal novelty, Aimee Semple McPherson learned to whip up crowds by speaking in tongues and delivering faith-healing demonstrations in which crutches were tossed aside and the blind were made to see. By 1922, she was breaking attendance records set by the biggest evangelical names at the time, such as Billy Sunday, the former baseball star. In San Diego, more than 30,000 people turned out for one of her events, and the Marines had to be called in for crowd control. There, McPherson laid hands on a supposedly paralyzed woman who rose from her chair and walked. The audience reached a frenzy.

The constant travel began to take its toll, and McPherson decided to settle down in Los Angeles, where she raised funds to build the Angelus Temple in Echo Park. She packed the 5,300-capacity building in services held seven days a week.

By the spring of 1926, McPherson had become a phenomenon — a household name across America. So it came as a surprise to the faithful on May 18, 1926, when McPherson did not arrive at the temple to preach the scheduled sermon and her mother stood in. By the next day, the entire nation was in shock at the news that Sister Aimee had disappeared and likely drowned.

But the prayers of many were soon to be answered: After a month of mourning and unending rumor, McPherson turned up in Agua Prieta, Sonora, a small Mexican town just south of Douglas, Arizona. She claimed to have walked across the "burning sands" of the desert to flee kidnappers and then collapsed. She was taken to a hospital, and in a phone call with the staff, Minnie Kennedy confirmed her daughter's identity by telling them of the location of a scar on her finger and of her daughter's ability to provide the name of her pet pigeon.

Once she'd recovered from her "state of collapse," McPherson gave a bedside interview, saying she'd been lured to a car after swimming and taken across the border by three Americans, including a man named Steve and a woman named Rose. She'd been drugged and held in a Mexican shack for weeks, she said, and her captors had planned on keeping her until they'd received a ransom of half a million dollars. But she foiled the plan, she claimed, when she sawed through the ropes that were restraining her and staggered 20 miles through the desert to Agua Prieta.

Minnie Kennedy rushed to Arizona to reunite with her daughter. "My God, Sister McPherson is alive," she told followers. "Run up the flag on the temple and send out the word broadcast. The Lord has returned his own."

When McPherson came home, a throng of more than 50,000 showed up at the train station to welcome her. In a massive parade featuring airplanes that dropped roses from the skies, the evangelist made a grand re-entrance. But despite the attendance of Los Angeles officials and dignitaries, not everyone was thrilled. The Chamber of Commerce viewed the event as "gaudy display," and Los Angeles District Attorney Asa Keyes called for an investigation into the evangelist's account of a kidnapping.

Within two weeks, McPherson voluntarily appeared before a grand jury as newspapers continued to trumpet accusations of fraud, accompanied by witness "spottings" in Northern California. Gaining the most traction was a story that centered on the fact that Kenneth Ormiston, a married engineer at the Christian radio station KFSG (owned by McPherson's church) disappeared just when McPherson did. The two worked together on McPherson's regular broadcasts. Police were dispatched to a cottage in Carmel-by-the-Sea, where Ormiston had been seen with an unidentified woman during McPherson's disappearance. Ormiston admitted to having an adulterous affair at the time of McPherson's disappearance, but denied that the stranger known as "Mrs. X" was her. After dusting the cottage for fingerprints, however, police found none that matched the evangelist's.

The headlines, gossip and innuendo continued throughout the fall, until a judge determined that there was enough evidence to proceed with the charges of conspiracy and obstruction of justice against McPherson. A jury trial was scheduled for January the following year. However, Keyes had begun to determine that some of his witnesses were unreliable, and he decided to drop the charges.

The kidnapping remained unsolved, and the controversy over a possible hoax went unresolved. Critics and supporters alike thought McPherson should have insisted on a trial to clear her name; instead, she gave her account of the kidnapping in her 1927 book, *In the Service of the King: The Story of My Life*. She would be mocked in the media for years, but the scandal did not diminish her popularity.

Even though the District Attorney recognized that he would have a hard time getting a conviction, the facts certainly warranted his interest in the case. Though McPherson claimed to have wandered for 14 hours across roughly 20 miles of cruel desert covered with mesquite, cactus, and catclaw to escape her captors, when she was found she showed no sign of having been through such an ordeal. Her shoes were not scuffed or worn; there were grass stains on the insteps (there was no grass in the desert through which she claims to have wandered); she was not dehydrated or sunburned; her lips were not parched, cracked, or swollen; her tongue was not swollen; her color was normal; her dress was not torn and bore no dust or perspiration stains. The dress collar and cuffs, though white in color, were barely soiled. Further, she was wearing a watch her mother had given her--a watch she had not taken with her to the beach!

106

Aimee told reporters that her ankles were bruised and torn by ropes from her captivity, but there had been no sign of such injuries when she was examined. An exhaustive search was made to find the adobe shack with a wooden floor where she claimed she had been held captive and which she described in detail to the authorities, but no such shack was found in a 46-square-mile area. Experienced desert men and trackers (one had ridden that country as a cowboy for 37 years, another for 20), who attempted to find her attackers, traced her footsteps, and they found where she apparently had gotten out of an automobile on a road not far from where she was found. The senior tracker testified that he examined every foot of the ground over which she had claimed to have walked and that her tracks had been found nowhere. As for the shack, he said: "I do not know of an adobe house such as the one described by Mrs. McPherson within a hundred and fifty miles of Agua Prieta, and I know every house in this vast area."

A grocery receipt signed by McPherson was found in a Carmel, California, cottage where it appears Aimee had met Ormiston during the time she was alleged to have been kidnapped. Several eye-witnesses testified that they saw the two together during that period.

The year after this episode, McPherson rejected the social taboos preached against by Bible-believing churches of that day. She bobbed her hair and started drinking, dancing, and wearing short skirts. In her early years she had preached against such things. Her choir director, Gladwyn Nichols, and the entire 300-member choir resigned because of her lifestyle. He told the press that they left because of "Aimee's surrender to worldliness – her wardrobe of fancy gowns and short skirts, jewelry, furs, her new infatuation with cosmetics and bobbed hair, all specifically condemned by the Scriptures"

McPherson continued to build her church right up until her death in Oakland, California, in 1944, from what the coroner described as most likely an accidental overdose (Seconol was found in the hotel room where she died) "compounded by kidney failure."

So, since Benny was so enraptured with Aimee, maybe he and Paula should have claimed they were kidnapped. It worked once, who knows? Better yet, Paula could have claimed to have been kidnapped by Benny. That would give her the flight-to-fantasy that she wanted and eliminate some of the competition at the same time. After all, she's no better than Benny when it comes to pulling off her con game in the name of God.

Paula is the queen of cons when it comes to begging for money from gullible, greedy Christians who think that if they somehow give large piles of money to the Laodicean false preachers and teachers, that God will 'send them a blessing' and give them piles of money, too. But guess what? It doesn't work that way. Not even close. And when it comes to 'holy begging' for your 'faith seed', Paula White can pimp it out like few others can.

In one YouTube video she gets all choked up with emotion, that she is able to twist the amazing resurrection story of Lazarus into a springboard for you to write her a check? Girl, she is *working* it. And not just any old check, no sir. She wants the exact amount of $1,144 because that's where in the book of John she is 'claiming your resurrection' from debt and financial oppression.

Paula is truly the blonde leading the blind and she has built a personal worth of five million dollars in the process. That's small change compared to Benny's $42 million but that's not important because everyone knows you can't buy love. Both proved in Rome, however, that with enough money, you can rent it.

"They're going to talk about you and write because it sells ragtag magazines," she said. "They're going to lie on you but God's going to tell you to keep your mouth shut."

Back in 2012 it should have been time for Jimmy Swaggart and Jim Bakker to move over and make room for Benny Hinn in the televangelist's wing of the Hypocrisy Hall of Fame, but it's starting to look like Hinn just might deserve a spot. The National Enquirer - admittedly not the most credible source of journalism, but one that has gotten this affair-type stuff right on more than one occasion (think John Edwards) – turned his world upside down and forced him to be on the defensive – lies and all.

At the time, Hinn issued a video in which he denied the allegations, and blamed Satan, other preachers and the media for his troubles. And, he ended his "friendship" with White, claiming it was too costly for his ministry. He couldn't fool the folks at Strang Communications, publisher of his books, who filed suit against Hinn openly claiming, ""Mr. Hinn was engaged in a public, romantic and otherwise inappropriate relationship with another high-profile minister, who was divorced." Hinn admitted trying to settle the suit out of court but that's not what innocent people do, Benny. Innocent people fight to prove their innocence, not pay someone off to be silent about it. In fact, EEWMagazine reported that, "But court documents claim Hinn acknowledged to his publisher "his inappropriate relationship" with White back in August and agreed that the publisher should be reimbursed for the book advances totaling $300,000, but Hinn failed to pay."

Filmmaker Anthony Thomas traveled across the world in search of a miracle, examining contemporary faith healing and the people who say they change your life. At one point they concentrated on Hinn.

"Well, this is the saddest thing about it, because you have a theology which implies that the more right you are with God, the more likely you are to receive a miracle. So you have people who come forward, who feel they've received a miraculous recovery and then go into a kind of denial. When their situation gets worse they stop going to the doctors, they stop getting further medical attention.

"And one woman who we were very close to, suffering from lung cancer, so wanted to believe that she was cured that she never saw here oncologist again. He (Hinn) heard about her death through us."

"The Catholic Church has laid down the strictest conditions for what is defined as a miracle," he added. "And I'll give you one very interesting statistic: Lourdes is a famous place of miracles, but they're no longer encouraging people to accept – expect a physical cure. Now, in the entire history of Lourdes, over 150 years, now you get 5 million people going there a day, so you can work out the numbers. Only 66 miracles have been confirmed. Benny Hinn claims more than that on -- at a single event."

One of my favorite Benny Hinn moments came with his healing of ex-heavyweight boxing champion, Evander Holyfield. Now Holyfield turned pretty much into a religious fanatic in the latter part of his career and maybe for that reason he decided to give Hinn a try. Having developed some heart problems, he appeared on Hinn's television program where millions heard Hinn announced, "The Lord is telling me right now. He is repairing Holyfield's heart completely." It was a big deal. Even Time Magazine carried the story. But then medical specialists discovered that the whole heart problem was because of an inaccurate diagnosis from Holyfield's internist. Holyfield later told sports writer Terence Moore that he didn't think Hinn had any influence on his so-called heart condition. "There really wasn't anything to heal," said Holyfield. "I didn't have a problem with my heart to begin with."

Known for his stinginess – remember, he didn't want to pay his publisher $300,000 and wound up with a lawsuit – when donations weren't up to par at the crusade where Holyfield's "cure" took place, he asked Holyfield to kick in $100,000 to help cover expenses. When Holyfield agreed, Hinn apparently realized he had a soft touch here and asked for the full $265,000 to cover the entire cost of the crusade. Holyfield finally paid it all for Hinn.

Inside Edition had an interest in Hinn for some time and kept an eye on his claims of healings. At one crusade Hinn claimed to have healted a mother and her two small children of AIDS. He was later confronted by *Inside Edition* who presented him with evidence that the woman and the children were not really healed. In fact, one of the children didn't even belong to the woman. Hinn's response was typical, "All I know is what she said. I was praying she would get a miracle and I put it on, showing me praying for someone with AIDS to give someone hope with AIDS."

When Larry King asked Hinn if he could cure people on the street, he responded, "Well, yes, but look, it's not as easy because you really need that atmosphere of faith." At other times, however, he stated that there had been people cured while driving on their way to the crusade or while waiting in line to enter.

On March 16, 1997, *Impact News* gave a couple of common examples of people who attend the crusades for healing. Linda Tyson brought her 17 year old son, Shandez who was injured in football and is now incapacitated in a wheel chair. She went to his crusade in Atlanta with much hope and faith. The first and second night she could not get in. Then Hinn prayed for Shandez briefly backstage and they went home still hoping for a miracle. Laura Twilly was dying of cancer and came to be healed. She was interviewed in a screening process. As often happens, she said she could not walk, but after attending she felt better and was very excited. Not truly healed, she walked with a new strength at the crusade; she died four weeks later.

Why are some accepted on stage while others are not? Larry king inquired about the screening process. Benny said, "I have doctors. I have people that are trained who make sure that the person is healed. I don't really pray for the sick. I pray for them, you know, after they are healed. On the program I pray for the sick when I say now stretch your hands. But in the crusade itself, they are healed just sitting there, see? And so they're checked. They're questioned. 'Do you know what's wrong with you?' And then the doctor, or whoever, will check as much as possible, of course. And, ah, you know the pain is gone and now of course when someone is healed of cancer or leukemia, or something, we will always say, 'Go back to

110

your doctor and make sure you really are healed because you really can't tell by just asking some questions.'"

Wait a minute, Benny. Why do you pray for the sick on your television program, *This is Your Day* and not at the crusades? You're not fooling anyone. You do pray for people to be healed during crusades, making such statements as, "If God will heal one he'll heal two, if he will heal two he'll heal three." How logical is it to attribute the sicknesses to demons and then cast them out of people who were already healed?

Are the demonized healed? When Benny pronounces that they will never be sick again or commands the sickness to go, what does that mean? Other faith healers call that "healing," so should you, Benny.

A few years ago after *Inside Edition* exposed such inconsistencies as when Hinn said, "We will not say they're healed or something like this, because how do we know they are healed. They're telling us they're healed, so we can't speak for the people." Then why do we hear that a left ear is being "healed," cancer is "healed," a blood condition is "healed," deafness is going and that sort of thing?

On the *Larry King Live* show, Benny shared a story about being sick with a head cold. He claimed that he turned on the TV and saw his own program. He explained, "I had a terrible cold one day. Oh, it was terrible! I couldn't breathe, it was terrible. I turned on my program . . ."

Larry King interrupted with a mock astonishment, "No. You cured yourself!."

Benny Hinn on the show said, 'Stretch your hands!' and I thought . . ."

Larry: "Come on, Benny!"

"Oh I thought to myself – so stupid you know for me to go and actually put my hands – and suddenly the Lord really spoke to my heart and said, 'The man on television is my anointed servant.' I went over and put my hands on the screen and yes; I got healed."

Benny claimed he was healed by his own video! I would find it more believable if he had breathed on himself. Seriously, if this is possible, people no longer need him in live crusades; they could just show his videos in hospitals and touch more people's lives with the power of God. A Benny Hinn video would be a greater miracle than the Apostle Paul's handkerchief? Why did the Lord say the man on the TV was anointed and not the live person? Obviously, Benny's promo was a pitch to the viewers to lend confidence in his ministry!

"Come on Benny!" are my sentiments also! Characteristically, Hinn tells people what they like to hear.

One has to ask why Hinn doesn't go visit hospitals where he could do the most good? Does his power to heal only function and big money crusades? Oh, but wait, Hinn does claim that he went to a Catholic hospital in Canada and conducted a service with some other penta-costal ministers. He claims that this hospital's chapel was filled with clinically ill, bed-ridden patients. The doctors and nurses watched as they anointed people. He said that it looked like an earthquake hit because the people were lying everywhere. His story went on into a miracle mystery tour of Benny's imaginations.

What Benny chronicled got investigated by G. Richard Fisher of *Personal Freedom Outreach*. He wrote, "Something of this magnitude probably never would have been forgotten at Sault Saint Marie General Hospital. How did it ever escape the attention of the news media? As described by Hinn, this could be the most incredible happening Canada had ever experienced. Many people could verify it, yet there is neither anyone at the hospital who remembers it as Hinn tells it, nor are there records to confirm the fact.

"The real story is neither extraordinary nor miraculous. Here is what actually happened. Our connection with the hospital got us the response, 'Benny who?' Director of community relations for Sault Saint Marie General Hospital, Lois C. Krause instantly denied all that Hinn claimed. She said it could not have happened in the way that Hinn's book described. She laughed after reading a copy of the story. No miracles occurred in the hospital as Hinn claims, she said, adding that no patients left that day due to miraculous occurrences. Some older staff members did recall Hinn's name but did not remember anything as extraordinary as Hinn's book describes. They did not deny the possibility that chapel meetings were held, but did not recall the meeting as recounted in Hinn's book, Welcome Holy Spirit. Mother Superior Mary Francis, also disputed Hinn's account. The hospital released this statement which included the following remarks: *'No such events have ever occurred at General Hospital. His pronouncements can neither be verified through the medical records nor by testimony by past or present personnel of this hospital. Mr. Hinn's claims are outlandish and unwarranted.'*

In his book, *The Confusing World of Benny Hinn*, Fisher declares that Hinn "embellishes truth and he fabricates, exaggerates and misrepresents events." He went to the hospital but the experiences did not happen anything like he claimed. Nothing supports the extravagant tales appearing in Hinn's books. If we are to offer any apologetics for him, perhaps he meant for the book to be listed as fiction.

Impact News, on March 16, 1997, presented Mr. Hinn with this question, "May I ask what your annual salary is?" Benny explained with difficulty, "Well, John, you knew that that would be private, but ah, I knew you would ask it.

"I can tell you this – um – if it wasn't for my book royalties, I'd be dead. But when Larry King asked about his income, he said, "People ask me what I do with this money from my books, for example, from my royalty. I give much of that away." At a revival in Hawaii he said, "Anything that sells, I don't get a cent. All the books, all the tapes, I get nothing. I just get one cent, that's it!"

Impact obtained a copy of his five year employment contract. It set Hinn's salary at $250,000 a year plus unspecified group benefits. Benny responded to another question, "So you're asking me if it's accurate?" (*Impact*: "If it's reasonably accurate.") "It's close." Later Hinn told *Impact* his yearly income including royalties was much more, between $500,000 and $1,000,000 a year. Two to four times as much is not close!

Hardly a man in history ever made so much money preaching "the Gospel!" Benny said softly, "I would love the day to come where, ah, I would live only on my royalties and would not have to take a salary from the ministry at all." Mr. Hinn has been quoted saying, "I have lost complete desire for anything to do with the world. My worldly desires are gone." On Larry king he said that he has needs while defending his opulent lifestyle, claiming that he gives much of his book royalties away. In truth, what comes through the ministry stays in the ministry. The week following the *Impact* program on *Larry King Live*, Larry asked, "Big salary?" Benny said, "Um. It's OK." Larry inquired, "Are you wealthy?" Benny said, "No, I'm not wealthy." What is Mr. Hinn's definition of wealthy or even well-to-do? He recently moved from the exclusive Heathrow Development to an even more exclusive Alaqua $685,000 home. On *Impact* he stated, "The home...the car, I paid for. The ministry pays nothing when it comes to home and car and all that." That sounds wealthy! His suits are tailored, his shoes are Italian leather, and his wrist and finger are endowed with gold and diamonds. He wears a diamond Rolex watch. How many people do you know who enjoy this kind of lifestyle that are not rich? Benny says, "What's the big deal, for goodness sake? What am I supposed to do, drive a Honda?" When Larry King asked about his Mercedes, he was not aware that Benny traded it in for a Jaguar.

DAVID ELLSWORTH

On *Larry King Live* he stated, "We don't force the people to give. People give out of their own freewill and it pays the bills." He asked the Lord to speak to the people of Hawaii, to give generously saying, "I'm asking the Lord to speak to many of you to give a thousand dollars tonight. Some can give even mor, at least a hundred dollars to help us." He cleverly lifted a greater offering, instructing the people, "If you have nothing to give but you really want to give something to the Lord's work, would you mind standing up. Now would you look around and see those standing around near you? Come on! Somebody get up and give them some money so they can give also. There's people standing up who have nothing to give. Somebody give them something to give so they can be blessed!" While freewill is involved there is a lot of coaxing. Once again we hear a double message.

With all the double talk and contradictions in his interviews, could anyone expect that he would tell the truth about Paula White? According to the Orlando Sentinel, "Hinn acknowledged to his publisher 'his inappropriate relationship' with White in August, according to the suit, and agreed that the publisher should get back its money, but he has yet to pay up."

Hinn's full-service ministry includes offering courses at the "Benny Hinn School of Ministry." While the inventory in his online shopping mall may not be as expansive as your typical Wal-Mart, he nevertheless offers up an impressive assortment of products, including art prints, health and healing books, Bibles, videos and cds, greeting cards, an angel keychain, a "Benny Hinn Ministries Dove & Globe Lapel Pin," and an "Ark of the Covenant" prayer shawl. There's also Max One, a product that "provides the most advanced glutathione support you can find-anywhere. Glutathione helps to strengthen the immune system, detoxify the body, fight intracellular inflammation, and neutralize many different types of free radicals." And there's lots more stuff.

Always believing he's right and in need of sympathy, he told one crusade, "Be glad you are not me. If I knew before I started the ministry that I'd be attacked like this, I would have said 'No. Lord thank you.' This is not the first time they do that to me."

With Hinn's 800 number flashing occasionally on the screen, he went on to complain about being scrutinized by the media at every turn. And he talked about being alone: "It's very, very difficult to talk about this, but I have to, otherwise people make up their own stories." He kept saying that there "are things we cannot talk about, but she [his wife] and I kept a clean life, that's a fact.

114

She and I kept a very pure life before God. We kept our marriage vows; there was nothing immoral ever, on her part or my part and I want you to know that to this minute, I am clean and so is she."

Hinn explained the presence of Paula White in his life. He started by saying that she was a member, along with her husband, of his church for nine years. "We got to talk. She went through a painful divorce, I went through a painful divorce. We found common ground to talk about stuff we could help each other in. And a friendship did develop. But hear this: no immorality ever whatsoever.

"These people out there are making it sound like we had an affair. That's a lie. That's a total lie."

Hinn told how the Vatican had made him a Patron of the Arts, and he went to Rome. He was asked if he knew any other potential donors. "Here's where I made my mistake. I let her come with me to Rome, so she can donate money. That was stupid on my part. And for that I do ask forgiveness, but that was an innocent mistake, nothing to do with stupid stuff. And then they have a picture of a bed, implying sex. That is terrible they done that."

In August of last year, Chrystal Whitt, writing at the Slaughter of the Sheep website, pointed out a contradiction in the stories Hinn and White were telling: "Hinn says that the Vatican truly did invite him to Rome, and he *let* White come with him so she could donate money. White said in her official statement that she was in Rome on ministry duties and that she and Hinn traveled to Rome separately. But, Benny Hinn says in the video that she went with *him*. This is a different story than they both told in their official statements (which, by the way, quickly disappeared from their sites)."

Recognizing a scandal in the making Hinn closed his video by saying that he had pulled back from his friendship with White.

Hinn's ministry, along with Paula White's and four other televangelists, was subject to an investigation into the ministries finances launched three years by Senator Charles Grassley (R-Iowa). According to Religion Dispatches' Sarah Posner, the investigation, which screeched to a crashing halt in 2012 "was initially launched to examine whether the ministries had abused their tax-exempt status by using tax-exempt funds for personal enrichment, [but] Grassley is not recommending any changes to the tax law to prevent such abuse, but rather a review by the Evangelical Council on Financial Accountability, which was formed in the 1970s."

A statement issued by Hinn's ministry cites the fact that the committee "recognized Benny Hinn Ministries for being responsive, transparent, and for demonstrating a high degree of integrity. " (Four of the six under investigation refused to co-operate with Grassley.) The Hinn statement said: "Throughout the inquiry process, Hinn personally led the effort to encourage greater transparency and more aggressive self-governance in his own ministry and encouraged others to follow that example. Detailed in the findings is the fact that Benny Hinn Ministries has consistently undertaken rigorous internal controls while utilizing exceptional outside sources to govern salaries. Pastor Hinn is not involved in setting or directing his own salary but has directed the ministry's board of directors to hire outside executive compensation firms to provide professional guidance. Further, he has instructed that such salary recommendations follow the most conservative recommendations of those compensation firms."

In a recent article titled "Benny Hinn's Buckets 'O' Cash," Bud Press maintained that, "Over the years, Hinn has mastered the art of rescuing his followers from their money. The mega-million dollar monster he created is greedy and voracious, and begs to be fed on a daily basis."

On his website, Press, Director of the Christian Research Service, had more to say about Hinn: "Since the early 1990's, Benny Hinn has established an incredible and unimaginable track-record of false prophecies, false teachings, false healings, and controversies, which is reason enough for him to be considered as the most prolific heretic of our day."

Boston summed it up by pointing out that despite the serial shenanigans of a number of televangelists, people are still tuning in and sending their money. "Consider Pat Robertson. Robertson has said so many extreme and bizarre things over the years that it's impossible to even keep a list anymore. Yet Robertson's audience has remained more or less stable, and like the Energizer Bunny, he just keeps going and going and going."

THE SCIENCE OF BEING CHRISTIAN

One would think that if a group calls themselves Christian this is what they would uphold. This is not true for Christian Science, which is neither Christian nor science.

The founder Mary Baker was born in Bow, New Hampshire, July 16, 1821 to a devout religious family (Congregationalists) with 5 other children. Her father, Mark Baker, was a Calvinist whom she strongly disagreed with later on in life. The disagreements were on the main points of Scripture such as judgment and eternal punishment. From this rejection of Scripture and circumstances of ill health she eventually sought out another understanding to the Bible.

Mary was married at the young age of 22 to George Glover in 1843 in Charleston, South Carolina. This was her only happy marriage that tragically lasted slightly longer than half a year as her husband died of yellow fever. She was left a widow, while being pregnant.

Later on after her husbands death a special meeting was convened for the purpose of paying the last tribute of respect to Brother George W. Glover, After interviewing Masonic authorities they found his records, he was honored "for his honorable record and Christian character and said record, with the seal of the Grand secretary." "His remains were interred with Masonic honors" This may explain the Masonic symbol used on the cover of her book, the cross through the crown, which Christian Science states are their trademark.

After his death Mary traveled back north and gave birth to a son whom she named George after her husband. It was from this time on she was in constant pain and became preoccupied with the question of health. Mary was a semi-invalid for years afflicted with a spinal weakness that caused her spasmodic seizures, other complications amounted to her complete nervous collapse.

Ruth Tucker writes, After Glover's death, she became involved in mesmerism such as hypnosis and the practices of spiritualism and clairvoyance.

In 1853 Mary remarried to a dentist, Daniel Patterson. This marriage was somewhat good, but Patterson was not a good provider; and some called him a womanizer. In 1866 he and Mary were permanently separated. 7 years later in 1873 Mary obtained a divorce on the grounds of desertion. Though her own references to this divorce imply that Patterson had been guilty of adultery.

It was during this time of her broken life and still in pain she heard of a man named Phineas P. Quimby in Portland, Maine. Quimby's fame was spreading as he was attributed to have done incredible cures without medicine. Seeking relief from her spinal illness Mary decided to go see to him (1862). She believed herself to have been healed by him. (Although she claimed she was cured by Quimby, her symptoms later returned).

Quimby was a metaphysician, he practiced a form of mind-over-matter healing, he called it Christian Science.

Ruth Tucker, *in her book Another Gospel writes* Mrs. Patterson (Eddy) developed a "psychic dependence" on Quimby, drawing on his spiritual presence, claiming even visitations by his apparition. This is not surprising as she thought highly of Mesmer and his discovery of animal magnetism at first.

She became an enthusiastic follower of Quimby, believing that he had rediscovered Jesus' own healing methods. She writes "In the year 1866, I discovered the Christ Science or divine laws of Life, Truth, and Love, and named my discovery Christian Science. God had been graciously preparing me during many years for the reception of this final revelation of the absolute divine Principle of scientific mental healing."

"It was in 1866 that the light of Science first came to me." Mrs. Eddy claimed she fell on the ice and injured herself. She later claimed that the fall brought her life with only three days to live (her physician denied such a diagnosis). On the third day she reported that after reading Matthew 9:2 she experienced a miraculous cure, "the healing Truth dawned upon my senses," and the divine healing ministry was born, this supposedly was an affirmation of Mrs. Eddy's own healing which led her to formulate Christian Science beliefs.

After Quimby's death in 1866, Mary determined to carry on his work. Though Christian Scientists reject the possibility that Quimby had any great influence on Mrs. Eddy's philosophy, researchers have proven that she did plagiarized his manuscripts and teachings. Mrs. Eddy did attribute most of her ideas to Phineas Quimby, even the name Christian Science did not find its origin in Eddy but came from Quimby who spoke of his system as "the Science of the Christ"; Mrs. Eddy turned the words around and called her system Christian Science. She stated, "We may say at once that, as far as the thought is concerned, Science and Health is practically all Quimby." (Quimby had even called his system Christian Science some years before Mrs. Eddy adopted the name in Feb. 1863).

118

In 1877 Mary had entered marriage for the third time to Asa Eddy who became her first disciple and Christian practitioner.

After 9 years Science and Health were first published in 1875 and Church of Christ Scientist was incorporated in 1879. Mary Eddy said, "It brought down a shower of abuse upon my head, but it won converts from the first." She later came to Boston and opened what later became "The Massachusetts Metaphysical College," where she said she taught some 4,000 students at $300.00 per student over a period of eight years (1881-1889). She had become an author of numerous writings publishing altogether 16 other books.

Christian Science has set up Reading Rooms through different communities these are small libraries of the local Christian Science, where members can go to read Eddy's works. If one attends a Christian Science service they will find no pastor, there are no ordinances. They have only lay readers and designated full-time practitioners who are both men and women able to administer the Church's healing techniques. The service will end with a reading of the Lord's Prayer (intermingled along the way with Mrs. Eddy's interpretations.)

At the heart of Christian Science is the power of divine healing. We should be aware that if any healing does occur, one should not interpret it as God's approval of their beliefs. There are healings that are not from God in various religions, so a change of sick or diseased condition is not the proof of a belief being of God.

Christian Science claims for itself that the Bible is its final source of authority. When one tunes into their TV presentation they will see them read from the Bible and then Mrs. Eddy's interpretation from her Science and Health. It gives the impression that they are into the Bible. But the fact is if one listens carefully everything that is said is reinterpreted to mean something other than the way it was written. They will "spiritualize" Biblical passages and the final authority *always* lies in the hands of Eddy's book.

When someone claims to be Christian there are certain fundamentals that they must adhere to. As a member they are not to belong to another church because theirs is where one would only find the truth. In the case of Christian Science, it has been said it is neither Christian nor science. In fact it only masquerades as Christianity for the individual that does not pursue what is meant by the inventor of this metaphysical system.

In Science and Health a statement is given to answer the question if they have any "religious creeds" "1. As adherents of

Truth, we take the inspired Word of the Bible as our sufficient guide to eternal Life." As we will see this is not the case at least to anyone who would apply good old fashion logic, and sound Biblical knowledge.

Mrs. Eddy claimed The Bible has been my only authority. I have had no other guide in "the straight and narrow way" of Truth." Yet Eddy claimed her own divine revelation was equal to the Scripture. This is common with all cult groups who add their own books or interpretations to the Bible. "I should blush to write of 'Science and Health with Key to the Scriptures' as I have, were it of human origin, and were, apart from God, its author. But, as I was only a scribe echoing the harmonies of heaven in divine metaphysics, I cannot be super-modest in my estimate of the Christian Science textbook.'" In her book The first Church of Christ Scientist and Miscellany it states "That Mrs. Eddy organized The First Church of Christ, Scientist, in Boston, Mass., devised its church government, originated its form of public worship, wrote its Church Manual and Tenets, and always has been is and is now its guide, guardian, Leader, and wise unerring counsellor."

As Eddy began her new religion she was put in an almost immediate position liken to a pope by being called a "wise unerring counselor." Though she denied those who called her pope she accepted the term mother, and claimed, "she is equal to Jesus Christ, a fulfillment of Bible prophecy of the woman of Revelation 12, the God-chosen revelator for this age, with a superior and final revelation to all that has gone before."

Divine Science then became the "final revelation" from God to man. Her book becomes the glasses the Bible is to be read through and the final authority for all members of the Christian Science religion. They needed her book to understand and "unlock" the Bibles true meaning. It was her mission to write Science and Health to give the world the "key" to the Scriptures so everyone was able to use them. In Science and Health she writes: "A Christian Scientist requires my work Science and Health for his textbook, and so do all his students and patients. Why? First: Because it is *the voice of Truth to this age*, and contains the full statement of Christian Science, or the Science of healing through Mind." So through her dark colored glasses the Bible would be reinterpreted to mean something the writers never meant for it to say. Her position more than insinuated that in 1900 years no one understood the word of God correctly until she came along to enlighten them.

"Its members can so protect their own thoughts that they are not unwittingly made to deprive their Leader of her rightful place as the revelator to this age of the immortal truths testified to by Jesus and the prophets" is a statement appearing in the Christian Science Journal, May, 1906.

She said, "In following these leadings of scientific revelation, the Bible was my only textbook." Is it? She had little regard for its contents. She said of the Scriptures "The Scriptures cannot properly be interpreted in a literal way ."

In the place of taking Scripture literally was an allegorizing method or more directly, *just plain making it up as you go*. She turned the word Adam into meaning *a dam* or obstruction. This suggests the thought of something fluid, of mortal mind in solution." To Eddy the meaning of Adam as red dirt was not the true meaning in Scripture even though this is the meaning of the Hebrew word. Eddy was bending the words to pour her own exclusive meaning into them. She had taken the route of many before her, specifically the Gnostics. Eddy's Christian Science denied the clear teaching of Scripture and in its place. She wrote the second chapter of Genesis was in error "false history in contradistinction to the true." Genesis had two distinct documents used in the writing of the early part of the Book of Genesis. The Elohistic and the Jehovistic. Genesis 1, representing the Elohistic document, describes man as having been created in the image of God; this account of creation is called "spiritual" and true. (The Supreme being called Elohim) Genesis 2, derived from the inferior Jehovistic document, represents man as formed of the dust of the ground; this account of creation is called false and in error. Elohim of Chapter 1 is the true God and Jehovah of chapter 2 to 5 "becomes a man of war" a tribal God to be worshipped, rather than love, the divine principle to be lived and loved.

That Gen.2 "Which portrayed Spirit as supposedly cooperating with matter in constructing the universe, is based on the hypothesis of error." That it was "the exact opposite of scientific truth" So out went Moses' record and Jesus ' affirmation of the Genesis account being accurate. She even said of Gen.3:22 "Behold man has become as one of us." This could not be the utterance of truth.

Her understanding of Genesis is seen by the question "Does life, truth, and love produce error, and hatred? Does the creator condemn His own creation?" In this she ignored the fact that the Bible does teach the creator condemning man because of his fallen state and did something about it, (which she further denied). In its place was substituted her solution instead of God's, and it was done in Jesus' name.

She also taught that the Bible has been corrupted, therefore Her own *Science and Health* is the "first book" which has been "uncontaminated by human hypotheses." She said the Bible has thousands of errors. 30,000 in the Old Testament, and as many as 300,000 in the New Testament. At times Mrs. Eddy would use the Bible to prove her point at other times she would outright deny it. With such little regard for the Binle one can only wonder why she used it at all. Yet Eddy would claim on the other hand "I therefore plant myself unreservedly on the teachings of Jesus, of His apostles, of the prophets-"

Exalting herself, and her revelation and new found religion she was able to claim "The true Logos is demonstrably Christian Science." Here we have her take a term applied to God and exalt her own religion to the status of God. We then can apply this statement to the first verse in the Gospel of John where the logos is found, reading it this manner: "In the beginning was Christian Science, and Christian Science was with God, and Christian Science was God. All things were made by Christian Science, and without Christian Science was not anything made that was made." And Christian Science has come into the world, when? Not when Jesus was here, but by Mrs. Eddy.

According to The Manual by Mary Baker Eddy, "To become a member of the First Church of Christ, Scientist, the applicant must be a believer in the doctrines of Christian Science, according to the teaching contained in our Christian Science textbook, Science and Health with Key to the Scriptures by Reverend Mary Baker Eddy. The Bible, together with Science and Health shall be his *only textbooks for self-instruction in Christian Science.*"

Eddy taught, Man already has everlasting salvation; there is no final judgment. We save ourselves; no one else can. "Universal salvation rests on progression and probation. No final judgment awaits mortals." Why call this Christian if every important thing the Bible speaks on is denied or changed. The fact is you can call it Christian but that doesn't mean it is. You can call it science but that doesn't mean its provable.

"Instead, the only hope of pardon and salvation for any person lies in that person eliminating all sin (false beliefs and the behavior they spawn) from his/her life."

She stated "All good ever written, taught, or wrought comes from God and human faith in the right." If this is true (which it is

122

not), then Christian Science must accept that many other religions and philosophies are from God, but they do not.

Question: Is there no sin? Answer- "All reality is in God and His creation. That which He creates is good, and He makes all that is made. Therefore the only reality of sin, sickness, or death is the awful fact that unrealities seem real to human, erring belief, until God strips off their disguise." So everything is subjectively interpreted, its true to you because you believe its true.

To Eddy salvation was a higher consciousness event and not through the cross "Final deliverance from error is not reached through paths of flowers by pinning one's faith without works to another's vicarious effort"

"In Christian Science it is plain that God removes the punishment for sin only as sin is removed, hence the hope of universal salvation. To lose the sense of sin we must first detect the claim of sin; hold it invalid, sin disappears, and its unreality is proven,"

Like other religions Christian Science has numerous contradictions within its own framework. Eddy claimed she received the revelation of healing when "the healing Truth dawned upon my senses." But then she rejects anything that speaks of the senses believing God is not communicated in any way through them. She states, "The physical senses can obtain no proof of God. They can neither see Sprit through the eye nor hear it through the ear, nor can feel, taste or smell spirit."

She took it upon herself to reform what she called "myths" of traditional Christian belief. This preconceived notion going back to her uncomfortable belief from her childhood. Her premise was that man is actually perfect and able to obtain the same Divine Mind that Jesus attained. Sickness can be eradicated once a person sees that pure thoughts will dispel the *illusion* of disease. As the one true church, members are encouraged to affirm that God is good and therefore good is God. In such a system evil cannot exist since matter (evil) does not exist. This is a Hinduistic concept that there is no good or evil, that life is an illusion. Her main concepts promoted had more an affinity to Hinduism than Christ's teachings. It is also docetic teaching from the gnostics, that matter is not significant and it is the spirit only that counts. An example of this is her teaching of man did not fall; death is an illusion. This is the very reason Jesus came to die for sin, it is reality and all of life's circumstances prove this, as did Eddy when she died in 1910. Mrs. Eddy's faith did not help her overcome death as she taught. Yet some of her followers did not think that she had died; Mrs. Augusta Stetson, in fact, wrote a letter in which she indignantly rejected newspaper accounts of her death, declaring in italics, "Mary Baker Eddy never died." Others hoped for her to resurrect, which never came. From her concept of matter being an illusion flowed out a direct denial of everything Christ came to earth, and suffered the consequences for.

Death is defined in the Glossary of Science and Health as follows: "An illusion, the lie of life in matter; the unreal and untrue. The definition continues: "Any material evidence of death is false, for it contradicts the spiritual facts of being." Death is only a "belief" which must finally be conquered by eternal Life. Life is real, and death is the illusion. It was described by her as a dream. "Man is incapable of sin, sickness and death." On the other hand she would say, "Christ came to destroy the belief of sin" which was interpreted as false belief. So for a healing to occur one only has to remove the false belief of the sickness.

If it is true that man lives, this fact can never change in Science to the opposite belief that man dies. Death is but another phase of the dream that existence can be material. The dream of death must be mastered by Mind here or hereafter life is real, and death is the illusion.

This is diametrically opposed to Scripture as Jesus and Paul called death an enemy, it was very real. If it was not real then there would be no need for a resurrection.

After she quotes the words of our Lord to His disciples, "Our friend Lazarus sleepeth; but I go that I may awake him out of sleep". Mrs. Eddy states that "He restored Lazarus by the understanding that he had never died," which contradicts the very words of Jesus a few verses later as Jesus finds that the disciples do not understand His use of the figure of sleep, He "said unto them plainly, Lazarus is dead" (John 11:14). Christian Science is also unable to understand but for a different reason.

"This then affected the way she saw the fallen nature in man and the world around her. She proclaimed sin, sickness, and death must be deemed as devoid of reality. "There is no disease, when the supposed suffering is gone from the mortal mind, there can be no pain." Disease is an image of thought externalized. The mental state is called a material state. Whatever is cherished in mortal mind as the physical condition is imaged forth on the body. "Man is never sick, for Mind is not sick and matter cannot be."

This is found not to be true as people do become sick, even in their mind (not just the brain) and it is not because of the way they think. It is not removed because they don't believe they are sick. Many people who are deathly sick walk around unaware thinking they are in good health, and they die.

"Sickness and disease are illusory, the product of a false belief, and not an actual result of sin."

"The cause of all so-called disease is mental, a mortal fear, a mistaken belief." Sin, which may in most cases be equated with evil, is a delusion, an illusion. "What is termed disease does not exist. It is *neither mind nor matter.*"

If something does not exist in both mind and matter it cannot have any affect on us. But then she contradicts this absolute statement by saying Disease is an image *of thought* externalized. "That all is mind, and that we too can overcome the false beliefs of mortal mind." If Sickness, and sin are the product of a false belief, to believe something means the mind is involved. Which she does at times agree, "his imagined disease is only the result of a false belief." "The cause of all so-called disease is mental, ..a mistaken belief."

"sin, illness, and disease are all illusions of the mind" All these statements show her confusion in saying something does not exist in "mind nor matter" and also saying they do. This was the dichotomy of her belief system in trying to erase the reality of sin, and evil in the world.

She summed up everything that is good is God, everything that is not is an illusion. She dismissed half of reality, the very one that Jesus came to rectify, the one that marred the human condition. She held that matter is not real but "the objective supposition of the Spirits opposite."

Christian Science claimed as absolute truth that evil is nothing, unreal, an illusion and a false belief. She also stated sin, sickness, and death has no real existence, they are only illusions, and that man is incapable of sin, sickness, and death. Yet she would also say that the Master "wrought a full salvation from sin, sickness, and death." "Christ came to destroy *the belief of sin*" and that salvation means "sin, sickness, and death destroyed." To her view this was all only a false belief that needed correcting. If this is so then why did she die? "The way to escape the misery of sin is to cease sinning, there is no other way." Her solution is to cease sinning which she believed is not real in the first place! The sin that is said to bring suffering, is just a false belief, and does not really exist yet one is to overcome sin which is not there in the first place. All by correct thinking.

How can we overcome this if "man *is incapable* of sin, sickness, and death." Are not beliefs real, and affect the way we live. This can only be attributed to the foreign factor of sin entering the human condition.

Then how can one know what she is saying is true? We would have to ignore all that we see and feel with the senses to live in this way. This all falls apart very quickly in even the simplest of things. For how could only the good be real and not the evil. Eddy was trying to deal with what befell her in her life and explain it all away without God's clear word. She literally stepped over God to come up with an alternate explanation. Like the three monkeys "see no evil, hear no evil, speak no evil", Christian Science minimizes sin by denying its reality and its real affect on the human condition, yet sin is ingrained in its teachings. The salvation from sin which she offered man is to not believe in it. Everyone dies proving sin is a reality. She died as well.

No place in her writings does more harm than her changing the biblical Christ. To Eddy Jesus was just a man, the perfect example for us to follow. He didn't die for our sins. The Christian Science Christ is not the same as Jesus but equal to "The divine manifest-ation of God, which comes to the flesh to destroy incarnate error".She even stated "Jesus is not the Christ." " Jesus meant; not that the *human Jesus was eternal*, but that the divine idea or Christ was and is so and therefore antedated Abraham, not that the corporeal Jesus was one with the Father." I don't know of anyone who claimed Jesus' flesh was eternal before his incarnation (until after he is risen). But certainly it was not a divine idea that conversed with Abraham and others.

Her Christ was the "Way-shower", the first human to understand the Divine Mind. "Jesus taught the way of Life by demonstration. There is but one way to heaven, harmony, and Christ in Divine Science shows us this way."

She held the view that Virgin Birth was a spiritual idea; and in agreement with other cults the Trinity is pagan: "The theory of three persons in one God (that is, a personal Trinity or Tri-unity) suggests polytheism, rather than the one ever-present I Am." God the Father-Mother; Christ the spiritual idea of sonship; divine Science or the Holy Comforter."

God, as the only author of man, has a perfect idea of man. Mary, according to Christian Science, was able to give birth to Jesus while a virgin because she was able to conceive of this perfect idea, this divine Principle dwelling in the bosom of God. Fully recognizing that "being is Spirit," Mary understood that the manifestation of God's perfect idea did not require a flesh and blood father. Born out of Mary's "self-conscious communion with God," Jesus was "endowed with the Christ," and was "the offspring of soul" rather than "of material sense."

Eddy succeeded in the first modern attempt to blend Christianity and what is known today as New Age philosophy. She distinguished between the man Jesus and the Christ. The man Jesus suffered on the cross; the Christ did not suffer anything. In the first two centuries of the Christian era there were individuals and groups who distinguished sharply between Jesus as a mere man, and Christ, as the divine spirit who descended upon Jesus at the time of his baptism and then left him again before He died." The Ebionites, Cerinthus, and other Gnostics all held this view and they were not considered part of the Church. Though the Gnostics believed the world was evil, Mrs. Eddy still maintained many similarities. Christian Scientists, may not agree on all points with them, but the teaching of separating Jesus and Christ, as the divine idea is the very much the same. The Christ spirit simply inhabited the body of the man Jesus. The Christ spirit had come to teach man the gnosis whereby he could free himself from bondage to the evil material world. Some even taught that Jesus did not actually have a body of flesh, but was pure spirit, and Christ did not die. The physical death and resurrection of the body were denied by the Gnostics as it is by Christian Scientists. Like the Gnostics to escape the illusion of the material, Eddy believed that knowledge of her revelation explained in her books became their salvation. Christian Scientists unknowingly find themselves in the company of a ancient heresy from the first century.

In her book *Science and Health with Key to the Scriptures*, she wrote a revealing statement that absolutely denied the Bible and the very words of Jesus "The material blood of Jesus was no more efficacious to cleanse from sin when it was shed on 'the accursed tree,' than when it was flowing in his veins as he went daily about his Father's business."

"One sacrifice however great is insufficient to pay the debt of sin." This is true if the Jesus who went to the cross was Mrs. Eddy's, but not the sinless Son of God from the Bible. The Bible makes it perfectly clear without the shedding of blood there is no forgiveness of Sins. This is taught from Genesis throughout. Since Mrs. Eddy did away with the sin factor there really was no need of the blood. Not only was there no need of God's cleansing she also stated, "Prayer is not to be used as a confessional for sin. Such an error would impede the true religion."

"If prayer nourishes the belief that sin is cancelled and that man is made better merely by praying, prayer is an evil." Since she did not believe she was a sinner so she had no need to pray for forgiveness.

She in its place taught, Jesus demonstrated the unreality of matter, that all is mind, and that we too can overcome the false beliefs of mortal mind, sin, illness, and disease are all illusions of the mind to be corrected by right thinking. The Jesus of Christian Science does not offer mankind redemption from sin by His death paying for sin in our place He "demonstrated; that divine Truth casts out suppositional error and heals the sick."

In place of the atonement "Jesus came to rescue men from these very illusions to which he seemed to conform: from the illusion which calls sin real, and man a sinner, needing a Savior; the illusion which calls sickness real, and man as invalid, needing a physician; the illusion that death is as real as Life. From such thoughts mortal inventions, one and all Christ Jesus came to save men, through ever-present and eternal good." In other words Jesus of Christian Science came to correct the teachings of Jesus of whom the Bible speaks of.

Eddy states, "Christ was not crucified. Jesus, being the man who possessed the Christ consciousness, was the one who went to the cross and who appeared to die. Thus, when the Bible appears to say that Jesus died on the cross and His body was laid in the tomb, it must be understood, according to the theology of Christian Science, that Jesus actually never died but was rather in the tomb denying death's reality."

Though Eddy perceived pain as non-existent, we find that she did not sit still and ignore it when she had it, she went to relieve herself of it. "Some years ago Mrs. Eddy herself had a tooth removed under local anesthesia. It caused her theories to be held up to ridicule in a good many quarters. In her reply she gave out this ingenious explanation: that the dentist's belief in the means he employed was a mental force which combined with her own-exerted in a different direction-and produced a painless operation as a logical, mathematical "resultant of forces."

Why go to a dentist in the first place, the pain was not there, it wasn't real.What would be the purpose of anesthesia to one who is enlightened, knowing that pain is an illusion.

"The sick unconsciously argue for suffering, instead of against it, they admit its reality, whereas they should deny it. They should plead in the opposition to the testimony of the deceitful senses, and maintain mans immortality and eternal likeness to God." Is the body lying when one feels pain or is it trying to tell you something is wrong. Imagine ignoring the signals of the body, such as when its hungry or when it is near a flame.

For her kind of reality it would be hard to find any valid proof. Her proof of this revelation was destroyed when she turned to doctors and they treated her with the painkiller morphine. She died in 1910. Christian Science continues to uphold her belief that Jesus revealed to people their illusion of illness and thus cured them, even though she was not cured and sought out a medicinal illusion. What is termed disease does not exist. It is neither mind nor matter."

Eddy stated "A man drinks poison and dies; but *it is not the poison that kills him*; vicious belief, or mortal mind, sends him to his long home. *If he only had been able to convince himself that the poison was pure, clear spring water, it would have done him no injury.* (NOTE: "If a dose of poison is swallowed through mistake, and the patient dies, even though physician and patient are expecting favorable results, does human belief, you ask, cause this death?

So let's get this concept straight; if you believe you drank poison but did not, you would die as if you did? Let me put this another way, If you thought what you drank was pure water and it was poison you would not die? How many people have died like this in history? I would think many.

Her solution was not to think about it, "The less mind there is manifested in matter, the better. When the unthinking lobster loses his claw, it grows again. If the science of life were understood the human limb would be replaced as readily as the lobster's claw-not with an artificial limb, but with a genuine one." While the lobster's claw can grow again, many animals tails do not. They certainly are not thinking of it growing anymore than a lobster. Maybe we should all get a third set of teeth since we don't think about it.

"The cause of all so-called disease is mental" organic disease does not exist, and it is blamed on the belief in sin They say that since our physical bodies do not exist, disease and death are only illusions. She went as far as to say "the danger of prayer is that it may lead us into temptation."

In divine Science, where prayers are mental, all may avail themselves of God as "a very' present help in trouble." Love is impartial and universal in its adaptation and bestowals. It is the open fount which cues, "Ho, every one that thirsteth, come ye to the waters." To Eddy love cured wrong thinking which then cured the false belief that one was actually sick.

Christian Scientists reject doctors of all kinds drugs and even vitamins and nutrition supplements. To Eddy this was breaking the first commandment. What they do is deny the material testimony of their senses. Their body is lying to them as it it is not the true reality.

The faithful Christian Scientist, when experiencing the "error" of illness, is to call upon the practitioner rather than a physician. If you go to a doctor you have no faith. While there are some cases of reported of healings there are many deaths as well. The Christian Science Church had 28 child deaths between 1975 and 1995, according to one study.

In the 1950's, there were 11,000 practitioners of this healing religion with about one million members, and by 1972 they had grown to 3200 churches. In 1976, scandal shook the cult with charges of financial, moral, and spiritual corruption among the top leaders. A major internal controversy occurred as some of the high ranking leaders of the Mother Church were accused by longtime members of "gross mismanagement, inexperience and lack of Christian ethics." One high-ranking CS consultant on security at the Boston headquarters, Reginald G. Kerry, accused the leadership of "an alleged lack of financial accountability and alleged instances of lesbianism among the top echelon."

In the late '80s and early '90s, the church once again experienced more difficulties due to negative media coverage of lawsuits, and financial difficulties. Then in the 1990's it was discovered that the church had secretly transferred millions of dollars from endowments and pension funds to help cover huge losses on their Monitor Channel [TV], which resulted in a reported loss of over several hundred million. "civil lawsuits brought against Christian Scientist parents who allowed their children to die of curable diseases by neglecting medical treatment A number of them went to court and some were publicized on TV by the parents who felt duped by this religious healing system and wanted to warn people. The members who practiced their religion were charged with manslaughter, murder, and child abuse for choosing prayer instead of medical treatment for illness."

In Minnesota, one four-week trial in 1994 levied a $14 million punitive damage award against the Mother Church, which a judge later reduced to $10.4 million. In 1995, the Minnesota Court of Appeals overturned this judgment. This court left intact $1.5 million in compensatory damages against the parents and two Christian Science practitioners. Now the Mother Church, has ruled contrary to its founder's strict philosophy, having revised its strong prohibition against medical treatment.

With a major decline in membership the future of Christian Science looked grim although they seem to be on a slight comeback as of late. The number of practitioners has dropped nearly 50 percent in the last three decades. The Christian Science Church has a national membership of 170,000 – way less numbers then they had first enjoyed. On their web page the group has approximately 2,200 branch churches in over sixty countries throughout the world. The majority of branch churches are in the United States (Approximately 1,600) and about 60 are found in Canada

Mrs. Eddy prophesied that, "in fifty years or less, Christian Science will be the dominant religious belief of the world." This certainly has not come true. However in the early twentieth century, the Mind Science religions as Unity School of Christianity, Religious Science, and the word /faith movement in the Christian Church can all attribute their theology in some way to Mary baker Eddy. One of the former practitioners was Emma Hopkins who was an independent Christian Science leader she taught Charles and Myrtle Fillmore who founded the unity school of Christianity. Christian Science never grew to the numbers by its contemporaneous movements such as Mormons and Jehovah's Witnesses probably because of its metaphysical slant easily identified as not biblical even by other cults.

Their publications are The Christian Science Monitor, The Christian Science Sentinel, The Christian Science Journal, The Herald of Christian Science, published in 12 foreign languages as well as in English Braille; (which seems to be an oxymoron from their own beliefs) and The Christian Science Quarterly, containing the Bible lessons studied daily by Christian Scientists. Mrs. Eddy's Science and Health is found published in a dozen languages besides English. Various other materials appear in numerous languages other than English. Christian Science has a weekly nationwide radio and TV program, which is also broadcasted outside the United States.

It is a fact that certain illnesses which are emotional or stress related in nature can be removed by the psychologically soothing effect of the practitioner's therapy. A good or new attitude seems to do wonders for some people. But the organic sicknesses do not have the same results. Again any seemingly miraculous results do not validate the belief system.

THE LOONY MOONIES

The infamous Reverend Moon was born in 1920 in what is now North Korea. Raised within a Christian household, he later turned to spiritualism and later claimed that on Easter morning of 1930, he had a visit from Jesus. In Young Oon Kim's *The Divine Principle and its Application,* we are told that Jesus "revealed that he (Moon) was destined to accomplish a great mission in which Jesus would work with him." Moon would later claim that Jesus told him that he would become the Messiah. When asked how he knew his spiritual visitor was Jesus, he replied that he looked just like his pictures. Now if that doesn't set off a B.S. alarm, nothing will.

Once he had gained popularity and a following, he instructed them that only he would be their spiritual guide. "You can do it even without the Old and New Testaments. You don't need them anymore."

After he and Jesus were spiritual penpals, Moon's next encounter was directly communicating with the dead. His "friends list" soon included Moses, Buddha and others. He may have unfriended some later, we don't know.

As often happens, one wacky cult is born of another. A group of loonies in North Korea got the idea that they were living in the new Jerusalem and a messiah would be coming from Korea. And so it was that as a 16-year-old, Moon went up on a mountain side and was in deep prayer when he received the call and refused it because he thought too much responsibility was involved. But influential voices like Jesus and some saints convinced him that he was to be the second Jesus on earth.

The story goes that way back in 1905 Moon participated in a séance and the quack operating the event channeled with some character named Fletcher. In the séance, the spirit Fletcher started to talk about Moon in pretty glowing terms and in fact, said that there was no need for Jesus to return – that he wouldn't return – because there wasn't any need. The world had Moon now. Long after that, Moon claimed to have the ability to project himself into the spirit realm to have chats with Jesus and a few chosen saints.

In Moon's book, (don't all wacko cult leaders need to write a book?) *God's Warning to the World* he wrote, "Early in my life God called me for a mission as His instrument. I committed myself unyieldingly in pursuit of truth, searching the hills and valleys of the spiritual world. The time suddenly came to me when heaven opened up, and I was privileged to communicate with Jesus Christ and the living God directly. Since then I have received many astonishing revelations." Wow, all that and he didn't even have a rock and a hat!

Moon died in 2012 but in the Unification Church manual, *Outline of the Principle - Level 4*, it says of Moon, "Only God really knows the kind of path he traveled. He freely communicated with Jesus and the saints in Paradise"

"When I was a teenager I had a trip to the Spirit world," he was to write. "I met Jesus. John the Baptist. When I came back the Bible took on an entirely new meaning. If you don't believe me go to the Spirit world and contact them yourself." I think we might need Benny Hinn for that one. After all, he called the Holy Ghost to be on stage with him. But Moon would probably have said he didn't need any help because later on he channeled through to his late son, Heung Jin Nim Moon.

More striking were revelations that a black church member from Africa was being possessed by Heung Jin Nim, who had been killed in a 1984 car crash at age 17. According to the Washington Post, church members were startled by the news, but they went along with it because it came from Moon. (they dare not go against Father) But as the bizarre story started to unfold the appearance and subsequent coronation of the unnamed Zimbabwean as Moon's son, some church members became skeptical, others had been working to quench rumors of theological differences inside the church.

The Zimbabwean, described as a baby-faced black man in his early 20s, has been a member of the church for the past three years. Last year he began claiming to hear the voice of Heung Jin Nim. After a church-sponsored investigation concluded that the man probably was Moon's son, he came to America and met with Moon. According to the Post, the man knew the answers to five questions only Moon's deceased son could have known, and thus won Moon's enthusiastic acceptance.

The entire organization of Moon's church was embarrassed when Moon's oldest son, Hyo Jin Moon, divorced his wife Nansook. It had been Moon himself who blessed them in marriage when Nansook was only 15-years-old. The truth was that Rev. Moon had selected Nansook as a wife for his soon on the recommendation of a psychic. There was further embarrassment when Nansook talked about abuse originating from her ex-husband's drug habit. She told of Hyo Jin Moon beating her when she was seven months pregnant and that when she told he divine in-laws of the problems and suffering, they did nothing.

Nansook was to later write, "Although Hyo Jin's family knew of his addictions and his abuse of me and the children, I received very little emotional or physical support from them. I was constantly at the mercy of Hyo Jin's erratic and cruel behavior." She also accused Hyo Jin of adultery, physical and mental abuse along with drug and alcohol abuse. Hyo Jin was to admit to his problem with drugs and drink.

That wasn't the only embarrassment. In 1982, 65 year old Moon, was convicted of failing to report $162,000 in income on his Federal tax returns. He appealed to the Supreme Court, but it refused to hear his case, and he began serving his sentence on July 20, 1984.

He spent 11 1/2 months in the medium-security Federal prison in Danbury, Conn., then was moved to the halfway house. He had to report to the house every evening but was allowed to conduct church business during the day.

Of course, good ole' Jerry Falwell, head of the Moral Majority, and the Rev. Joseph Lowery, president of the Southern Christian Leadership Conference, called on President Reagan to pardon Mr. Moon. They said government was increasingly intruding in religious matters.

What the Unification Church presents publicly and to their members are two different things. It's intentions of strengthening the family through strict moral discipline and serving the needs of humanity seems wonderful commendable and even Christian. That is on the surface and what they want you to see, but the true Unification Church is a mind control cult of no equal.

Moon teaches some outright bizarre things about Jesus. His body was invaded by Satan, and He was killed. Therefore, even when Christians believe in and become one body with Jesus whose body was invaded by Satan, their bodies still remain subject to Satan's invasion. In this manner, however devout a man of faith may be, he cannot fulfill physical salvation by redemption through Jesus crucifixion alone.

For Moon, Jesus' death was failure. For Paul, it was the central point of the Gospel, the purchase of salvation, the guarantee of liberty from both sin and the Law -Moon has stated with reference to Jesus nature Jesus was this Messiah, the second Adam. But he doesn't end there, John the Baptist is also a failure. Moon teaches, "Abraham was the father of faith, Moses was a man of faith, Jesus

135

was the son of man, trying to carry out his mission at the cost of his life. But they are, in a way, failures."

Moon in Jesus' place teaches: "I am now making a prototype of the perfect family, accomplishing what Jesus could not do." It is after many great spiritual battles with Satan, Moon achieved perfection and became one with God, qualifying him to be Jesus replacement.

Mr. Moon himself said of himself, "I had to accomplish all left unaccomplished by my predecessor. When you think of that, you must feel indebted to me and cannot lift your face before me."

Moon's goal to start a new human race under his leadership. "I must save America. I know the direction that human kind must go, and I, with the help of God, will lead the world there. My wife and I can now stand on a worldwide foundation as true first true parents." Adam failed to accomplish this task. Jesus, the second Adam, also failed in this mission. Thus, according to Moon, full salvation requires a "completer." When Jesus failed to accomplish his purpose "it became God's desire to send another Messiah, a second son here on earth."

Moon's own Kingdom of God on earth will be established by what he identifies as the "third Adam". The "third Adam" is Rev. Moon and that he has already begun to establish God's kingdom. "He [God] is living in me. I am the incarnation of Himself. The whole world is in my hand, and I will conquer and subjugate the world."

Moon teaches "Through adultery, the archangel who became Satan stole the intended bride of heaven." According to Unification doctrine, however, they failed in this mission as Eve succumbed to the seduction of the archangel, Satan, having sexual intercourse with him. Her eyes were then opened and, realizing what she had done, she attempted to correct this by having relations with Adam, prior to God's appointed time. Eve successfully seduced Adam and, after having sexual relations with her, his eyes were also opened and he felt fear and shame over what he had done. Eve did all this when she was 16-17 years old. Moon teaches that if she had only made it to the age of 21, then she would have been perfect- and her children with Adam would have been perfect. Sure Rev, and she could legally buy beer.

Moon's speeches which span a lifetime consists of thousands of volumes, all recorded as it is to them Holy Doctrine. Moon's teachings, his belief system are far beyond the scope of just an article or a book to address. We can take note that everything he says counters what the bible says almost 100%.

Here from a speech that appeared in Midweek of march 19th of this year with a 2 page ad we find the most ridiculous revelations yet. I read a lot of cult material in my research but much of what he said are so graphic, bizarre and disgusting it boggles the mind how the paper allowed this to go to print. So I cannot mention it all and it certainly was not pleasant to read.

"What did Adam and Eve plant in the garden of Eden? It was the seed of free sex. Can that be denied. That is the reason they covered their lower parts."..."If the fruit of the tree of knowledge of good and evil were a literal fruit, then Adam and Eve should have covered their mouths or their hands. So why did they hide their lower parts? Reverend Moon is an intelligent man. I am not doing what I am doing because I am inferior to you.. It cannot be denied

He has even the audacity to say "No one throughout history has known God better than I do."

Rev. Moon has bluntly said, "I know the established Christian theology. I know the enemy, but the enemy doesn't know me. Thus the enemy has already lost the war." In some ways he is right , we have numerous people who have become comrades with him despite his claims to be the Messiah and God. There are those who will side with anyone as long as the money comes in. Then there is the prestige of being seen with a modern day moral leader, a martyr for a cause. But can anyone come to this conclusion after reading some of his material where his focus is on sex. He was more a disguised liberal, who is false messiah, prophet/teacher that had in essence gained the whole world and in reality lost his own soul. But then that was Jesus' words and we don't need Him anymore, we have Moon!

In 1995, more than 720,000 people were married via satellite at 545 sites in over 100 countries, 10,000 were American. Two-thirds of the participants were renewing their vows. Moon and his wife spent over a year matching people for their perfect marriage. This was done using photographs categorized by sex, age and nationality." This blessing does not come free or even what one would pay a minister in a normal ceremony. This is the Rev. Moon who specializes in marriages. It cost Japanese couples $29,000 each Americans paid $2,000. I guess he charges by the nation's economy. "Church officials say the money goes for satellite charges and the costs for 200,000 African couples, but a number of Protestant churches in Korea said that the ceremonies, which have brought the church $1.3 billion throughout the years, are just a way for the church to make money. Worldwide, there has been more than 360 million couples who have accepted Reverend and Dr. Moon's (his wife) blessing on their marriage.

In one of his ceremonies Whitney Housten was to sing for a fee of almost a million dollars but canceled at the last minute being sick. Louis Farrakhan appeared on stage giving support by his presence there seemingly finding solace in this Messiah wanna be.

So what is the mystique of the marriage performed by Rev, Moon? "What is the meaning of the Blessing? Blessing means coming from God through the True Parents." Since 1960 the Blessing has been offered because this is when the "marriage of the Lamb" prophesied in the book of Revelation happened. Moon married his second wife Hak Ja Han who was a 17 year-old devoted follower of his religion. Rev. Moon claims that his wedding to Hak Ja Han appointed them as the true parents of mankind.(Some say this is wife #2 others report her to be wife #4 as he divorced the first three) Moon died at the age of 92, and his widow was 69, 23 years his junior.

"After the Blessing the couples spend a period of time, usually forty days, abstaining from sexual contact, and during this time each spouse prepares in a prayerful way for a pure, new start to married life. After this period of time, a three-day ceremony is performed privately by the husband and wife, thus completing the process of the Blessing."

In January of 2000, Moon's second youngest son (of thirteen children) Young Jin Moon, committed suicide by jumping from the 17th floor of Harrah's Casino/Hotel in Reno, Nevada. Instead of finding fault in his son, the Moonies representative Tyler Hendricks said, "It is because the members didn't fulfill their responsibilities, that is why Moon's son is dead. This is a tragedy."

One can only wonder if it was the pressure of being Moon's son or depression of being Moons son? Moon had selected Young Jin Nim's wife and married him giving the "Blessing" to both of his sons Hyung Jin Nim, Young Jin Nim together in a joint ceremony.

One of Moon's daughters, Ye Jin, is said to have denounced her father while another, Sun-Jin, left her husband only weeks after having received her "blessing."

The Unification Church is one of the most bizarre mind control cults in all history. The Unification Church has successfully done a PR job to have the public be unaware of their teachings and support their cause. With family values in the forefront this is all the public knows about them. Most people are totally unaware of the true teachings of the Rev. If people were able to read his speeches and his theology which he claims is true Christianity), they would be aghast.

It has been estimated, conservatively, "that those Moonies [Unification Church members] on the street corners, in shopping malls, and in supermarkets, selling candles and flowers, yield for the Church over a million dollars every five days." Moonies take in over ¾ of a billion dollars a year from their workers selling trinkets and flowers. I'm sure you have drove pass their flower stands many times. But this is not where they get their money to support their 350 companies worldwide.

Through deceptive recruiting techniques and calculated false teachings one can become indoctrinated quickly into the unification church. Members are stripped of their critical thinking ability and made into Moons religious activists within a very short time. They can worked up to 18 to 20 hours on average, all 7 days a week. They are so busy that they either have no time or are not allowed to see their family and friends. They have become part of the New Messiah's family.

This is the family of Mr. And Mrs. Moon becomes a dedicated army, a growing number of young people soliciting donations for the Unification Church. Typically, a donation was requested in exchange for an item such as candy or flowers, to aid some endeavor or organization. These are often fictitious needs, which they allegedly represent. These fund raising tactics, are still used today on an unsuspecting public, and continue to help fund the efforts of the Unification Church. They will usually say they are here attending the college as a foreign exchange student as they ask for help. I have found them to be less then genuine in their presentation.

If you find Unification church workers that you see looking tired, thin, spaced out like no one is home. This is because they work long days with often little sleep. They are known to take 7 and 21 day fasts of water and are malnourished. But this is all done by choice in their service to the new Messiah.

Unfortunately there are Christians and others who ignore his new age science fiction and look at the causes promoted by his organization, just as Louis Farrakhan and Jerry Falwell did.

Christian leaders have been criticized for what some perceived as drawing too close to the Unification Church over the years. Tim LaHaye, Christian author and head of the American Coalition for

Traditional Values, came under fire for accepting a gift from Col. Bo Hi Pak. The Col. a former Korean C.I A. officer, who is president of the Washington Times newspaper, and who just happened to be Moon's right-hand man. Since then, a number of pastors from a broad spectrum of denominations have received free trips from CAUSA, a Unification Church-funded a organization which has pumped millions of dollars into anti -communism efforts in Central and S. America. Some well known names have also been speaking at CAUSA rallies (Jerry Falwell is a favorite who spoke at a conference in Miami which was co-sponsored by CAUSA).

In 1994 Falwell accepted $3.5 million donation from one of Moon's front organizations (the Women's Federation for World Peace). This was to bail out Falwell's Liberty University. "Robert Parry writing for I.F magazine and the Los Angeles Times, revealed that moon had funneled the donation through the Christian heritage Foundation (CHF) a non profit that had purchased the school's then 473 million dollar debt."

Because Falwell became friends with Moon, he attended and spoke at gatherings about which the Unification Church has this to say, "Southern Baptist church leader Rev. Jerry Falwell sincerely praised Father as the world leader establishing true love. Jerry Falwell and people of conscience in America are beginning to recognize the contributions and sacrifices Father has made for America. For the first time in 40 years, Able-minded people like Jerry Falwell are testifying to Father."

The degree to which Moon involved himself with high profile personalities can be seen by the roll of speakers at events sponsored by Moon's organizations. Some of the more highly visible celebrities were: Maureen Reagan (daughter of former President Reagan); former President Gerald Ford; George and Barbara Bush; comedian Bill Cosby; Marilyn Quayle (wife of former vice-president Dan Quayle); Republican vice-presidential candidate, Jack Kemp. Even knowing the Moon connection, Kemp continued to speak at Unification sponsored functions.

Other participants have included Olympic gold medalist and speed skater, Dan Jansen; wife of the late Martin Luther King, Correta Scott King; ABC News anchorwoman, Barbara Walters; film actor, Christopher Reed; astronaut, Sally Ride; and former British Prime Minister, Sir Edward Heath. Also speaking were highly visible religious and Christian leaders such as Robert Schuller, Senior Pastor of the Crystal Cathedral (not surprising); Ralph Reed, executive director of the Christian Coalition; Beverly LaHaye, president of Concerned Women of America. Ralph Reed and singers Pat Boone and Family, Jack Kemp and others shared the platform with both Mr. and Mrs. Moon.

Particularly disturbing during her speech, Mrs. Moon taught that Jesus was, not the virgin-born son of Mary, but rather the illegitimate son of Mary and her cousin's husband, Zecharias. But this is not new teaching but standard Unification Church theology. In his February 7, 1995 address in Washington D.C., Moon stated, "Who was the father of Jesus? Zachariah." He continued, "The result of the relationship between Zachariah and Mary was the birth of Jesus Christ."

In lists of names, Barbara Walters and Bill Cosby publicly expressed their concern when they learned the event was hosted by Moon. Walters has stated she will never again speak at an event sponsored by Moon. Cosby tried to back out of his commitment when he learned of Moon's involvement. He ended up performing after being threatened with litigation for failing to honor his contract, but gave only a short performance and refused to be photographed with Moon. Many others have distanced themselves from him once they became aware of hidden teachings and agendas. But his popularity continues today among the unsuspecting and unknowledgeable.

Cal Thomas was present at a CAUSA (a Unification front group) seminar in San Francisco, asked to comment from the floor, reacting to the unchristian theories put forth, he shocked participants by standing and saying, 'I am a follower of Jesus, who said he is the Way, the Truth, and the Life, and no man comes to the Father except by him.'"

Then there is Former President and Mrs. Bush. The Canadian magazine, Maclean's, maintains Bush is the most outspoken defender of involvement with these front organizations. While he been requested by many concerned Christians, former Moon members, and even anti-cult organizations, that he stop lending himself to Moon's causes, the former President has continued to speak at Moon/Unification sponsored events. Sun Myung Moon launched a new Spanish language newspaper for the whole of Latin America, with the backing of guest George Bush who praised Moon's respect for editorial independence. Bush then traveled with Moon to Uruguay to help him inaugurate a seminary in the capital, Montevideo, to train 4,200 young Japanese women to spread the word of his Church of Unification across Latin America. Bush was

141

reported by the *Washington Post* to have been paid $100,000 for his appearance.

In 1995 more than 50,000 people paid from $105 to $196 each to attend a Bush speech at the Tokyo Dome in Japan, in an event sponsored by Moon's organization. I guess George Sr. didn't agree with his son's axis of evil.-

Cynthia Lilley (who is the founder of MOMS, Mothers Opposed to Moon) speaks out on the children have been recruited into the Unification Church/cult. "All these people should know better. My daughter would tell me over and over how in their recruiting films, they would show Moon with Bush to impress young people. They use the films of Moon and Bush and other celebrities to reassure parents that it is okay that their children are on the streets selling flowers 18 hours a day."

Moon lived in the U.S. for more than 30 years and was the CEO of a private company, the Tongil Group, with interests in construction, heavy machinery, munitions, and much else. A subsidiary of that company is the biggest distributor of raw fish for sushi in the U.S. The Tongil Group has its own newspaper, the *Washington Times*, as well as a football team and a ballet company. The size of Moon's fortune is a closely guarded secret, but was thought to be around $1 billion dollars. He was undoubtedly the richest messiah in history.

Yet first and foremost Moon was the leader of an outrageous sect founded on his claim to be the reincarnation of Jesus Christ, destined to rule the world. "God is living in me and I am the incarnation of Himself," he once declared. "The whole world is in my hand and I will conquer and subjugate the world." In 1976 he said in a speech that was recycled last week by the Church, "After my death millions of people in the spirit world and here on earth will testify to my deeds, and to what I have done in history; in eternity I know that my deeds will shine. I intend to surpass the suffering of all the past saints, so as to not only dwell among them but rise up above them."

In 2004 he told a grand audience on Washington's Capitol Hill that long-dead emperors, kings, and presidents, including Hitler and Stalin, had declared "from beyond the grave, to all Heaven and Earth that Reverend Sun Myung Moon is none other than humanity's saviour, messiah, returning Lord and parent."

Moon founded his church amid the squalor and misery of Busan, a rough Korean port town, in the wake of the Korean war, claiming that Jesus had appeared to him years before to explain that the crucifixion had prevented him from completing his work, and had given him the task of doing so, by spreading his blessings to create a world of faithful, sinless couples and families.

Moon blended the most enticing elements of the available traditions with the panache of a top chef: the Christianity of the conquering Americans, made palatable to his Korean flock by a neo-Confucian stress on weddings and families, spiced with a dash of pseudo-Buddhist mysticism. No wonder Christian churches in the West rejected his efforts to unify them.

But Western kids were another matter. Steve Hassan was a 19-year-old college student with a high opinion of himself as an "independent thinker," but one day, he told the Guardian, "three women, dressed like students, asked if they could sit at my table in the cafeteria. They were kind of flirting with me. I thought I was going to get a date." He says they lied to him, flatly denying they belonged to a religious group; in fact, they were missionaries for the Moonies, and quickly he was hooked. "Within three months I was a cult leader. I got very deeply involved, and I got to the point where I was being told to think about what country I wanted to run when we took over the world."

"Love-bombing" Moonie co-eds have gone the way of bell-ringing Hare Krishnas. And although the Unification Church still stages the occasional mass wedding, and tens of thousands attended Moon's funeral, the reported pressure on new members to recruit and raise funds has eased: today's Moonies live in their own homes and the Church is allegedly underwritten by the business empire.

Today the most high-profile of the old-time secretive sects is Scientology. It continues to respond belligerently when challenged—to the assaults by Anonymous, to Vanity Fair's story about young actresses being auditioned for the job of Tom Cruise's wife, to the acclaimed new film by Paul Thomas Anderson *The Master*, in which Philip Seymour Hoffman plays a character that Anderson admits was based on Scientology founder L. Ron Hubbard. But that's another looney and yet another story.

Psycho Pentecostals

Wherever you are, on any given Sunday, you can find a Pentacostal Church because it will be the loudest and certainly one of the wackiest. Boisterous singing, clapping hands, shouts of "Amen!" and "Praise the Lord!" loud enough for God to hear.

Pentecostalism started in Los Angeles at a place called the Azusa Street Revival in which people, led by a preacher named William J. Seymour, believed that the fervor of the service would bring them to speak in tongues and witness miracles. Seymour was the son of slaves and certainly had some awareness of the old African belief systems. The events within a Sunday service ae strikingly similar to what Wikipedia tells us about some African religions.

"West and Central African religious practices generally manifest themselves in communal ceremonies and/or divinatory rites in which members of the community, overcome by *force* (or *ashe, nyama*, etc.), are excited to the point of going into meditative trance in response to rhythmic or mantric drumming and/or singing. One religious ceremony practiced in Gabon and Cameroon is the Okuyi, practiced by several Bantu ethnic groups. In this state, depending upon the region, drumming or instrumental rhythms played by respected musicians (each of which is unique to a given deity or ancestor), participants embody a deity or ancestor, energy and/or state of mind by performing distinct ritual movements or dances which further enhance their elevated consciousness. When this trance-like state is witnessed and understood, practitioners are privy to a way of contemplating the pure or symbolic embodiment of a particular mindset or frame of reference."

Like their African counterpart, Pentecostals often convulse and become enraptured as they speak in tongues and generally lose control of themselves. Seymours earliest congregations were primarily blacks and although historians never mention it, Pentecostalism clearly appears to bear African trademarks.

A 2011 Pew Forum study revealed that 44% of all Pentecostals are in Sub-Saharan Africa while 37% are the Americas.

Certainly the basic principles of Christianity are found in the Pentecostal doctrines with few modifications. They are heavy on baptism even though they don't always agree on how it should be done. Most of the typical Christian practices are duplicated except that grape juice is used at the administration of communion.

Where the Pentecostals get truly off the rail is in their belief in healing. One of the reasons their meetings are so raucous is that they pray for a healing to occur – and they don't know much about silent prayer – and then the preacher and others put their hands on the afflicted and ask that devils be cast out or that the illness be cured. Usually there is an anointing with olive oil. Basically, what you have is a whole church full of Benny Hinns calling on God to do something special just for them.

Now all this is made possible because once a person is baptized into the Pentecostal Church, they receive "gifts." These divine presents include the ability to speak in tongues – a kind of gibberish that no one understands, not even the person speaking it – that leads us to the question about why speak it at all?

The gifts of prophecy, tongues, interpretation of tongues, and words of wisdom and knowledge are called the vocal gifts. Pentecostals look to 1 Corinthians 13 for instructions on the proper use of the spiritual gifts, especially the vocal ones. Some teach that the gift of tongues is equal to the gift of prophecy when tongues are interpreted.

David Cloud in his *The Pentecostal-Charismatic Movement: Its History and Error* states: "Those are the terms we have heard frequently at Charismatic conferences, such as those in New Orleans in 1987, Indianapolis in 1990, and St. Louis in 2000. The tongues that I heard in these conferences were not languages of any sort but merely repetitive mumblings that anyone could imitate. Larry Lea's "tongues" at Indianapolis in 1990 went like this: 'Bubblyida bubblyida hallelujah bubblyida hallabubbly shallabubblyida kolabubblyida glooooory hallelujah bubblyida.' I wrote that down as he was saying it and later checked it against the tape."

I can't imagine by what reasoning – or lack of it – Pentecostals fail to recognize that "speaking in tongues" mentioned in scripture refers to normal, known languages of that time. In fact, those tongues are actually listed. They might even look up the word "tongues" in the Greek. As you will find, "glossa" simply means "languages." When the Bible speaks of "tongues," it always is referring to a known, earthy, established language – never some mysterious, unknown, hocus-pocus, mumbo-jumbo. The 100% phony tongues which the Pentecostals practice is not found anywhere in the Bible. Even the carnal Church of Corinth wasn't foolish enough to speak in some crazy language that even the speaker didn't understand. This is clearly evidenced by Paul's constant mention of the necessity of an interpreter. No one could interpret the garbage which Charismatics are babbling even if they tried. They admit that they don't even know what they're saying. You have to really try hard to come up with a line of BS like that!

One articulate friend once told me, "Pentecostal churches are very participatory. "We believe in backing up the preacher." I've heard said many times. I've been to a Pentecostal church a few times as an atheist, and it's always a very awkward situation. The congregation doesn't just sit there. They're going to get up, stand on things, shout praises, dance around, waving their hands in the air to inspirational, upbeat music, and yes, often times 'speak in tongues' (or get a case of the la-la-la's as I like to call it). Defining a typical Pentecostal service as a 'Jesus orgy" would not be too much of a stretch.

The Pentecostals have produced their share of fakirs and snake oil salesmen. William Branham. He was the amen-shouter who predicted that the Rapture and end of the world would take place in 1977. Shades of the Watchtower, no? But like ole' Joe Smith, he claimed an angel taught him the method by which he could detect diseases in people. A serious ailment would bring tremors to his left hand.

F. F. Bosworth said in his *Gifts of Healing Plus, The Voice of Healing,* "When the afflicting spirit comes into contact with the gift it sets up such a physical commotion that it becomes visible on Brother Branham's hand, and so real that it will stop his wrist watch instantly. This feels to Brother Branham like taking hold of a live wire with too much electric current in it" On one occasion he "resurrected" a fish that had been killed by a friend.

Who can forget Kathryn Kuhlman, another Pentecostal phony who claimed thousands of cures during her crusades but not one could be proven by medical examiners. But Kathryn had a touch of Aimee McPherson in her and while pastoring in Denver, Colorado, she had a fling with another evangelist, Burroughs Waltrip. The problem was that Waltrip was married but that was soon taken care of when he left his wife and kids and married Kathryn. Desertion, adultery, lies – all appeared to be acceptable by Kathryn Khulman as she continued to spew her holy words. To her credit, however, a few years later Kathryn claimed that God had given her a choice between the man she loved and her service to His calling. Being the noble, obedient soul she was, she chose God and all the cash she could rake in from her revivals. As for Waltrip, his wife was abandoned with two kids to support and all his bills to pay. He never sent the court-ordered child support payments and finally died in a California prison for having bilked a woman out of her money.

Perhaps the king of the Pentecostal wackos was A.A. Allen who Benny Hinn claims was a great evangelist and healer! This fruitcake once claimed that a woman lost 200 pounds instantly during one of his healing services. Later he claimed to be able to "raise the dead" and told his followers that they needed to completely believe that God could resurrect their lost loved ones. He stopped this only when some refused to bury their recently lost loved ones.

Allen built his own 2400-acre community called Miracle Valley, in Arizona. His vast evangelistic empire took in about $3.5 million annually, a massive amount of money for that time. Allen was arrested for drunk driving during a revival in 1955. He divorced his wife in 1967, in spite of the fact that she had stood by him during the many troubles he had brought upon himself, and three years later he died alone at a motel in San Francisco while his team was conducting a crusade in West Virginia. He was 59 years old and he died alone, an alcoholic and a fraud.

And then there was Oral Roberts. Who can forget Oral telling his followers that he was going to fast until he had enough donations to build a tower at his university. Always dramatic, rarely truthful, he was nonetheless one of a kind.

More than sixty years ago Roberts predicted that Jesus was returning that year – 1950. Four years later he modified his claim with the announcement of "a coming together of God's anointed for the final revival."

The cover of the March 1952, issue of *Healing Waters* featured "three great medical doctors congratulating Oral Roberts." One of these was identified as Dr. J.H. Miller, "outstanding medical doctor and president of a medical society of over 20,000 physicians." When an inquiry was made to the American Medical Association by two Presbyterian ministers, it was learned that there was no record of these "great medical doctors." Presbyterian pastor Carroll Stegall, Jr., attended Oral Roberts' crusades and did follow-up interviews of those who were supposedly healed. He testified that there was no basis to support Roberts' claims. Writing in 1955 in the *Presbyterian Outlook*, Stegall concluded: "I have never seen a vestige of change. I challenge any honest investigator to follow my technique and see whether his findings do not agree with mine." Referring to the Pentecostal healers in general, Stegall said:

"So far from curing, they often kill. Far from blessing, their arrival in a city is rather a curse, a misery, a racket, a destruction of faith in simple people."

In 1956, Mary Vonderscher died twelve hours after appearing on Robert's television program to testify of her healing. In January 1959, a 64-year-old man died during a campaign in Oakland, California. In May 1959, a three-year-old girl died during a healing crusade in Fayetteville, North Carolina. An elderly Indian woman died on her way to that crusade. In July 1959, a woman died after believing herself healed in a Roberts crusade.

Another popular Pentecostal "faith healer" of our day is Morris Cerullo, who took over the Heritage USA properties after Jim Bakker was convicted and sentenced to prison. The September 1992 issue of the *Evangelical Times* contained the following information about Cerullo healing crusades:

"Miss Audrey Reynolds attended a Morris Cerullo healing crusade in London and believed she was healed of a brain abnormality. She stopped taking her medicine and, as a result, suffered a fatal brain seizure. Sir Montague Levine, the Southwark Coroner, told the inquest, 'It was a tragedy that she went to this meeting and thought she was cured of everything. Sadly, it led to her death.'

Foundation magazine, published by the Fundamental Evangelistic Association of Los Osos, California, wisely warns: "Multitudes have been discouraged and led astray by so-called faith healers such as Cerullo. Their paths are strewn with heartbreak and confusion. I realize that many feel it is wrong to speak publicly against supposed Christian preachers such as this, but this type of thing is a great wickedness. It is a serious matter to claim that God wants to heal every sickness."

Back in 1944, the Supreme Court ruled that parental authority cannot interfere with a child's welfare, even in cases of religious expression. "The right to practice religion freely," the court concluded, "does not include liberty to expose... [a] child... to ill health or death."

That decision hasn't stopped 38 states and the District of Columbia from providing religious exemptions in their civil codes on child abuse and neglect. These exemptions can prevent Child Protective Services from investigating and monitoring cases of religion-based medical neglect and discourage reporting. Seventeen states have religious defenses to felony crimes against children. And 15 states have religious defenses to misdemeanors.

But while much of the criticism directed toward faith-healers lands on Christian Scientists, there are a number of other denominations that also discourage members from turning to modern medicine. One is the Church of the First Born, a network of more than 100 small Pentecostal churches sprawling across 20 states.

In defense of its faith-healing practices, the Church of the First Born cites biblical verse James 5:14: "If any be sick, call for the elders of the church, let them pray over him, anointing him with oil in the name of the Lord."

In 1983, Rita Swan founded Children's Health Is a Legal Duty (CHILD), an organization that lobbies against state laws that protect parents who choose faith over modern medicine. In 1998, she decided to team up with pediatrician Seth M. Asser to investigate the child fatalities associated with faith healing.

The two began reviewing the deaths of 172 children where medical care was withheld on religious grounds. Their study showed that 140 of these children would have had a 90% likelihood of survival had they received routine medical care. CHILD estimates that since 1976, at least 82 children linked to the Church of the First Born have died from lack of medical treatment.

Like so many other court rulings, the *Prince v. Massachusetts* decision has been marred by contradictory rulings, state versus federal discrepancies and legal ambiguity. Does the Supreme Court ruling stand independent of the Free Exercise Clause? What about the First Amendment's Establishment Clause? Should this constitutional argument be extended to all denominations that practice faith-based healing?

The answers to these questions will differ depending on who's giving them. But there is one piece of literature that should be taken from the Court's 1944 decision: "Parents may be free to become martyrs themselves, but they are not free, in identical circumstances, to make martyrs of their children."

Over the past decade or so, a number of children born into the Church of the First Born have met untimely deaths. While these incidents may have gone underreported and under-investigated in the past, the Internet has afforded the public an opportunity to learn more about these children and their deaths. Here are the histories of five such children.

Travis Rossiter, 39, and Wenona Rossiter, 37, were convicted of first and second degree manslaughter in the death of their daughter, Syble after the 12-year-old died from untreated diabetic ketoacidosis. In Oregon, where the family is from, the sentence conviction carries a 10-year mandatory minimum sentence.

As *Medical Daily* reports, Syble suffered from type 1 diabetes, formerly known as juvenile diabetes, a condition in which a person is unable to produce insulin. Without insulin therapy, type 1 diabetes is fatal. The most common cause of death among pediatric diabetics is diabetic ketoacidosis, which is caused by a buildup of fat metabolites called ketones. Symptoms include vomiting, dehydration and confusion, eventually leading to coma and death if left untreated.

The Rossiters assumed Syble had come down with the flu. "I always prayed that God would allow the body to naturally take care of itself. I had no idea – the day my daughter died – that the body was destroying itself. Instead of taking care of itself. I had no idea," Wenona said on the stand. "It's been hard," she said about listening to testimony in the trial. "Especially hearing from the doctors. It just tore me up inside that as a mother, I had no idea that that was going on."

At the time, local Police Captain Eric Carter insisted the 12-year-old "had a treatable medical condition and the parents did not provide adequate and necessary medical care to that child."

Travis Rossiter told a detective that doctors are for people who don't believe strongly enough in God. Wenona Rossiter's own brother died of untreated leukemia at the age of 7. When prosecutors asked if she believed it was God's will for her daughter to die, she said yes.

With insulin therapy administered through injections or an insulin pump, people with type 1 diabetes can live a long, normal life.

In another case, Russel Bellew, 39, and his wife Brandi, 36, were arrested in February 2012 for the death of their 16-year-old son, Austin Sprout. Austin fell ill in December and began suffering from flu-like symptoms. Rather than taking the teenager to see a doctor, his mother and stepfather chose to pray for his recovery. Austin's condition continued to deteriorate for over a week, until he eventually died. An autopsy revealed that he died from an infection from a burst appendix.

In exchange for pleading guilty, "faith healers" Russel and Brandi Bellew were placed on probation for five years. The couple has six other surviving children. At first, the court ruled that the children would be closely monitored by the state's Department of Human Services. Any time a child misses a day of school due to illness, the family must consult a doctor, the *Register-Guard* reported. A few months later, however, the children were removed from the home and became wards of the state.

Brian Sprout, Austin Sprout's father and Brandi Bellew's first husband, died in 2007 of sepsis after seeking prayer instead of medical treatment for a leg injury.

At the time of Austin's death, his uncle Shawn Sprout defended the congregation's practice of faith healing. "We trust in God for everything. We trusted him to take care of our illnesses and heal," he proclaimed.

Greg Swezey, 48, and his wife JaLea, 46, accepted a plea deal in 2012 that spared them jail time but holds them responsible for the death of their 17-year-old son, Zachary, who died in 2009 of a ruptured appendix. His parents had originally faced second-degree murder charges.

After falling ill, Zachary was bedridden for days with a fever, diarrhea and vomiting. His parents claimed they gave their son the option of going to the hospital but he declined.

The family called for church elders from Olympia and Spokane who anointed the ailing teenager's body with olive oil and prayed over him.

Doctors confirmed that an appendectomy would have saved Zachary's life. Appendectomies are relatively safe and simple procedures that have dramatically reduced the mortality rate attributed to acute appendicitis. Over the past 50 years, the rate has dropped from 26% to less than 1%.

In 2012, JaLea Swezey pleaded guilty to third-degree criminal mistreatment and received a suspended sentence. Greg Swezey was charged with second-degree criminal mistreatment. His case was continued for two years.

Swezey's charge was later reduced to third-degree criminal mistreatment under the condition that he commit no felonies over the following two years, and he also received a suspended sentence. During his testimony, Greg Swezey claimed he did not know until minutes before Zachary died on March 18, 2009, that his son was dying.

Susan Grady, 43, was sentenced to two and a half years in jail for the 2009 death of her 9-year-old son Aaron, who died of complications from diabetes. Grady was convicted for second-degree manslaughter in the boy's death. The maximum penalty for second-degree manslaughter is four years.

In an audio-recorded interview, Grady told Broken Arrow Police, "I felt like God would heal him," *Tulsa World* reported. Grady continued, "We just believe that prayer works."

"I didn't want to be weak in my faith and disappoint God. I don't believe what I did, with the way I believe, was wrong. I try to have faith and do what I feel is right," she added.

Aaron lost 16 pounds in six days, which Michael Baxter, a pediatrician involved in the case, said proved that the boy "suffered from child neglect."

On May 12, a jury convicted Dewayne and Maleta Schmidt of reckless homicide in connection with the death of their 2-day-old daughter, Rhiana Rose. Rhianna was born breech with the umbilical cord wrapped around her neck. She turned blue and stopped breathing three times before dying of puerperal sepsis, a common infection at birth that is easily treated with antibiotics.

"My clients are being prosecuted as a result of their faith in God—their religious beliefs. 'They didn't fail to act. They acted. They acted in accordance with their religious beliefs," said the couple's defense attorney.

Deputy prosecutor Matt Solomon said during an interview away from the courtroom, "Parents do have some rights. Those rights don't extend to this area where you're talking about reckless conduct."

Instead of seeking medical attention for his daughter, Dewayne Schmidt called church elders to pray for Rhiana. Both parents were sentenced to six years in prison, but the penalty was later reduced to one year each at a work release facility, with each of them serving 6-month terms alternately so that one parent could be at home caring for their other children.

Following the conviction, prosecuting attorneys asked that the couple's other two children be ordered to receive medical care if needed. The judge stopped short of granting the request but appointed a guardian to notify the court about possible health concerns.

"I thought we lived in a country where I had freedom of religion, but I've come to realize it's only if it agrees with everyone else's," Maleta Schmidt said. "I can't believe it ever came to this."

Judge Margret G. Robb later wrote that "Parents, while free to make martyrs of themselves, are not free under identical circumstances to make martyrs of their children," citing the Supreme Court's 1944 decision.

It's easy to demonize these parents, to say that if they really loved their children, they would have done something more than pray. But even CHILD founder Rita Swan admitted that the Schmidts' love for their baby was "undeniable." In the birth announcement for Rhiana, Maleta Schmidt prepared a photo of herself and her baby, tiny ink footprints and a poem to Rhiana, reading:

"You are more perfect than I could've hoped for, More beautiful than I could've dreamed, More precious than I could've imagined. I love you more than I could've known."

Religious indoctrination is not something that's easy to stray away from. Strict legal repercussions for failing to get one's child medical treatment will help encourage parents to act in accordance with the laws. But perhaps the law would be most effective if coupled with an internal push for reform. Rita Swan was a former Christian Scientist herself; she left the church after her young son died without medical attention while a Christian Science practitioner prayed for him.

The topic of faith healing can be debated in legal jargon forever, but any responsible parent knows that a dying child cannot be condemned to prayer alone. That sounds mean and tough and I intended it to. Watching your own child suffer should stir any parent to want to make whatever effort is reasonable and even in desperation, it should be clear that prayer alone does not heal. I don't care how many claims are made by phony evangelists or the rock and roll churches, prayer isn't the answer to all things. How many prayers have you had answered personally? How many things you prayed for as a child were later yours? Prayer is the personal communication to ease the soul of the individual but only a moron would sacrifice their own child on the altar of such ignorance.

The only thing the promised cures of all the fakes and their crusades have done is filled cemeteries. And without conscience, they can drive away in their BMWs and Mercedes from the misery they help perpetuate. There is nothing special, blessed or holy about them. Their touch contaminates far more than it ever cured. They are criminals who escape judgement only because they cower under the shield of the freedom of religion.

And yet – thousands flock to the message of hope. Many go because they have no hope left within their lives. If a messenger has come among them, they will go to witness and hope even more. And that's what evangelists are – peddlers of hope. The prey upon every weakness, every desire and dream, every last shred of expectation and ask the mindless crowd to share within them in their pretense. These are people of evil and they spawn evil in their words of threat and consequence. They are the worse of the worst and the lowest of the scum.

STUPIDISM WITH SNAKES

Many will claim that those utilizing live snakes in their Sunday services should be included in the section on Pentecostals, and perhaps they're right. These are Pentecostal folk but they step over the loony line so far that they deserve their own place in our examination of Stupidism.

Locked in the beautiful Appalachian Mountains are communities of simple people, connected to nature and devout in their somewhat primitive way. These are the snake handlers, those who gyrate on Sunday mornings with their hands filled with menacing, deadly serpents because one verse at the end of the Gospel According to Mark. "And these signs will follow those who believe: In my name they will cast out demons; they will speak with new tongues; they will take up serpents; and if they drink anything deadly, it will by no means hurt them; they will lay their hands on the sick, and they will recover."

It is of no importance to these people that the verse they use to risk their lives is not original to the Bible. You'd have a difficult time finding a theologian who did not agree that "the snake verse" was added to Mark long after the formation of the New Testament. It is not found in any manuscript prior to the fourth century. Early third-century theologians like Origen and Clement of Alexandria also make no mention of the last 12 verses of Mark – all much later additions.

That does not deter devoted serpent handlers. "For scholars of religion, the questions surrounding the Mark 16:9-20 passage are extremely important for questions of canon formation and scriptural authority," explained Yolanda Pierce, scholar of religion at Princeton Theological Seminary. "But for those who believe that the version of the Bible that they physically hold in their hands is the true, literal, and unchanging word of God, it's pretty irrelevant if that particular Mark passage was added later than the other chapters."

If you haven't noticed by now, almost all of these religious movements and sects were founded by some pretty shady characters. The idea of putting snakes into the sermon came from yet another on-the-edge loony. George Went Hensley started out as a self-made minister in the Appalachian hills, having experienced a "religious conversion" in 1910. On the basis of his interpretation of scripture, he came to believe that the New Testament commanded all Christ-ians to handle venomous snakes.

155

Hensley was part of a large family that had moved between Tennessee and Virginia before settling in Tennessee shortly after his birth. Following his conversion, he traveled through the Southeastern United States teaching a form of Pentecostalism that emphasized strict personal holiness and frequent contact with venomous snakes. Although illiterate, he became a licensed minister of the Church of God (Cleveland, Tennessee). in 1915. After traveling through Tennessee for several years conducting Church of God-sanctioned services, he resigned from the denomination in 1922. Hensley was married four times and fathered thirteen children. He had many conflicts with his family members because of his drunkenness, frequent travels, and inability to earn steady income, factors cited by his first three wives as reasons for their divorces.

Hensley was arrested in Tennessee on moonshine-related charges during the Prohibition era and sentenced to a term in a workhouse, from which he escaped and fled the state. Hensley traveled to Ohio where he held revival services, though he and his family rarely stayed long in one location. He established churches, known as the Church of God with Signs Following, in Tennessee and Kentucky. His services ranged from small meetings held in houses to large gatherings that drew media attention and hundreds of attendees. Although he conducted many services, he made little money, and he was arrested for violating laws against snake handling at least twice. During his ministry, Hensley claimed to have been bitten by many snakes without ill effect, and toward the end of his career, he estimated that he had survived more than 400 bites. In 1955, while conducting a service in Florida, he was bitten by a snake and became violently ill. He refused to seek medical attention and died the following day. Despite his personal failings, he convinced many residents of rural Appalachia that snake handling was commanded by God, and his followers continued the practice after his death. Although snake handling developed independently in several Pentecostal ministries, Hensley is generally credited with spreading the custom in the Southeastern United States. Somehow, that doesn't seem to be a very attractive legacy. Even so, according to ABC News, an estimated 125 churches practice serpent handling in the United States, most of which are concentrated in rural Appalachia, although some are as far away as Canada.

The short-lived National Geographic series "Snake Salvation" featured snake-handling preacher, Jamie Coots, 42, and his small but enthusiastic congregation that jumped in a spasmatic dance while speaking in tongues and grasping chattering Timber Rattlers.

In February of 2014, however, Coots was bitten by a rattlesnake during the church service and died two hours later. 22-year-old serpent handler Andrew Hamblin watched his mentor die in his arms. Jamie, a third-generation snake-handling pastor and the star of the National Geographic reality show, had been bitten by a four-foot rattlesnake during a service at his church, the Full Gospel Tabernacle in Jesus Name, in Middlesboro, Kentucky. He had been bitten by his snakes eight times before and survived, but the ninth bite, which had severed an artery in his right hand, killed him quickly.

"I didn't think it was going to hurt him because I had seen him bit there before," said Andrew, describing the night that Jamie died. Andrew and Cody, Jamie's son, followed the preacher into the church bathroom, where he told them that his face felt like it was burning.

"As I was moving behind him he said—and he didn't have any fear in his voice, he didn't sound like he was in pain—he said, 'Lord come by,'" said Andrew. "And then he said, 'Oh God no.' I thought that odd, and when I unbuttoned his right shirt sleeve, he looked at me, he looked me right in the face, and he said, 'Sweet Jesus.' Just as calm, just as peaceful as you'd imagine."

"Then he looked past me, and his eyes glazed over, they shut, and Jamie never spoke a word again. He never opened his eyes again. He started to slump, and I said, 'Dad.' And I knelt behind him, and when I did, I felt something wet, and his bowels had released, (he could have left that part out) and he was dead. He took his last breath in my arms."

He doesn't mention, of course, that emergency workers tried to convince Coot's family to let them take him to a hospital, but his wife and son refused.

"He always said, 'Don't take me to a doctor,'" his son Cody told reporters. "It was totally against his religion."

Well, know what, Cody? I would prefer to have my father alive and forever angry with me than dead because of some bogus belief founded on a false verse in the Bible. Jamie Coots didn't die of a snake bite. He died of collective ignorance – his own and all that surrounded him.

While it seems unsurprising that a serpent-handling pastor might die of a snakebite, particularly since they tend refuse treatment for their bites, it is less so than it seems. Seemingly more

157

surprising is that this was actually Coots's ninth rattlesnake bite. At the bottom of this seeming mystery is the fact that rattlesnakes rarely inject large doses of venom into non-prey like humans, and largely for this reason, even if left untreated rattlesnake bites carry nearly a 97.4% survival rate in humans. (This is a 1/40 chance of dying, which is extremely serious, and this rate is improved to 99.7% while other serious complications can be avoided with rapid medical treatment, so do not refuse medical treatment if bitten by a rattlesnake, obviously!) Coots's son identified that something about this bite was different than the others, and a good guess for that is the quantity of venom the snake injected into him. Obviously, knowing that there is a 97.4% survival rate to a rattlesnake bite takes some of the faith-inducing mystery out of the situation, but what about less likely medical "miracles"?

Because the chance of surviving a rattlesnake bite is so high, the miracle in this case already appears busted, but what if Coots had been bitten instead by the most venomous snake in the world, Australia's fearsome inland taipan, which packs an 80% untreated mortality rate. Would surviving this snakebite be a miracle? (Note: The African black mamba, the second most venomous snake in the world, because it more reliably injects fatal doses of venom, has an untreated mortality rate of very nearly 100%).

But Coots survived eight untreated rattlesnake bites. Isn't that something shocking enough to be considered miraculous? Not quite. He had nearly an 81% chance of surviving them, assuming independence of the circumstances in each bite. To have had a cumulative survival chance equal to a single bite from the inland taipan, Coots would have needed 61 rattlesnake bites. But even surviving that more venomous encounter would hardly have counted as a miracle.

In Coots' case, there were no miracles. All the speaking in tongues and laying on hands couldn't change the venom moving through his veins. His death should have been a message to the congregation that something was wrong with their most basic doctrine – they cannot pick up snakes and be bitten and nothing happens as Mark promised. It should have been a lesson taught long ago. Ralph Hood maintains that there have been "over 100 documented deaths" among the snake handlers. Robert Winston claims the number is 120. Paul Williamson, professor of psychology at Henderson State University submits "91 documented snake bite deaths."

Following Coots' death, Andrew Hamblin took up the task of pastoring the loonies and his Sunday snakes. His calling wouldn't last too long, however, because he was arrested for the possession of the 53 illegal snakes, but in the end he was not indicted. The snakes were not returned to him, however, and initially the snakes found a home at the Knoxville Zoo. Many had already died, and the remaining snakes were diseased and did not qualify to be on display permanently at the zoo. The snake remains will provide valuable insight for researchers who will study their bones. Snakes in captivity bring additional insight to the data not available from snakes captured in the wild.

So, while it might seem to observers that this is the end of snake handling in Appalachia, it is clear to residents that this is not so. It appears from Hamblin's remarks that the church has continued its snake-related worship services in Tennessee with the view that they were divinely protected from prosecution. Viewers of this National Geographic program would remember that one of the fond recreational activities of many of the congregants is snake hunting, and replacing the snakes will be no trouble at all. People Magazine quoted a judge who ruled in one of these cases: "If the court thought that a trial would act to deter future snake handling in church, my decision would be different," Bell District Judge James Bowling Jr. wrote to the county attorney. "But you and I both know that this practice is not going to stop until either rattlesnakes or snake handlers become extinct."

The loonies are far from extinct. Ralph Hood, professor of psychology at the University of Tennessee at Chattanooga, tells that church followers not only handle snakes but speak in tongues, handle fire, and drink a poisonous mixture of strychnine and water during church services. "They see these acts as obedience to God. The motivation is belief in eternal life. Not simply the here and now. Hence to be obedient to God, even in such a risky behavior as handling, assures eternal salvation."

Successful snake handling, or "victory," he added, "is an emotional and sometimes ecstatic experience of perfect obedience and assurance of the protection of the Holy Spirit. Even bites and death are proof of obedience and a holy life."

It's an extreme and—in most states—illegal kind of worship, one that lives on the far-out edges of Christianity, where life, death, and eternal salvation are indistinct, and greet you together when you walk into the church house. After initially gaining popularity in the early 20th century, serpent handling fell out of fashion around the 1940s, after a rash of lethal snake bites during church services. (About 90 pastors have died from snake bites since 1900, according to some studies. Most states now have laws against using snakes in religious practices, not to mention laws against housing and transporting poisonous reptiles. But despite, or perhaps because of, this risk, serpent handling is experiencing a resurgence driven by a new generation of young, charismatic pastors like Andrew, who post snake-handling photos on Facebook and invite strangers— including the media—to come watch their services.

Andrew Hamblin speaks of his ministry with a tone of inspireation. "I didn't grow up in a serpent-handling church. I grew up in a Baptist church. We spoke in tongues, we danced, we sung, and we believed in the Holy Ghost, but we didn't take up serpents. Then I saw it on TV one time, in a documentary, and I started getting books and watching videos—I wanted to know what makes these people tick. They were just like we were at my grandpa's church, but they took up serpents, they handled fire, they drunk the deadly thing. I wanted to know if this was real or not. So when I was 17 years old, I convinced some people to take me to Jamie's church, and he went into a box and pulled two rattlers out, and you could just feel the power of God in that church house. I said then, "This has to be real." And I prayed and I fasted, and finally, a year to the day later, the Lord moved on me and let me do it, he let me handle them. And I've been doing it ever since.

"It's an indescribable feeling to feel the power of God move on somebody to take up a serpent. I've seen the sick healed, I've seen devils pass out of people, I've seen miracles, I've seen unexplainable things happen — I've seen all sorts of things that God has done through people. It's a way of life. We live this every day. We live close to God.

"When God moves on you, there are only one or two reasons that you are going to get bitten. One is that to get bitten and not suffer, and that's a sign to the people for some reason. That was like me last night—I got bit, and I didn't feel a whole thing. We had three people get saved last night, gave their hearts to God. Now on the way home, I fainted, and my finger's a little sore this morning, but other than that, I am just fine. The second reason would be that it would be your appointed time to die that day. I believe that we all have an appointed time to die, whether it be by cancer, by snake bite, by car wreck, or by plane crash."

Julia Duin is a great writer and longtime investigator of the snake handlers. The last I heard she was preparing a book about them. But I was taken by her article in the *Washington Post Magazine* about Mack Wolford, a snake-handling Appalachian preacher. It said in part:

"For years, this tiny church in an unincorporated hamlet of 1,191 souls has been world-famous for its death-defying handlers of serpents. Reporters, researchers, photographers and TV crews have come here to track Pentecostals who brandish poisonous snakes, drink strychnine and play with fire as a testimony of their faith. Each Labor Day weekend, the church has hosted a well-documented "homecoming" for snake handlers, who believe that Mark 16:17-18 mandates that true Christians 'take up serpents and if they drink anything deadly, it will by no means hurt them; they will lay hands on the sick and they will recover.'

"Wolford's mission in life is to make sure that this custom, which he learned from his parents, survives for another generation. 'Anybody can do it that believes it,' he says. 'Jesus said, 'These signs shall follow them which believe.' This is a sign to show people that God has the power.'

"Though snake handling is condemned by mainstream Pentecostal denominations, Wolford believes that 21st-century Christianity desperately needs people willing to exhibit such signs. And he's willing to do so despite having been bitten four times — and despite watching his snake-handling father die an agonizing death.

"If you read down into the story, it gets really poignant. It's easy to see people like this as utter crackpots (and by the way, I wonder if people like Julian Baggini, who sneer at the Roman Catholic Church's claim to have the authority to rule on the authenticity of religious revelation, understand that without such authority, there is no basis on which to tell zealous religious folks that no matter what they think, God does not want them to pick up rattlesnakes). But their journey to the radical fringe of Christianity comes out of a savage desperation.

Wolford, the rattlesnake-rubbing divine profiled by Duin, was later bitten in church by a rattler and died. She describes the event:

"At one time or another, we had handled [snakes], but we had backslid," his sister, Robin Vanover, said Monday evening. "His birthday was Saturday, and all he wanted to do is get his brothers and sisters in church together."

And so they were gathered at this evangelistic hootenanny of Christian praise and worship. About 30 minutes into the service, his sister said, Wolford passed a yellow timber rattlesnake to a church member and his mother.

"He laid it on the ground," she said, "and he sat down next to the snake, and it bit him on the thigh."

Time and time again, the deaths of preaches and congregation members have proven that there is no divine immunity to the sanke bite. No one is healed during the church service, especially from a snake bite. In reality, snakes have been more effective in reducing over-population than in healing the sick.

Mark Twain said that "Faith is believing what you know ain't so." That pretty well describes the faith of the snake handlers. With a long roster of dead preachers, they have to realize that something is wrong with their most basic beliefs. But how can they be convinced? Still, we might say to the snake-handlers, regardless that this passage appears in the Bible, why are you paying so much attention to this one passage in Mark? What does it matter? Their answer would certainly be: it's in the Bible and the Bible is the word of God. It is fair to ask, then, why do you take this passage literally and ignore other passages, such as cutting off your hand if it offends you (Matthew 5:30)? Or why do you not tie a millstone around your neck if you harm a child and jump in the sea (Mark 9:42; Matthew 18:6; Luke 17:2)? Yet, asking snake-handlers to take literally every passage in the Bible does not mitigate against taking the passage in Mark 16:17-18 literally.

It is certainly not a Christian approach simply to counsel the snake-handlers to scoff at the passage or ignore this passage or suggest it does not belong in the Bible. The necessary approach is to find an alternate interpretation of this passage that fits within the broad Christian tradition of biblical interpretation, which does not always prefer literal interpretation. Better than literally writing the passage out of the Bible ought to be an attempt to make sense of the passage spiritually. The literal reading of the passage, frankly, is the most obvious reading of the verses, but it need not be the only way to read these verses.

There are five "signs" listed in Mark 16:15-18. Out of these five "signs" many mainstream Christians would accept casting out demons (such as Catholics - at least through the formal rites of exorcism - and many evangelical Protestants), speaking in new tongues (charismatic Catholics, Pentecostals and other charismatic Christians), and healing the sick (Catholics, mainstream and evangelical Protestants). But it is only a very few who take seriously the other two "signs," namely, picking up poisonous snakes and drinking poison. Why? Why do most Christians ignore these two signs?

Some might argue that casting out demons, healing the sick and speaking in new tongues have a more substantial biblical basis. Jesus' ministry is full of him casting out demons and healing the sick, as the first two chapters of Mark alone attest. The examples in the four Gospels are too numerous to mention. Speaking in tongues is also attested in Acts 2 and in 1 Corinthians 12-14. What does the rest of the NT say about drinking poison and snake-handling?

Just as Jesus never intended to produce an incalculable number one eyed, one armed followers when he said to poke out your eye and chop off your hand if they lead you to sin, so too, when the NT speaks of handling snakes and drinking poison harmlessly, hyperbolic language is being used. Common sense should make it clear that Jesus never intended the physical handling of snakes and the drinking of poison in the literal sense but that's hard to get across to someone who believes each word in the Bible is true and original. It's hard to get across to someone who knows nothing about the characters forming the history of their snake-handling beliefs.

Take a look at Alabama preacher Glenn Summerford. In 1991, Summerford was convicted of attempted murder for allegedly forcing his wife at gunpoint to fake a suicide note and stick her hand into his cage of poisonous snakes, which he utilized during his church services. Sentenced to 99 years in jail for his vicious attack on his wife – who miraculously survived – the preacher unsuccessfully attempted a jailbreak in 2003, escaping for 45 minutes before being re-captured.

•

Five Tennessee children were orphaned at the hands of snake handling in 1998, after the practice claimed their father John Wayne Brown Jr., a preacher who suffered a fatal snake bite in an Alabama church. The children's mother? Also dead from snake handling, bitten in 1995 attending a Kentucky religious revival. Brown's five children were taken in by his parents, who have their own snake-handling church in North Carolina.

•

In 2004, Rev. Dwayne Long was leading a service on Easter Sunday in his southwestern Virginia Pentecostal church when the rattlesnake he was holding recoiled and bit his finger. Long refused medical treatment and died the next day.

•

Are snake handlers fit to be foster parents? A Kentucky agency didn't think so in 2007, when Jason and Tammy Barrett had their licenses revoked after refusing to stop attending snake handling services. In response, the Barretts sued the foster care agency for discrimination, claiming the agency violated their constitutional rights when it revoked their license and took custody of the foster children in their care.

In the early years of snake handling as a form of worship, it was generally accepted that a lot of snake-handling was vaudeville flash, with little risk of actual death. The snakes used were considered "docile," and it was always rumored they had been defanged, or at least "milked" beforehand to exhaust them of most of their poison. Supposedly, you could make a pretty penny from popping a snake's fangs through a bit of cheesecloth stretched taut with a rubber band over a mason jar. Many parishioners said that nearby hospitals would purchase the subsequently expelled venom to produce antivenom, adding to skepticism surrounding the "spirituality" of snake-handling. And when there was news of a snake handling preacher dying from a bite, it brought little more than an exasperated head shake — no one ever thought it wasn't dangerous, most thought it was idiotic.

The poverty and geography of Appalachia fosters a desperate, insular kind of faith, and in the common context of poor health, the spiritual and corporeal congeal into a complex delusion of "miracles" and inexplicable, supernatural forces. These tales filter down through the generations and believing them means there is no need to research for the truth. It is easier to accept and most do.

One apologist issued the fierce defense of snake handling in this form: "Don't even try to approach us and convince us to forsake our experiences, especially if you have not ever tried it nor even bothered to understand it. We don't care what your fallible ministers say against serpent handling. We have our revelation, many of you don't. We don't care what your cult prophets or gurus say against serpent handling. We rely on the Holy Ghost and Jesus Christ to give us the Word of God only - not any exterior fallible men.. There is no other name under Heaven to which a man can be saved by and that name is Jesus Christ - not Moses, not Elijah, not Buddha, not John the Baptist, not the Watchtower, not Joseph Smith, not Mohamad. Just JESUS. Snake Handlers are some of the toughest Christians around. Don't even try to sway us.. God has given us revelations and experiences that many other Christians

164

can't comprehend due to their ignorance and rejection of it. There is no real way to describe it in words unless you cross the line yourself. We are Apostolic Holiness Pentecostal Christians who love Jesus, who love all of His Words and look to Him as the ultimate authority in our day to day practices."

Somehow it just doesn't sink in that the most fundamental part of their doctrine is based upon the words of some Catholic monk in the fourth or fifth century – not Jesus. The same can be said about the missionary movement of the Mormons and the Jehovah Witness – again based upon the same group of verses that did not come from Jesus, rather from the pen of some zealous early Christian. There was no command from Jesus to "go into the world and teach the gospel to all creation." It just didn't happen. Like it or not – it didn't happen.

What this tells us is that the snake handlers are true fundies but not very heavy on the academics. It's apparent that they know nothing of the Councils of Nicaea and the construction of the Bible. They obviously are unaware that Constantine ordered that, "Search ye these books, and whatever is good in them, that retain; but whatsoever is evil, that cast away. What is good in one book, unite ye with that which is good in another book. And whatsoever is thus brought together shall be called The Book of Books. And it shall be the doctrine of my people, which I will recommend unto all nations, that there shall be no more war for religions' sake."

In other words, there is no way to know if any of the New Testament represents an original document. If the "good parts" of several books were combined into one, all were corrupted. And yet, that was the command of the emperor and you can rest assured that it was obeyed.

To take a verse from the Bible and upon it form an entire belief system is nothing less than ridiculous. To believe in each word and mandate as true in its most literal form is absurd. If we did that, we would be killing homosexuals and non-believers.

Exodus 31 verse 15 tells us: "For six days, work is to be done, but the seventh day is a Sabbath of rest, holy to the Lord. Whoever does any work on the Sabbath day must be put to death. I guess that means we should go down to Walmart on any Sunday and gun down all the workers there. Come to think of it, isn't a preacher working when he gives his Sunday sermon? Throw him in with his snakes.

The idea that the Bible can be taken literally produces folks like the Pentecostals, Ken Ham, all the phony evangelists, the young earth wackos and the like. And as long as the concept survives, it will continue to produce followers that are one egg short of an omelet.

Dan Sewell wrote of his experience with the snake handlers in candid terms:

"You have your skeptics on everything," said Pastor Charles McGlocklin of New Hope, Ala., who's been handling snakes for more than 20 years. "I don't put people down for not believing. I'm just a poor country boy, and it's hard for me to explain to a well-educated man like you. But I know that it's real."

America's snake-handling practitioners--as many as 3,000 strong – meet in plain little out-of-the-way churches, defying mainstream church tradition, skepticism and ridicule, legal crack-downs and death itself to prove their faith. It is religion done raw and raucous.

"A lot of people are going to church to have a place to go on Sunday and say they went to church. They're trying to make salvation like going to a fast-food restaurant," said McGlocklin. "You've got to get down on your knees and separate yourself from the world, and really have an experience with God."

The numbers of faithful are believed to be in a slow decline. But there remains a dedicated core of followers, many from several generations of snake-handlers, some who have had relatives die of snakebite.

Even suffering the painful bites and venom rarely discourages believers – one, Dewey Chafin of West Virginia, says he's been bitten 118 times while handling thousands of snakes since 1960. And there are newcomers, like two recent converts at the Kingston church.

"My friends think it's like devil worship; it's like we're worshiping the snakes or something," said Michelle Tancrede, 15. "It's hard to explain. But you can feel it."

"I don't have a lot of friends left anymore," added Branden Neitz, 24, who said he's left behind his life of drugs, booze and heavy metal music. "Some of 'em think I'm pretty strange."

Today, said Steven Kane, a University of Rhode Island anthropologist, there are regular snake-handling services in Ohio, Michigan and Indiana, among others. The churches are usually called Pentecostal Holiness, but are independent. They are fundamentalist, but vary: Some say women can wear makeup, some object. Others disagree on what it means when a handler is bitten. Various biblical verses spur some to handle fire and tread barefoot on snakes besides handling them and drinking poison.

166

There is no knowing when the next service will be a snake-handler's last. For 77-year-old Kale Saylor of Kentucky, the final service was March 12. A rattlesnake bite claimed his life three days later. He was at least the 74th victim of a snake-handling service in this century. Even Hensley, the first snake-handler, died of snake-bite in 1955.

Dewey Bruce Hale, 40, died in the south Georgia town of Enigma on Jan. 15, nine hours after being bitten in church by a rattlesnake he had taken there. Berrien County Sheriff Jerry Brogdon was chagrined to learn that Hale refused medical treatment. He died at his home, surrounded by fellow faithful who prayed with him but didn't call authorities until after his death.

"One of the hardest things is they had probably 100 people sitting there watching a person die," Brogdon said.

He added: "I don't agree with that, but this is their belief, and I respect that. He died doing what he believed in."

Free-lance journalist Dennis Covington, a Birmingham, Ala., native, attended his first snake-handling service while covering the 1991 trial of Glenn Summerford, a minister convicted of attempting to kill his wife by forcing her hand into the box of rattlesnakes he kept for services.

A middle-aged man with an appetite for danger, interest in his own Appalachian roots, and a desire for more vibrant spirituality than he found in urban churches, Covington was drawn inexorably into the snake-handling world.

He attended eight churches in six states, and became a snake-handler himself. As recounted in his new book, *Salvation on Sand Mountain*, Covington even mulled becoming a minister.

Covington, who insists he would "never be so stupid or desperate enough to pick up a rattler just to make a good book," thinks often of the "anointing" that followers say is a divine feeling. "It was a complete absence of fear, a sense that I was being obedient. When I actually picked it up, everything started to fade; the congregation, the church, started to fade out.

"That's when I understood there is power, there's a spiritual ecstasy in the believer giving up a sense of self."

Covington, sitting up on the sofa of his comfortable suburban home, added: "I was anointed by the Holy Spirit. A psychologist or a medical doctor might have a different explanation. I don't much care about what they say."

Several states outlawed snake-handling in the 1940s and some practitioners were jailed. But the snake-handlers saw themselves as martyrs, much like the early Christians, and many simply became more determined.

It is still outlawed in some states, but prosecutions are rare. Authorities are sensitive to charges that they are infringing on religious freedom, and some are leery for other reasons: A North Carolina sheriff was hospitalized two weeks after being bitten by a snake during an arrest in 1985.

There are less risky aspects to the services. Once the snakes are returned to their boxes at the Church of the Lord Jesus Christ, the pace slows. There are readings from six biblical verses that refer to serpents, then singing of country gospel, a sermon, and "testifying" by congregants about their faith.

Regardless of the dismal history of snake handlers and the estimated 100 deaths, some ask why are the handlers bitten so rarely, and why are so few of those snakebites lethal? Considering how many people attend the churches and actually handle the snakes, the bites and deaths are somewhat rare. The answer might lie with some snake experts who strongly suggest that a snake's reluctance to bite a religious serpent handler may have more to do with the creature's poor health than with supernatural intervention.

The herpetologists at the Kentucky Reptile Zoo have been following the activities of Pentecostal snake handlers for years. They have watched hours of video of snake-handling services and examined snakes used in church.

"The animals that I've seen that have come from religious snake handlers were in bad condition," says Kristen Wiley, curator of the Kentucky Reptile Zoo, a facility in the town of Slade that produces venom and promotes the conservation of snakes. "They did not have water. The cages had been left not cleaned for a pretty long period of time. And the other thing we noticed is there were eight or 10 copperheads in a container that was not very large."

What's more, she says there was no fecal material in the container, which indicated the snakes were not being fed. Riley says a snake that may be dehydrated, underweight and sick from close confinement is less likely to strike than a healthy snake. Moreover, the venom it produces is weaker.

She says snake-handling preachers who don't take care of their snakes are "setting themselves up for a safer encounter during their services when they use a snake that is in bad condition to begin with."

One of the pastors they leveled criticism was the late Jamie Coots, who regularly took up serpents in his Full Gospel Tabernacle in Jesus Name in Middlesboro, Kentucky.

When experts visited the snake room behind Coots' house, there were about 30 snakes — mostly timber rattlers and copperheads — crowded into glass cages. He said he waters them regularly but that his supplier of live mice and rats moved away. And many of the snakes wouldn't eat anyway.

In a follow-up call, they asked him how long his snakes usually live. "Average is probably three to four months," Coots said.

The Kentucky Reptile Zoo reports that well-cared-for snakes live 10 to 20 years or longer in captivity.

Coots rejected the criticism. "People who don't believe in it are gonna say anything to try and discredit us, you know, to say that it's not God actually doin' it," he says.

Coots was arrested in 2008 by the Kentucky Department of Fish and Wildlife for trafficking in illegal venomous snakes. He was convicted and fined. Later he possessed permits to keep and transport snakes legally.

An entirely different view of religious snake handling comes from Whitfield Gibbons, an authority on snakes of the Southeastern U.S. at the University of Georgia.

"I think most snakes, a rattlesnake or a copperhead, if you are gentle with them after they've been in captivity and [you] pick them up gently, they won't bite you. So, it wouldn't matter what [your] religious belief was," Gibbons says.

Perhaps all the snake dancing and handling in Coots' old church has finally come to an end since the owner of the building has evicted the current preacher and his flock and reclaimed the place for other, more reasonable activities.

Despite the theories, one snake was healthy enough to kill Coots and that should serve as conclusive evidence that what these people call anointed, I call insane. The worst thing about the snake handlers is their stubbornness – their unwillingness to learn some historic truths about the singular verse on which they base their entire sect philosophy. They would call that devotion – and I call it ignorance.

THE TOM CRUISE CULT

He had achieved success beyond his wildest dreams; wealth, fame and the adulation of thousands of devoted adherents. Yet for the last five years of his life, L. Ron Hubbard, founder of Scientology, dwelt, a virtual prisoner of his own paranoia, a recluse in self-imposed exile, on a ranch in the desert of Creston, California. Surrounded by a handful of trusted aides, he handed over the running of his multimillion dollar empire to a chosen few. Even his wife was cut off - after she got out of prison after serving a sentence for her part in the notorious Snow White case, she never saw her husband again.

We start to see just how complex and confusing Scientology is when we look back on the Snow White case and the role of Mary Sue Hubbard who had enormous influence within the Guardian's Office of the organization. From its establishment in 1966 to its demise in the early 1980s, the Guardian's Office (GO) of the Church of Scientology carried out numerous covert operations and programs against a range of perceived opponents of Scientology in the United States and around the world. The GO sought to discredit, destroy or otherwise neutralize – or "depower", in Scientology jargon – any group or individual that it regarded as anti-Scientology.

Through both her role in the Guardian's Office, and the subsequent drama known as Operation Snow White, one can see Mary Sue at her most powerful, a power realized through her connection to Scientology's Founder (L Ron Hubbard), and, tragically, at her lowest ebb.

Mary Sue was appointed Guardian World Wide in March 1966 (and subsequently given the role of Controller). L Ron Hubbard created the Guardian's Office with the purpose 'to sweep aside opposition sufficiently to create a vacuum into which Scientology can expand.'

A list of the significant operations conducted by the Guardian's Office would include:
- Operation Bulldozer Leak
- Operation Bunny Bust
- Operation Cat
- Operation China Shop
- Operation Devil's Wop
- Operation Freakout
- Operation Italian Fog

170

- Operation Keller
- Operation Orange Juice
- Operation Snow White
- Operation Speedy Gonzales
- Operation Street-Man
- Operation Yellow
- Project Mayor Cazares Handling
- Project Power 2: Vatican Passport
- Power Project 3: Normandy
- Project Power 4: Tricycle

Mary Sue was granted a lot of power, due to her role in the Guardian's Office. However, it was this power that was to cause her downfall. Out of all these operations, one in particular stands out. Operation Snow White, where Scientology through its Guardian's Office infiltrated and burgled offices of the Government of The United states of America.

Operation Snow White was the Church of Scientology's name for a project during the 1970s to purge unfavorable records about Scientology and its founder L. Ron Hubbard. This project included a series of infiltrations and thefts from 136 government agencies, foreign embassies and consulates, as well as private organizations critical of Scientology, carried out by Church members, in more than 30 countries; the single largest infiltration of the United States government in history with up to 5,000 covert agents. This was also the operation that exposed 'Operation Freakout', due to the fact that this was the case that brought the government into investigation on the Church.

The FBI raided GO offices in Los Angeles and Washington in 1977, leading to the conviction of eleven Scientologists for their roles. This list included Mary Sue Hubbard. In October 1979, she was fined $10,000 and jailed for five years. Due to appeals, Mary Sue started her jail term in 1981.

L Ron Hubbard lost confidence in the GO, despite the fact that he was the ultimate authority within the Church of Scientology, and they had therefore been acting on his orders and wishes. He particularly turned on Mary Sue.

Ex-member Ken Urquhart stated, "Hubbard abandoned her, and made it quite clear within the organization that he had abandoned her. He was totally prepared to allow his wife to go to jail for crimes he was equally guilty of.

"After the FBI raid I was put to work making up reports to show that he did not know what was going on. In other words, I

171

was to cover his ass. He was privy to almost all of it and was as guilty as Mary Sue."

The Guardian's Office was eventually dismantled. It now operates under the name Office of Special Affairs, answerable to Religious Technology Center, headed by David Miscavige.

Mary sue Hubbard died in November 2002, an event which went unreported by the Church of Scientology to its members. In fact, they have gone so far as to remove her name and contribution from many Scientology publications.

'The Book of E-Meter Drills', a book she helped compile, now no longer makes mention of her contribution. The Policy Letter, 'PTS Type A Handling', which was originally written by Mary Sue, now no longer credits her. The book 'A History Of Man' used to state, at least up until 1980 'this work is dedicated to Mary Sue Hubbard who helped'. It now no longer states this."

Having helped coin the term 'Scientology', and serving as one of three trustees in the first incorporation of The Church of Scientology, Mary Sue ended her life forgotten by the organization that she contributed to for close on thirty years. She had already been forgotten by her husband, L Ron Hubbard.

Mary sue had this to say about L Ron Hubbard, "To my dear husband, auditor, teacher and our Founder go my thanks and acknowledgment for having given the most precious gifts of Freedom and true Beingness to me and my fellow Man. Without him, none of this would have been possible; and so to Ron goes my everlasting gratitude for having provided for all of us the Road to Clear."

Fearing indictment in the Snow White case, Hubbard fled to the desert in the early 80s, leaving behind his role as de facto controller of the Scientology empire and taking with him only a handful of trusted aides, mostly those now-grown messengers from the Commodore's Messenger Org, who had, in some cases literally, grown up under the Machiavellian tutelage of Hubbard, and became his emissaries to the empire he oversaw.

Of these former messengers turned executives, the future head of Scientology, David Miscavige, was amongst those angling to take control of the church upon its founder's death. But despite chronic ill health, the founder lived on, leaving Miscavige - and others, including Terri Gamboa, Vicki Aznaran, Lyman Spurlock and Norman Starkey – in a state of flux. They controlled the church, for all intents and purposes. But their authority came only through their appointed - some say self-appointed - role as the controllers of

172

Hubbard's communication with the world. But events, as we shall see, were spinning out of control for these so-called young rulers of Scientology.

Also omnipresent during Hubbard's final years were Pat and Annie Broeker, a couple who lived with Hubbard in Creston. While their official duties were to take care of Hubbard's welfare, as those closest to Source, they became important players in the operation of the church itself, given their enormous influence over Hubbard as his day-to-day caretakers. On a more practical level, Pat Broeker, in particular, oversaw the financial dealings between Hubbard and the church, and eventually became such a trusted friend that Hubbard named him as successor, the Loyal Officer who would look after his church after his passing.

On January 24 1986, under circumstances that can at best be characterized as 'suspicious', L. Ron Hubbard died. Although his condition had been steadily deteriorating for years, even the coronor noted that there were irregularities surrounding his death, including the presence in his body of vast quantities of Vistaril, a powerful ani-psychotic medication. Just days before Hubbard's death, his personal physician, Scientologist Gene Denk, left for a gambling vacation in Las Vegas with some of Hubbard's top aides, including Gamboa, Miscavige and wife, and the Aznarans. By the time he returned, there was nothing he could do. Hubbard died, and the battle for control of his legacy, which had been simmering for years, took centre stage.

Hubbard left behind a vast corporate empire, including millions of dollars worth of copyrights and trademarks, as well as a personal fortune rumored to be in the hundreds of millions. Rumour, though, is all that is available - the vast portion of Hubbard's riches were buried far inside the Church of Scientology ledgers, safe from the prying eyes of the IRS, which had been threatening an audit of Hubbard for years, right up until his death. But even leaving aside his personal fortune, Hubbard's legacy was rich - and there was no shortage of people eager to take a cut.

The day before Hubbard died, his will was redrafted. Gone was the reference to Pat Broeker, who had been the executor in the previous will. The new executor, who would oversee the transfer of all Hubbard's intellectual property to a trust known as Author's Family Trust-B, and from there, into the newly created vessel, the Church of Spiritual Technology, was Norman Starkey, a longtime Church of Scientology heavyweight who had earned the animosity of many now-disenfranchised Scientologists during the days of the

Missionholders' Conference in 1982, when David Miscavige and the young rulers first made waves as the new power behind Hubbard's throne. Gone, too, was Norton S. Karno, Hubbard's former tax lawyer whose presence weaves through the story of the Church of Scientology like an invisible, but unbreakable thread.

Starkey became Hubbard's executor, and David Miscavige took the reins of power as effortlessly as he had disposed of his rivals to the throne in previous internal skirmishes. There was no explanation for this last minute changing of the guard. But it was not long before those most likely to raise questions about the new regime - Pat and Annie Broeker - disappeared from the eye of the storm as though they had never been. With the Broekers out of the picture, there was no one who could pose a significant threat to Miscavige, and, like one born with the divine right of kings, he took his place as titular head of the church, highest ranking officer and ruler of the Scientology empire without firing a single shot. He remains there to this day.

The world, however, has moved on - and now, some of those same people who were present during the last days of L Ron Hubbard have come forward to tell what they know. Day by day and thread by thread, the real story of what happened at the end of his reign is slowly emerging.

The story behind the story of the Church of Scientology resembles a tale from the heyday of the Mafia far more than a religious organization. The evidence can be found in that many ex-members write of their experiences anonymously for fear of reprisals. Here is one example:

"I was a member of Scientology for many years. The only counseling I ever received was from official, authorized Scientology. A few years ago, at the hands of some of it's most trained members, I went through a devastating experience that left my mind and spirit shattered. I was no longer a whole person. Only now, am I able to even talk about it. Stories like mine are the exception, rather than the rule. However, mine is not the first, nor will it be the last.

I am posting this anonymously because I do not wish to be 'outed.' I am doing better, but I need time to continue healing in private. Of Course Scientologists in the Office of Special Affairs International (OSA Int) and Religious Technology Center (RTC) will recognize who I am because it was under their care that this happened.

"The story I wish to share began almost three years ago in 1996. I did not know it at the time but my saga began eight weeks after Lisa McPherson died on December 5, 1995, in Clearwater,

174

Florida. Several aspects of my story are similar, if not the same as Lisa's both of our doctors were Scientologists, we were given the same vitamin and herb concoctions as well as the Drug Chloral Hydrate, and both of us had complete mental breakdowns including hallucinations. Luckily, there were some aspects that were quite different, especially our endings.

"Lisa and I had both been long term Scientologists. I had spent over 10 years on Scientology staff (the Sea Organization) as a full time employee or staff member in one of their organizations. Several of those years were spent in Scientology International Management (Int.). After leaving the Sea Organization, I spent another ten years as a public Scientologist with varying degrees of activity.

"While I was a Scientologist, I encountered many conditions and situations within the church that I disliked or disagreed with. However, I rationalized them and placed them into perspectives that allowed me to feel I could and should continue as an active member. I guess I always hoped that these conditions would eventually be changed for the better.

"By the early 1990's, I found my hopes were wearing thin and my doubts and disagreements weren't so easily put to rest. I took some Scientology courses intending to get these doubts and disagreements resolved. Instead, the doubts got stronger.

"Towards the end of 1994, I received a call from someone at OSA Int. who wanted me to join a new group that "Wolly" had started on the Internet. (Note: "Wolly" is the name that staff at OSA Int. use for Larry Wollersheim, a former Scientologist.) She wanted to know what "Wolly" was up to. I turned her down, saying that I did not know my way around the Internet.

"However, her call made me curious and I soon learned how to get 'online'. That was how I discovered the Internet. During 1995, I found and read many court cases, court decisions, affidavits and press information in support of and against Scientology.

"While this information answered a lot of questions for me, it neither eased my doubts nor made me a stronger Scientologist. I took a few trips into AOLA (the Advanced Scientology Organization in Los Angeles) and CCLA (the Celebrity Center in Los Angeles) to get some help in sorting out my feelings. These actions did not help either.

"A few of the points that I wanted sorted out were:

"1. If Scientology was supposed to clear the planet, how come it cost so much? Most of the people that I knew in the regular middle class world, couldn't afford the lower levels of Scientology - much less the higher levels of "clearing'. Due to its prices, it seemed to be more of an elitist group than one working to help mankind. I knew of one member who had already paid $300,000 and he was being told he needed to purchase another $60,000 to get to the first level above Clear.

"2. Where was all the money going? Looked to me like a huge portion was going to lawyers to handle court cases to handle the people that were hurt by the exorbitant amounts of money being charged for services. And they needed to charge those exorbitant amounts of money because their lawyers cost so much.

"3. Was it really a religion? When I first joined I was clearly told that the 'religion' label was used only for tax and legal reasons, and that no one had to change their personal religious affiliation to be a member. During my 20 years as a member, I had only ever been to one Scientology church service. Once I tried to find a Scientology service to which I could take my children. One Scientology organization told me that they held a small service while people ate their lunches during a break in a Scientology Training Course. Another organization spent their Sunday mornings putting on a very large social Brunch, that they heavily advertised and promoted. I did hear that one organization had a service on Sunday nights that was pretty good. So I packed my children up one Sunday night and went. There was one other person standing in front of the building where we had been told the services took place. It was a dark, locked up building. We both went into the main lobby of the building next door. After asking several staff, who knew nothing about a Sunday service, we found one gentleman who casually said, "Oh, no, that was cancelled tonight". End of my foray into Scientology Services for my children.

"4. If Scientology was a religion, what were the group's beliefs about God. I had thought that my Scientology counseling would bring me a better understanding and a closer relationship with God (the divine, universal, whatever you call it), but here I was 20 years later, having experienced the highest levels of Scientology counseling, and I didn't feel any closer to God. Most of the Scientologists whom I knew personally did not believe in God. But, was that their decision as individuals, or was that due to Scientology's influence over them? I attempted to find out. That was when I discovered the massive editing that had been being done on Scientology materials. The one book in which I found some clear LRH references to the religious basis on Scientology (Notes on the

Lectures), I had to buy in a used book store because the Church had "cancelled" it.

"5. How come there were always these "Enemies?" I had done some projects for both the GO and OSA Int, and during those projects had the opportunity to spend some time with a few of these "SP's" and "Enemies". I did not find them to be the ogres that Scientology portrayed to its members. In fact, most of them knew of some valid point of outrageous Scientology behavior that led to the creation of their discontent or anger. In other words, from my point of view these enemies were being created by the very group that held itself up to be the 'victim'.

"These were a few of my feelings and concerns, as I wandered about the Internet.

"Around New Years 1996, I realized that I had to tell my husband how I felt, even though it was a High Crime to tell another Scientologist about one's disaffection with Scientology. I also told him that I might not want to be a Scientologist any longer. He was visibly upset and very clear with me that that would be a problem for him. I knew that if I continued in my current direction, my marriage and children could be at risk. So I stopped talking about my feelings.

"On Monday, February 5, 1996, I received a call from a member of OSA Int. who I knew personally. She wanted to meet with me. I met with her and her associate in the boardroom of OSA Int. on Hollywood Blvd. To my amazement, they handed me a private E-mail message I had sent to someone several months earlier. Scientology had declared this person a Suppressive Person, meaning that the Church had dismissed him from membership, severed his ties to the Scientology and to active Scientologists, and forbad all Scientologists to have anything to do with him. The person, in his message to me, marveled that I, a Scientologist in good standing, still trusted and communicated with him. I replied that I did not distrust him personally, but that I was concerned about the spies that I was certain that Scientology had positioned closely to him.

"The two women at OSA Int. never admitted how they obtained my private E-mail message. I told them I was not hiding anything, in that I had signed my real name to it, and knew they had observers and spies everywhere. I also told them about my visits to AOLA and CCLA to try to sort out my thoughts and feelings about Scientology, including some thoughts I had recently resolved.

"I told them that I disagreed with many of the operations that OSA Int. instigated against its so-called "enemies," as they were unethical. I disagreed with the Scientology mindset, "the end justifies the means," that governed their actions and decisions, including those I had personally been involved in or had personal first hand knowledge of.

"They really did not seem interested in my point of view, but instead zeroed in on specific names I mentioned, wanting to know if I had talked with this or that person, all of whom, of course, were on their enemies list.

"They offered to help me sort through my doubts and confusions. They said that a wonderful auditor, whom I had known but hadn't seen for many years, had been studying my folders and that she wanted to help me.

"I was not adverse to an offer of help, so went in for a D of P interview. Only to find out it was not a D of P interview like any I had ever had, but more like an interrogation. I was asked if I knew people who are off the bridge. Did I know anyone who is an SP? How bout people I chat with? How bout what I think??

"I returned home numb. I didn't want to talk about it. I knew if I refused their 'handling' I would be declared, and I knew my marriage (and other facets of my life) were at risk if I got declared. That night I happened to get a call from a Scientology friend of mine. She was troubled. Her Org (AOLA) had ordered her to disconnect from her best friend (disaffected as a Scientology member, but not a declared enemy). Her husband told her that if she didn't disconnect, she wouldn't be moving on the bridge and if she was not moving on the bridge, he could no longer be married to her.

"I felt I was in a similar corner to her and that I had no choice but to appear at the scheduled 'session' the next day. I call it a "session" because it was not an interview; the interview had been done the previous day. It was meant to be an informal interview before the more 'formal' auditing began.

"The next day the two OSA Int. women walked me back into the auditing room to meet the auditor. They followed me into this tiny auditing room. At first I looked at these three women and their stern faces and wondered if this was about to be a "Gang Bang Sec Check" that I had heard about years ago. But it wasn't, and they soon left me alone with my auditor.

"What transpired over the next several days was like no 'auditing' I had ever experienced. 'Grueling' is a word that comes to mind. The sessions were hours long, and went on for several days.

"I remember on the second day, the auditor had me read these different bulletins to show me that this was truly for my benefit and that these sessions were not meant to be an inquisition or to 'attack' me. The auditor said that she really cared about me and that this was being done to help. But then she would begin yelling at me over something I said or that she disagreed with.

"For example, I remember telling her about something that I had done to a suppressive person that I considered to be an overt, only to be yelled at. She shouted at me that what I had done couldn't possibly be an overt, that 'You cannot commit overts on Suppressive People.'

"We had several disagreements about the definition of an overt. I said that I did not agree with the definition, "Greatest Good for Greatest Number," as it had been used to justify a lot of wrong actions I had done. I said that I felt that "Do Unto Others," or 'what goes around comes around' had immensely more validity for me, and I used them to decide if I transgressed. The auditor vehemently disagreed with my point of view as it did not comply with either Hubbard's or Scientology's beliefs and, right in the auditing session, this led to several more yelling episodes.

"These 'session days' lasted about a week. When I wasn't in session, I talked very little. I felt numb all the time. Although I tried, I could not sleep. I forced myself to eat in order to "pass a metabolism check," the needle phenomenon that shows your body is rested and fed and allows the session to begin.

"At night I would feel these 'sessions' repeating constantly in my mind. It was like the session never ended. I brought the auditor home with me. She was in my mind, disagreeing with me, screaming at me, and digging into my head.

"This was the longest session I had, about six hours. I remember desperately wanting to leave. However, I was on one of the upper floors of OSA Int. When I pictured the difficulties in getting past my auditor as well as the hallways and stairs that had cameras everywhere and were always full of staff and security guards trained to prevent "session blows", I ended up remaining. I spent most of those six hours sitting in the tiny auditing room sobbing, or doubled over a trash can with the dry heaves.

"I went to sleep. Around 2 AM I was awakened with the cracking of my mind, my self, my soul. I don't know how else to describe it, other than my mind broke. I was driven to do something, but I did not know what. I was yelling at my husband, but it didn't feel as if I was yelling the words.

"I left the house running. My husband, who was chasing me, caught me before I left the driveway. I paced around the car and tried to touch the trees. My husband calmed me enough to get me back into the house.

"I was scared to death. Something had happened to my mind and I knew I was now in a different place. My husband called OSA Int. and spoke with my auditor (who happened to be up at 2AM)... She spoke with my husband and then myself. All I remember of our conversation was her saying 'There is no tech to handle this'. I remember feeling as though I was off in the distance, while thinking, 'she could at least have lied to me...'"

Decades ago the U.S. Government experimented with mind control methods. They could have saved a lot of money and simply used the Church of Scientology playbook. This is the king of cults, the most subversive form of controlling members with a dictatorial framework that violates ever concept of human rights.

The First Amendment to the Constitution states in part:

"Congress shall make no law respecting an establishment of religion, or prohibiting the free exercise thereof; or abridging the freedom of speech, or of the press; or the right of the people to peaceably to assemble, and to petition the government for the redress of grievances."

Thomas Jefferson, who possessed more than a passing familiarity with and passion for such freedom, underscored the importance of this protection saying, "Our most fundamental liberties depend upon the freedom of thought and the freedom of expression; and you cannot limit either one in any way without destroying both." In recent years, scientology has attemped to style itself a champion of the first amendment and of the liberties and freedoms it promises to us all. But beyond its protestations of alleged intrusions against it's own freedom to defraud, coerce and conspire, the cult behaves in a manner which is inimical to freedom.

To support this statement, let us examine the behavior of scientologists with regard to the subject of the freedom of speech and belief.

According to scientology policy it is a High Crime and a Suppressive Act for a scientologist in good standing to remain in communication with any person who has been declared to be a "Suppressive Person." What this means, of course, is that a scientologist's right to freedom of speech is abrogated – at least it is limited in that one cannot exercise free speech with respect to declared Suppressive Person's. Savvy scientologists might argue that they accept this limitation knowingly and willingly and thereby retain full freedom of speech. But Jefferson's caveat stands: one cannot limit this freedom in any way without destroying it. And, in fact, a scientologist who wishes to exercise full freedom of speech, risks the consequences that accompany violation of the above cited offense. One can, of course, be declared a Suppressive Person oneself for continuing communication to another declared Suppressive Person.

The point here is simply this: regardless of the arguments that can be made supporting such a limitation of free speech, it must be recognized that scientology advocates this significant abridgement of this freedom for its members. Though they cite historical, religious precedents for strict codes of conduct, etc., this fact remains. When it comes to talking to people who have been declared Suppressive or discussing the faults of the group, scientologists are simply not free to do so.

To understand the force with which scientology attempts to impose this limitation of the freedom of speech, one need only consider the consequences of being declared a Suppressive Person and expelled from the church. When one is thus declared, one suddenly finds oneself cut off from everyone with whom one has lived, loved, worked, and played.

This is precisely what happens (or what is supposed to happen) to a scientologist who is declared to be suppressive. This is disconnection. Think about it for a minute. Think of it in terms of your own life. Imagine that you live in a community heavily populated by scientologists.

We now know something about L Ron Hubbard and what a creep he was – no, coward is a better word – to abandon his wife and run and hide, trembling with the idea of a federal indictment. But what about the rest of this lunatic fringe group? Just what do they believe and why do they surrender their entire faculties to an organization that makes North Korea look like Cancun?

According to their official literature: "Scientology is a religion that offers a precise path leading to a complete and certain understanding of one's true spiritual nature and one's relationship to self, family, groups, Mankind, all life forms, the material universe, the spiritual universe and the Supreme Being."

It claims to have roots in the beliefs of "all great religions" and thus encompasses "a religious heritage as old and as varied as Man himself" and could be considered 50,000 years old.

Scientology begins with the concept that man is "basically good, and that his spiritual salvation depends upon himself, his fellows and his attainment of brotherhood with the universe."
The fundamental principles are threefold:

- Man is an immortal spiritual being
- His experience extends well beyond a single lifetime
- His capabilities are unlimited, even if not presently realized.

According to the church, people believe in scientology because of an "absence of answers" from science. They claim scientology supplies "workable methods of application, that made it possible for Man to reach the ancient goal he has been striving toward for thousands of years: to know himself and, in knowing himself, to know and understand other people and, ultimately, life itself."

Scientology means "knowing how to know". It is a contraction of the Latin *Scio* ("knowing, in the fullest sense of the word") and Greek *logos* ("study of").

These loonies at least rank a step above Jehovah Witnesses in one category – they celebrate holidays. Sure, L. Ron Hubbard's birthday in March, the Anniversary of the first publication of Dianetics in May, and Auditor's Day in September. Whoopee!

They believe the spirit can alleviate "injury, trauma or discomfort" by "putting the spirit in communication with the body". The church advises a method of detoxification involving saunas, exercise, vitamins, the drinking of oils, as well as light jogging."

It was reported Katie Holmes was not permitted to made a noise during childbirth, for fear of having a negative affect on her newborn daughter.

They believe life is compartmentalized into eight "dynamics". The First Dynamic, experienced by babies, is explained as an "urge towards existence" and the Eighth is an "urge toward infinity". They call a spiritual being "Thetan", meaning "the source of all life or life itself".

They have a concept of God or Supreme Being, but no set dogma. They explain: "Scientologists take the maxim quite to heart that God helps those who help themselves."

They believe in "past lives", with a person being born again. One cannot progress unless "aberrations" from past lives are dealt with. The concept of heaven or hell therefore relates to a future life, with experiences being earned by behavior. "In other words, the individual comes back," they say. "He has a responsibility for what goes on today since he will experience it tomorrow."

182

Scientologists believe children are spiritual beings occupying young bodies, and should be given the same respect as adults. Tom Cruise and Katie Holmes were reported to treat their daughter Suri as a young adult, allowing her to make her own decisions. Of course, Tom Cruise later admitted that Katie Holmes filed for divorce in part because of his involvement in the controversial Church of Scientology. When an attorney asked if Katie had left him to protect their daughter from Scientology, Cruise became very angry. He first responded that he found the question "offensive," saying, "there is no need to protect my daughter from my religion." But when lawyers pushed the question again, asking if his ex-wife ever indicated that she left because of the religion or because she wanted to protect their daughter from Scientology, Cruise responded:

"Did she say that? That was one of the assertions, yes."

Cruise also admitted that his 7-year-old daughter is no longer a practicing member of the religion. This is a huge admission since anyone who leaves the faith is considered a "Suppressive Person" and is cut off from all members of the church, including their immediate family.

When Holmes and Cruise divorced back in 2012, many of Scientology's defectors spoke out claiming that the church seemed to be playing favorites and bending rules when it came to Cruise and his family. Former Scientologist Samantha Domingo (whose ex-husband Placido Domingo, Jr. spoke out and left the church after officials tried to make him "disconnect" from her when she was labeled a "Suppressive Person") told Vanity Fair that the way Holmes blindsided Cruise with the divorce and enrolled Suri in private school would be automatic grounds for disconnection if Holmes were married to any other Scientologist.

Domingo said that even if Holmes left Cruise to protect her daughter from the church, he likely won't give up on bringing her back to the religion.

"According to Scientology doctrine, Katie has denied Suri her spiritual eternity in the church. There's no chance for her now," Domingo explained to Vanity Fair. "Why would Katie deny their daughter her spiritual freedom? How suppressive is that? If [Tom] loves his daughter, he will never give up on [Scientology]. He will try to use every means available to help his child, and he does think he's helping his child, but he's also helping the church control his life."

In his deposition, Bauer's lawyers asked Cruise if both he and the church now consider Holmes to be a "Suppressive Person" after leaving the church.

"That is a distortion and a simplification of the matter. I don't want to just give an oversimplification of religious doctrine," he said. However, he did agree that the definition of a Suppressive Person listed on the church's website was accurate.

Holmes is not the only big name to come to grips with scientology. Screenwriter/director Paul Haggis, who is known for his work in *Million Dollar Baby*, *Crash* and other Hollywood films, spent more than half his life in the Church of Scientology. But in 2009, Haggis (who is now 62), left the cult after 35 years because of its homophobic ways. That year, the cult's San Diego branch came out in support of Proposition 8, the ballot initiative banning same-sex marriage in California. Haggis, who has two lesbian daughters, refused to keep quiet. In an open letter to Scientologist official Tommy Davis explaining his reasons for leaving, Haggis asserted that he could not be a part of a group that would "support a bill that strips a group of its civil rights." Haggis was also quite critical of "disconnection," a practice in which Scientologists are encouraged to discontinue all contact with relatives and friends who are deemed hostile to the cult.

Beyond Belief author Jenna Miscavige Hill, who is the niece of Church of Scientology head David Miscavige, was raised a Scientologist and was once a member of Sea Org, considered the most elite group within Scientology. But after leaving the cult at 21, Hill became one of the cult's most outspoken critics. Hill has described her Scientology upbringing as both abusive and controlling. Scientology children, according to Hill, were required to work 14-hour days seven days a week, and she was discouraged from associating with children who weren't part of Sea Org. At the age of seven, Hill says, she was forced to sign a pledge that she would serve Sea Org "for the next billion years." (Scientologists believe that one obtains a new body after death, although they reject the Hindu and Buddhist views of reincarnation.)

Given how many openly gay people there are in the entertainment industry, it is ironic that the homophobic Church of Scientology goes out of its way to recruit actors and musicians. Actor Jason Beghe, a former Scientologist who is now one of the Church's most scathing critics, said he began to question Scientology after a member implied that a car accident he suffered was the result of his friendship with a gay man. But that incident was only the tip of the iceberg when it came to Beghe's crticisms of Scientology. Beghe, who began taking Scientology courses in 1994 and was once described by David Miscavige as "the poster boy for Scientology," left the cult in 2007, and from 2008 on, he has been asserting that Scientology harms members psychologically by convincing them their lives are meaningless without it. Scientology, Beghe has stressed, is great at breaking up families. He bluntly described how "dirty and underhanded" the Church of Scientology can be when, according to journalist Tony Ortega, he asserted, "They say they're not a turn-the-other-cheek religion. No, they're a knock-you-down-and-kick-you-in-the-balls religion."

When actress Leah Remini, now 45, publicly announced her departure from the Church of Scientology in July 2013, she had much to say about how controlling the cult could be. Remini, who was a Scientologist for 30 years, stressed that no one was going to tell her who she could and could not associate with, and she has been critical of the policy of disconnection as well as Scientologists' practice of labeling critics "suppressive persons" (a term L. Ron Hubbard used to defame anyone he considered hostile to the goals of Scientology).

When entertainment industry veteran Sylvia "Spanky" Taylor was part of Scientology's Sea Org, one of her duties was recruiting celebrities. Taylor was a close friend of actor John Travolta, one of Hollywood's most famous Scientologists, in the 1970s, and she recruited Priscilla Presley. But Taylor saw how nasty the Church could be when she was sent to the Rehabilitation Project Force, a prison-like place where Sea Org members are sent for "rehabil-itation." In *Going Clear*, Taylor recalls that at the RPF, she was sleep-deprived and was forced to perform "arduous physical labor"while pregnant. After giving birth, Taylor says, she was not allowed to see her baby daughter (at the RPF, children are considered a distraction). Taylor has alleged that when she was suffering the abusive practices of the RPF, Travolta avoided contact with her despite the fact that they had been close friends in the past. Taylor left Scientology in 1987, but continued to work in the entertainment industry.

Florida resident Sara Goldberg, one of the ex-Scientologists interviewed in *Going Clear*, spent 37 years with the Church of Scientology and became a high-ranking member. But her relationship with the organization went sour when she was given an ultimatum: either disown her son, Nick Lister, or risk being labeled a "suppressive person." Goldberg had raised Lister and her daughter Ashley Lister Epstein as Scientologists, but when Lister associated with Scientology critic Matt Argall, he was deemed a "suppressive person." Goldberg refused to "disconnect" from Lister, and in 2013, she was declared a suppressive person. Epstein "disconnected" from her own mother rather than go against the Church.

As a high-ranking Sea Org executive, Tom DeVocht, another interviewee in *Going Clear,* had close contact with David Miscavige. But since leaving the Church of Scientology in 2005 and being declared a suppressive person, he has been one of the cult's most vehement critics. DeVocht alleges that his sister Nancy, a Sea Org member, was sent to Rehabilitation Project Force for seeing him after he left the Church. She has since disconnected from him at the Church's insistence. DeVocht alleges that he has been under constant surveillance by the cult since leaving and has described Miscavige as a tyrant.

Actress Diana Canova was once heavily involved in the Church of Scientology, and for years, she was afraid to leave the Church because of her fear of retaliation. Eventually, Canova left because she "was so fed up with being afraid." Canova felt that she was being financially exploited by their expensive "auditing" sessions. The Church of Scientology, which is staunchly opposed to conventional psychiatry and psychology, has a bogus form of "spiritual counseling" it calls auditing — and it's not cheap.

At one time, actor Larry Anderson was among Hollywood's most vocal proponents of Scientology. Anderson spent 33 years in the Church of Scientology and was featured in the cult's promotional film, *Orientation,* in 1996. But Anderson left the Church of Scientology in 2009 after becoming increasingly critical of the high cost of auditing sessions. Anderson, who has described Scientologists as "sheeple" and auditing as a major rip-off, has asked the organization to return $150,000 of his money.

As a prominent member of Sea Org, Marc Headley worked closely with one of Hollywood's most famous Scientologists, actor Tom Cruise. But in 2005, Headley left because he feared being sent to the Rehabilitation Project Force. In 2009, his book *Blown for Good: Behind the Iron Curtain of Scientology* was published. Headley was declared a suppressive person and members of his family who were still active in the cult were ordered to disconnect from him.

Super millionaire Rupert Murdoch characterized scientologists as a "Very weird cult. Something creepy, maybe even evil, about these people." Among those "creepy" people are Cruise, Travolta,

Kirstie Alley and Will Smith. Lisa Marie Presley finally decided to bail out of the lunacy.

Fortunately, there are some ex-members with courage. Among the numerous court cases, reports and rumors involving scientology are allegations of human trafficking, holding people against their will, members cutting ties from their families and forcing a woman to have an abortion.

The church says: "Like all new ideas, Scientology has come under attack by the uninformed and vested interests. The so-called controversy of Scientology is merely the bitter old resisting the ambitious new."

The Church has its own cruise ship, the MV Freewinds, based in Curacao, for the most committed members. A former member claims she was held against her will on board for twelve years and forced to do hard labor.

An Australian senator called Scientology a "criminal organization" and accused it of embezzlement and blackmail.

Nora Crest, a former top female Scientologist who worked with some of the Church's prominent members like John Travolta and Tom Cruise, opened up about the three years she endured in a Scientology prison. The 39-year-old was forced into the Rehabilitation Project Force (RPF) because she kissed another girl. The RPF is another name for the secret labor camp in a remote Southern California suburb where Crest was forced to endure horrifying working and living conditions.

"It was the most horrific time of my life," Crest said. "I was battered and bruised, pushed around and nearly died trying to leave the Church, and all because I had the audacity to desire another woman."

The Church's founder, L. Ron Hubbard, believed homosexuality was an "illness" and "perversion" that could be "cured" with the help of the Church.

"We would stand in an empty trash can while various people poured buckets of iced water over your head and were shouting at you about what crap you were," Crest said.

The squalid living conditions in the camp reflected the horrible treatment of inmates in the prison.

"The rooms had bugs and cockroaches," Crest said. "The bunks were dirty mattresses with rusty springs dating back to the '50s. Disgusting conditions become the norm and you think that's what you deserve and that you are what they say you are: a worthless piece of shit."

Crest continued with more painful details: "We'd be made to wait in line for the food to be distributed, there'd be around 250 people. When the doors opened, there was large stands of burger and fries and people would be diving at them, it was like a scene from *Lord of the Flies,* elbowing, punching each other, ripping hamburgers from one another, screaming in each others' faces, then running off with the food to corners of the room like rabid animals and eating it quickly."

After two years, Crest begged to leave the camp, but the only way out was to admit she "was a degraded human being." The RPF also continued to incessantly interrogate Crest with thousands of questions regarding her stance on the Church, making sure she wouldn't speak out if she were to leave.

"It was one of the worst days of my life and I had to wait for three months for their decision while being convinced to stay on a daily basis," Crest said. "They threatened to split my family up and that I could never speak to my mother or sister. Ultimately I changed my mind and decided to stay, they'd broken me again."

Crest was later caught laughing and joking with another inmate, and was brutally punished for attempting to leave her interrogation session regarding the interaction.

"I was trying to get to the door and got five feet from it, but they were grabbing all parts of me and dragging me down. At one point, I had 13 people on my body and was pinned to the floor. I was kicked and punched, my face was covered in blood. I was screaming."

Crest was only able to escape the prison by drinking a bottle of bleach in an act of desperation. After she was released from the hospital, she "was forced to sign a waiver" that said she wasn't going to sue to speak out against the Church. "I said it all to the camera," she said. "I didn't care, I just wanted to go home."

Monique Rathbun has never been a member of Scientology but is the wife of an ex-high-ranking official in the organization, Marty Rathbun, who left the church under hostile circumstances 11 years ago.

In a 2013 suit she filed in Texas, Monique said that the church — which she called a "notorious, multi-billion dollar cult" — had harassed her and her husband, and had them under surveillance, on orders from the church's controversial leader, David Miscavige.

Rathbun claimed a legal win after the Texas Third Court of Appeals denied the church's legal appeal of a ruling from a lower court. The church in 2014 filed an "anti-SLAPP" motion in the ongoing litigation, saying that the religious-based conflict was protected under free speech.

After the initial motion was shot down by Comal County District Judge Dib Waldrip, the church appealed to the Third Court of Appeals — which denied the church's request, saying it had not proven that Rathbun's claims were "based on, related to, or in response to" their protected free speech.

Leslie Hyman, a member of Monique's legal team, said that "we are very pleased that the court saw through the church's attempt to recast into protected activity Monique's complaints of stalking and harassment and the church's attempt to shield its wrongdoing with a Texas statute not meant for that purpose."

As RadarOnline.com previously reported, Marty Rathbun — a one-time "inspector general for ethics" who defected in 2004 after 27 years in the church — slammed Miscavige as having "a complete narcissistic psychotic personality" in a disposition, and compared him to notorious historical figures Adolph Hitler, Joseph Stalin and Ayatollah Khomeini.

"That doesn't connote hate or dislike, it just is what it is," he said. "There's parallels in their behavior that are very direct."

So we have a gestapo with a egomaniac chief running a religious organization that should be based at Guantanamo. The don't have members, they have victims and they have brainwashed them so effectively and completely, that they don't even know they're being manipulated and robbed of their very being.

Unlike other religions, which are primarily based around books and stupid statues, like Jedi Knights, Scientologists use advanced, futuristic technology to "audit" its members. Auditing is the process whereby Scientology ministers cure spiritual upset. They do this using an instrument known as an "electro-psychometer", or "E-Meter". It is an electronic device used to test the mental state of an individual. The E-Meter does this by running a small electric current through a person's body, and reads the "mental image pictures" flowing through the "Thetan". The area of spiritual trauma is then pinpointed by an "Auditor", via the E-Meter's readout.

Within Scientology there are several governing bodies. The Office Of Special Affairs directs the legal affairs of the Church, and works to expose violations of human rights, and close down Internet sites which are particularly critical of Scientology. The alleged secret purpose of the OSA is as follows:

"1.To provide early warning of threats to Scientology or its leaders.
2.To discover the extent of information on Scientology held by governments.
3.To unearth compromising information on opponents of Scientology. "

Another semi-secret division of Scientologyis the Flag Service Organization. Based upon a 450 long ship, off the coast of Florida, "Flag" deals in advanced spiritual training and auditing. Another division, The Sea Organisation, is composed of the most dedicated Scientologists in the world - a bit like the Jedi Council, in The Phantom Menace. Like Flag, it is run from a number of ships, and members must sign a token billion-year contract dedicating their life to Scientology.

Those within the upper echelons of Scientology are privy to a number of scriptures and texts that are kept from public view. These texts are said to deal with very advanced levels of spiritual counselling, and are kept hidden because "premature exposure could impede spiritual development".

Scientology is supported financially by its members. Though it runs a small number of free churches, the path to spiritual enlightenment does not come cheap. Perhaps explaining the high number of millionaire celebrities who are advocates of Scientology, those wishing to "go Clear", can expect to be asked for a donation of at least $5,000. More intensive "processing" can cost up to $30,000.

Then again, The Church Of Scientology actively courts high-profile celebrity members, and has set up special "Celebrity Centres" around the world, offering Dianetics services to "artists and professionals in such fields as the performing arts, fine arts, sports and business." You know - high-profile people with lots of money, basically.

As well as Travolta and Alley, other confirmed celebrity Scientologists included Priscilla and Lisa Marie Presley, singer Al "Moonlighting Theme Tune" Jarreau, and - shocker! - Nancy Cartwright, who does the voice of Bart Simpson.

Among those who have opposed Scientology are the psychiatric profession, the US security services, and "Germans".

Some former Scientologists have claimed that the Church held them against their will. One Lisa McPherson was allegedly held for 17 days against her will, before dying while in the custody of the Church. The state of Florida has subsequently filed charges, while

McPherson's family have sued for imprisonment and wrongful death. Several high-ranking Scientologists were convicted for stealing government documents, while founder L. Ron Hubbard himself was once convicted of fraud by a French court.

According to the Church's doctrine, anyone who speaks out against Scientology "Cannot be granted the rights and beingness ordinarily accorded rational beings."

In one of Hubbard's early writings on Scientology doctrine, The Creation Of Human Ability, the author discusses "R2-45". Not a character in Star Wars Episode 2, R2-45 is actually described as "a highly effective process for exteriorization, but its use is frowned upon by this society at this time". This isn't terribly surprising, given that "exteriorization" is Scientology speak for "being killed". Opponents of Scientology have alleged that R2-45 is a codename used when ordering the murder of opponents. Perhaps he's an assassin droid, or something.

However, not all of Scientology is scary; some of it is just plain stupid. Scientologists believe they have been being reincarnated for four quadrillion years - before the creation of the universe even. Scientologists seek a return to this "energy state", and seek to become an "operating thetan" - a being who, like Ben Kenobi after he died, is comprised entirely of energy, but is capable of causing physical events through sheer force of will.

It gets better. According to Hubbard, the planet Earth - then known as "Teegeeack" - was once part of a Galactic Federation along with 76 other planets. However, 95 million years ago the Federation was suffering from over-population, and so the Federation's evil ruler, Xenu, captured billions of alien species, transported them to Earth, and killed them all by detonating the planet's volcanoes using hydrogen bombs, and then harvested their spirits. Hubbard called this "Incident II" (Incident I being the creation of the universe, or something like that). The Sea Organisation's insignia carries 22 stars, relating to the 22 planets which had their populations decimated by Incident II. Most Scientologists will not even say the name "Xenu", and others will allegedly pretend they've never even heard of him.

The robots of scientology accept this bullshit without considering that L Ron Hubbard was the author of no less than sixteen science fiction novels. If this part of the scientology belief system isn't from a science fiction imagination, nothing is. If we choose to put the whole of religion in perspective, we must consider the absurdity of a man who walked on water, raised the dead and oddly prayed to himself. If you think it's offensive that I call alleged biblical miracles ridiculous, you should ask yourself whether or not it's ridiculous to insist that Muhammad flew on a winged horse. Or that the earth was hatched from a cosmic egg? Or that Xenu, the dictator of the Galactic Confederacy, brought billions of his people to earth 75 million years ago and killed them using hydrogen bombs? These are all religious beliefs of others, but that doesn't mean calling them ridiculous is an insult - it's an objective fact until proven otherwise.

There can be little doubt that of all the stupidism to be found in religion, Scientology must rank as the most dangerous. Its followers are the Stepford Wives of all congregations. Like governments, it maintains its influence through fear, keeping members in a state of terror just as phony as was the Cold War or much of the modern terrorists scenarios. It is the perfect church for masochists and those wanting to return to infancy when they had everything in their lives controlled and governed for them. Beyond that, it is surely the dark face of religion itself. The ugliest history found within the pages of faith are combined and concentrated in Scientology. I personally do not believe that hell exists – but confess that I hope it does if for no one else than the creators and keepers of Scientology.

CULTS THAT KILL

A polygamous Mormon fundamentalist group who, under the leadership of Ervil Morrell LeBaron, killed the majority of their enemies. Using their religious doctrine, they justified each murder, leaving a bloody trail of misery wherever they went. Although LeBaron died in prison, the killings did not end. He left his children a hit list, and they continued to work through his list long after he died. Many people still remain in hiding in fear of being brutally murdered by The Church of the Lamb of God.

The Mormon faith used to preach and practice (don't kid yourself, it's still practiced) polygamy as a part of their doctrine. Despite this, polygamy was outlawed in the U.S in 1862 and the mainstream Mormons finally removed it from their practices around 1890. This decision did not sit well with many fundamental Mormons, and they soon fled the U.S into Mexico where they formed polygamous groups or colonies. It was here in Mexico that many families set up to begin their life of freedom, including the LeBaron family.

Alma LeBaron claimed to hear the voice of God of many occasions, claiming it was God who told him to take a second wife and move them all to Mexico. Throughout the family, mental illness ran rampant, infecting the majority of the children spawned by LeBaron. Their daughter Lucinda was prone to so many violent outbursts that her parents kept her chained by the ankle to a hut, in fear of the damage she was capable of. Lucinda's brother Ben spent a lot of his life in and out of mental asylums, before finally committing suicide in 1978. Another son named Wesley began preaching that Jesus was coming back to Earth in a giant spaceship, whilst their nephew Owen declared that God had told him to have sexual intercourse with the family dog.

In 1924, Alma Dayer LeBaron moved both of his wives and their eight children across the border into Mexico, started a farm called "Colonia LeBaron" in Galeana, Chihuahua. A year later, Ervil Morrell LeBaron was born. The family lived and worked as farmers, and Ervil spent many of his childhood days working in the fields with his brothers. As the bothers grew older, they began to travel across Mexico, searching for new members for their branch of Mormonism.

Alma died in 1951, and he passed on his leadership to one of his sons, Joel. Ervil quickly became his right-hand man and new members began flocking to the group. Soon, they opened a primary school, alongside a nursery, communal farm and a kitchen, with Joel working amongst his followers. Ervil, on the other hand, concocted the work schedules and did very little physical labor. He claimed it was his role as their spiritual leader to not work like them, but to study the scripture and prey instead. Many members grew tiresome of Evril's attitude, noticing his penchant for luxurious items and women.

Ervil LeBaron grew into a handsome, masculine young man, who stood tall at 6 foot 4. His thick, sandy coloured hair complemented his deep blue eyes, attracting women across the country and contributing to his growing confidence and ego. Staring relentlessly into people's eyes, he would quote from the book of Mormon confidently, whilst convincing women and girls alike that God had told him to marry them. His wives would become a necessary nuisance to him, deemed necessary to birth his children, who would in turn become his footsoldiers.

Ervil began preaching his own messages in 1967, teaching members that is was he, not Joel, was the head of the 'celestial authorities.' This, combined with the attitude of Ervil had become too much for his brother Joel, and he denounced and discredited all teachings of his younger brother. In a bitter fury, Evril retaliated, claiming:

"I know as sure as the Lord lives that my program is the only one that will put over the kingdom. And I also know that there are men in leading positions in this work who oppose me. And I tell you that blood will have to run to settle our differences." This would prove to be the end of the brothers' leadership, as Joel released Ervil from his position within the church.

Ervil LeBaron quickly set up his own group, of which he preached a strong doctrine and subjected his followers to acts of sheer brutality.

In Ervil's teachings, he began with the basic Mormon teachings that there are three grand orders of priesthood, but gave detailed support of his own ideas, which were new and unheard of in any other Mormon sect. He published a leaflet entitled: *Priesthood Expounded*, which delved into the details of how LeBaron's supposedly legitimate priesthood authority. The first paragraph of the piece demonstrated how Ervil's insights were superior to all other religious doctrines:

"If we LeBaron brothers are so fortunate as to be able to explain these things correctly, in this time of confusion and turmoil, when all others of our time have utterly failed to do it, then let every man and woman sit in silence and put their hands on their mouths, recognise where authority is, and cease to speak evil of the servants of God."

In 1962, Ervil introduced the doctrine of *Civil Law*, which declared that many of the principles of the church could be re-established with as much force as necessary, including deadly force. Whilst Joel agreed that this law could perhaps come in useful in the future, Ervil was wanting to put it into action immediately.

After Joel had Ervil removed from their religious group, Ervil went on to create his own religious sect in 1971, called The Church of the Lamb of God with a new and harsher set of doctrines. By the following year, he was preaching that he was "the one mighty and strong", and with his domineering appearance, and charmingly confident mannerisms, people believed him. It was August of that year when Ervil began openly declaring that "Verlan and Joel will be put to death!" and it only took until the 20th August for Joel to be attacked by the group and shot in the head. The next brother in line to take over from Joel was Verlan, and he took control of the Church of the Firstborn of the Fullness of Times; becoming the next target for Evril and his followers.

Ervil was a key suspect in his brother's death, and to the surprise of the authorities, on 13 December 1972, he handed himself in. He was found guilty on November 8th, but walked free after serving only one day of his sentence when the higher judges overturned the verdict.

After his release, Ervil's teachings become even more focused on hatred, anger, and exposing betrayers "to hot lead and cold steel" and sending his opponents a "one way ticket Hell." The practice of harsh punishments and violence continued throughout the years, with Ervil assuring his followers that cataclysmic events would happen by 3 May 1977, and his former church led by his brother would be obliterated. Despite up-scaling his plans for the murder of his brother, Verlan, they day came and went without and blood spilling.

In June 1979, Ervil LeBaron was finally caught by the authorities in Mexico and sent to the U.S where he was convicted of ordering the death of Rulon C. Allred. He was sentenced to life imprisonment and sent to the Utah State Prison where he began writing his 500 page book entitled: *The Book of the New Covenants.* It was to be his last piece of writing, and also his most infamous, as he listed more than 50 people who he deemed needed to be assassinated, including ex cult members and prison officials.

Ervil was found dead in his cell on 16 August 1981, and it was later determined that he has suffered a mass heart attack. In a twist of irony, his brother Verlan was killed on the same day in a car accident in Mexico, but many family members feel that this was no coincidence. Whilst many people now felt safe that Evril was dead, their hope was misguided. One by one, the people listed in the final writings of Evril began to disappear and it became apparent that the Church of the Lamb of God had not finished their path of destruction.

Further deaths implemented by the group:

- Issac LeBaron, son of Ervil. He testified against his father in court and died in a suspicious suicide in June 1983.
- Ervil's wife, Lorna LeBaron was attempting to leave the group when she was strangled and buried in a shallow grave.
- Arturo LeBaron, Ervil's eldest son was gunned down in December 1983.
- Gamaliel Rios was shot in the face with a .45 automatic by new leader Heber LeBaron, Ervil's 20-year-old son. His body was dumped in the desert and has never been recovered.
- Ervil's twelfth wife, Yolanda Rios was strangled to death in May 1984
- Ervil wrote about three men in particular that he wanted dead, labelling them as traitors. Mark Chynoweth, Duane Chynoweth and Ed Marston were all former cult members, and at 4pm on 27 June 1988 they were simultaneously murdered, alongside Chynoweth's 8-year-old daughter Jennifer. All four bodies were found in a variant of locations, each of them riddled with bullets. Whilst Jennifer was not part of the plan, she was deemed as a potential witness and was shot directly in the mouth.
- The authorities were on the case quickly, and one by one, the killers were dragged in for their part in the recent murders. Their names include:
- Heber LeBaron
- Patricia LeBaron
- Douglas Lee Barlow
- Richard LeBaron
- Cynthia LeBaron,
- Aaron LeBaron
- Jacqueline LeBaron

- Despite the majority of the killers being behind bars, many people on Evril's 'hit list' still remain in hiding, in fear that they may be shot like so many before them.

•

On the other side of the world, Ugandan cult leader, Joseph Kibwetere who masterminded a ragic inferno in which 780 people, including 47 children, died in early 2000, is still Uganda's most wanted man.

Kibwetere led the cult, the Restoration of the Ten Commandments of God. He is still wanted in connection with the death of the fire victims plus hundreds more victims found in mass graves, assassinated before the tragedy. It is believed that when two predictions for the end of the world failed to take place, some were disenchanted and wanted their money returned since part of the cult mandates was to surrender all earthly goods to the cult leaders.

According to one witness, Kibwetere fled the compound the day before the church and all the victims inside were put to flames.

The Ugandan Government has maintained that police is working with Interpol to track down Kibwetere and his accomplices.

The Restoration of the Ten Commandments, popularly known as Kibwetere cult, was led by Joseph Kibwetere, Credonia Mwerinde, Angelina Mugisha, Fr. Joseph Kasapurari and Fr. Dominic Kataribabo.

At first it was assumed that the Kanungu massacre was mass suicide by the members of the cult who were convinced about going to heaven through fire but later it was established that it was planned and executed by the cult leadership.

Before dust could settle after the Kanungu tragedy, it was discovered that many more people belonging to the same cult had died and been secretly buried in other camps outside Kanungu including Bushenyi and Buziga near Kampala.

By the end of March the death toll of the cult members had risen to about 1000 people. The Kanungu tragedy and its aftermath invariably generated national and international concern.

Joseph Kibwetere was a primary school teacher by profession and at one time an Assistant Supervisor of Schools in Mbarara Catholic Diocese.

He had about 16 children including three he had got outside marriage. He was recruited by Credonia Mwerinde together with two other women, Angelina Mugisha and Ursula Komuhangi. The cult leader ordained 'bishop' of the cult Movement for the

197

Restoration of the Ten Commandments of God in 1991. He was Mwerinde's right hand man. He separated with his wife in 1992. Credonia Mwerinde was born in Kanungu at Kateete, Nyabugoto, the place where Kibwetere's camp was situated. (She donated her father's land at Kateete as the cult's base) Mwerinde became a key figure in the cult's leadership and was put in charge of all programmes.

She was known as the 'programmer' among her followers and religiously as 'Ekyombeko kya Maria' (the Virgin Mary's structure). She was believed to represent a message from the Blessed Virgin Mary.

The whole cult revolved around a belief that some people were talking with God through visions and had received warnings from the Blessed Virgin Mary about the end of the world by the year 2000 (apocalypse).

The followers were not supposed to go to hell if they strictly followed the cult (The Movement for the Restoration of the Ten Commandments of God).

For the devout Christians the whole concept of 'okubonekyerwa' (getting heavenly visions) was very appealing. The cult talked of the doomsday. According to their former preacher, Martino Nuwagaba, they preached as far back as the Easter of 1992 about how on that "last day" snakes as big as wheels of tractors and big blocks of cement will fall from heaven onto the sinners. They preached of three days of consecutive darkness that will engulf the whole world and how only their camps were supposed to be safe havens, something reminiscent of the biblical Noah's Ark.

It is said that even sealing the church doors and windows by nail before setting the church on fire was to create that darkness situation that was a prelude to the apocalypse. They promised their followers that when all this happened, everybody would perish except their followers and that whatever remained on earth would be theirs alone and that they would then start communicating directly with Jesus.

Followers believed in this so much so that they considered themselves the most privileged people on earth. Leaders warned the cult members about the end of the world and the visions. The cult and its leaders violated human rights (the right to education, health, property, marriage, freedom, speech, parenthood, childhood, etc.).

The leaders rarely recruited close relatives or neighbors. They separated families, including children, and took them to different camps in a new environment where they would not socialise easily. They used to erect fences around their buildings/camps. The fences would be opaque enough to prevent those outside from seeing what was happening inside. They created total detachment between their followers and the society around them. Producing children and having sex among followers even between spouses were strictly forbidden. Leaders instilled too much fear among their followers. It relied on deception, prophecies and lies through selective readings of the Bible. The Bible was usually read out of context. Apart from the leaders, other members of the cult were not allowed to talk. They used signs to communicate among themselves and to their cult leaders. They had a tight day's schedule that kept the followers extremely busy so that there was virtually no time to discuss, not even in signs. They tried to keep within the law and be close, very friendly and generous to the authorities, which helped them to avoid any suspicions from the state.

They usually travelled at night so they could not easily be noticed even by neighbors. They did not own their own transport/vehicles. They usually hired vehicles to travel, they were therefore not easy to identify. They used to command all followers to sell all their property and bring all the proceeds to the cult leaders.

They used to burn property under the pretext that the Blessed Virgin Mary was annoyed with the owners. They created a property-less and helpless society of followers who became totally dependent on the cult and had nothing to fall back to. They fully exploited the general view among Ugandans that religious people are always innocent, humble, harmless and peace-loving which helped them plan and carry out mischief and crimes without being detected at all.

Cult members got completely detached from their 'non-believer' relatives. Therefore the latter could not follow, know or detect what was going on in the cult camps. All cult camps were terminus so that there would be no passers-by.

The cult leaders have thus far escaped capture and are believed to be up to their old tricks in Kenya. Members of a religious organization whose leaders re believed to be remnants of Uganda's Kanungu doomsday cult, have invaded western Kenya, causing panic among the residents and concern to the government. Members who escaped a government crackdown are suspected to have seeped into

Kenya and established massive following under a different name in the western districts of the country.

Police in western province reported that they were investigating the religious body which, they accused of inciting followers to burn down houses of non-members, and stopping their children from going to school. The sect is also said to be claiming that the World will come to an end soon.

A recent report by human rights groups operating in western Kenya and eastern Uganda, warned that an emerging religious group calling itself, "Choma," Swahili for "burn," could be an off-shoot of the Kanungu sect.

•

The mysterious circumstances surrounding the dramatic "transit" of fifty-three members of the Order of the Solar Temple (OTS, *Ordre du Temple Solaire*) in Switzerland and in Québec in October 1994 spawned an unprecedented wave of public speculation and conspiracy mongering. The subsequent death of sixteen people in France in December 1995 and of five more in Québec in March 1997 have only added to these conspiratorial speculations. Ironically, Joseph Di Mambro, Luc Jouret, and those who, over the course of months, methodically prepared their own deaths and the deaths of dozens of others were quite concerned about the impact their departure would have on the public mind and spent many hours creating a kind of legend that would survive their earthly exit. Why else would they have felt the need to send manifestos justifying *post mortem* their decision not only to order members but also to television stations, newspapers, and some other correspondents (including the author of this article)? The Swiss investigators found a tape, dating probably from the spring of 1994, in which one can hear the core group discuss the "departure." There is a telling exchange between Joseph Di Mambro and Luc Jouret:

> JDM: People have beaten us to the punch, you know.
>
> LJ: Well, yeah. Waco beat us to the punch.
>
> JDM: In my opinion, we should have gone six months before them – what we'll do will be even more spectacular.

"More spectacular": such are the words used by Joseph Di Mambro himself. A movement such as the Solar Temple cannot escape its media-saturated era. It worries about its public image until the very hour of the "crowning of the work," to use its own vocabulary. Many fringe movements tend to cultivate a very high estimation of their own importance, and the OTS was no exception.

The core members of the group understood themselves as an elect people who had incarnated periodically on Earth since ancient times in order to fulfill a cosmic mission. They had gathered together for that purpose and were ready to sacrifice their lives for its sake. Especially toward the end, some internal texts disclose these grandiose perspectives:

"Do you understand what we represent? We are the promise that the R[osy] C[ross] made to the Immutable. We are the Star Seeds that guarantee the perennial existence of the universe, we are the hand of God that shapes creation. We are the Torch that Christ must bring to the Father to feed the Primordial Fire and to reanimate the forces of Life, which, without our contribution, would slowly but surely go out. We hold the key to the universe and must secure its Eternity."

In reality, like so many other movements that see themselves on the cutting edge of cosmic progress and who assign to minor events in their own history a global significance, the Solar Temple was in fact a tiny (and actually declining) group whose claim to cosmic importance would have been viewed as dubious by most commentators. But through a sensational act of self-immolation that compelled the attention of both popular and academic observers, the leaders of the Solar Temple came close to creating a durable legend for their esoteric order.

Unfortunately for the order's leaders, documents exist which, when analysed carefully, begin to deconstruct this legend. If everything had worked as Di Mambro planned, no trace would have remained. Nothing, not even the bodies themselves, would have been recovered: "We will not let our bodies dissolve according to nature's slow alchemy, because we don't want to run the risk that they become soiled by frantic lunatics." The Solar Temple's thorough preparation for their mysterious exit, however, could not take into account certain technical problems: some of the devices intended to start the fire did not function properly, which made it possible for the investigators to seize a large number of written documents (in part found on computers that survived the fires relatively unscathed) as well as video and audio cassettes belonging to the group's archives. It is upon these sources that this article is in large part based.

Joseph Di Mambro was born in Pont-Saint-Esprit, in the French department of Gard, 19 August 1924. At the age of sixteen, he began an apprenticeship as a watchmaker and jeweller and very soon became fascinated with esotericism. In January 1956, he joined the

Ancient and Mystical Order Rosae Crucis (AMORC), to which he would belong until at least 1968. In the 1960s, he apparently established links with several persons who would later play a role in OTS history, including Jacques Breyer, the initiator of a "Templar resurgence" in France in 1952 to which several groups, including Di Mambro's OTS, trace part of their roots.

Several major points of doctrine, as well as an embryonic circle of disciples, began crystallizing during the 1960s. After visiting Israel and dealing with legal problems in Nîmes in 1971 related to swindling and writing bad checks, Di Mambro set himself up in Annemasse, near the Swiss border. In 1973, he became president of the Center for the Preparation of the New Age, which was presented as a "cultural center for relaxation" and a yoga school. The center became a full-time job by 1976. That same year, eight people (seven of whom resided at a common address) formed a building society and purchased a house named "The Pyramid" at Collonges-sous-Salève, close to Geneva. Of these eight people, four would lose their lives in October 1994. The building society in fact sheltered an esoteric activity: the consecration of the Temple of the Great White Universal Lodge, Pyramid Sub-Lodge, was celebrated on 24 June 1976. Internal documents show that, of the fifty-three believers who died in October 1994, at least twelve already belonged to the group by the end of 1977.

The next step commenced on 12 July 1978 with the creation of the Golden Way Foundation in Geneva. This foundation would remain at the very heart of activities undertaken by Di Mambro's various groups over the ensuing years. Thanks to substantial financial sacrifices made by several members, the foundation bought an attractive property in a suburb of Geneva that was the site of meetings open to non-members. The Golden Way Foundation was above all a front for a nucleus of people called simply the "Fraternity," who took part in esoteric rites in a communitarian setting. This communitarian ideal played a role in attracting people to the group and also led later to disappointments when the gap between the ideal and the reality of everyday life became untenable for certain members. People belonging to the "Fraternity" held all assets in common; along with them lived people belonging to what was called the "Community," who kept their income, paid a rent, and bought tickets for food and beverages. In the context of the 1970s, it was only one attempt among many others at developing an ideal communal life. Indeed, one member who joined at that time

202

had lived in the New Age community of Findhorn, Scotland, and was hoping to find something similar in the Golden Way.

Excerpts from an account given at a 1994 OTS meeting provide us with retrospective (and no doubt idealized) glimpses into the experiences of the pioneer members of the brotherhood:

Meeting at first in a house which they called "the Pyramid," where every evening was devoted to rituals and meditation, they later moved near Geneva, to a large property which was discovered to be an ancient Templar command post. There, living in a perfect fraternity where all was equally shared-salaries were put into a common fund and everyone received in return an equal share-they devoted all their free time to the cause of spirituality. Daily ceremonies quickly became operational at the highest degree, even more so because hermeticists, alchemists, and spiritually elevated people joined in. The Masters of the beyond regularly manifested themselves, with a presence visible, audible, and olfactory.

The Golden Way Foundation had impressive headquarters, but in order to spread its ideas on a larger scale the group needed a communicator. Enter a Belgian homeopathic physician, Luc Jouret (born 18 October 1947), who was likely introduced to Di Mambro by one of the victims of October 1994. On 30 May 1982, Jouret and his then wife were "accepted in the Golden Way" and took the oath of "Knights of the Rosy Cross." Di Mambro confided to some members at the time that Jouret had charisma and, being a physician, would be taken seriously; therefore, he should be pushed into the limelight, while Di Mambro would remain discretely backstage.

From that moment on, Luc Jouret became the propagandist for the group. Beginning in 1983, he gave lectures in Switzerland, France, and Canada. Cultural clubs were created and, from 1984 to 1990, the organization operated as a tripartite structure involving

> (1) public lectures and seminars given by Jouret and a few others under the label of Amenta;
> (2) an exoteric structure, the Archedia Clubs, for those wishing to go further; and finally, for a limited number of candidates,
> (3) an initiatory order (organized as the esoteric counterpart of the clubs) called the "International Order of Chivalry, Solar Tradition."

Obviously, the group hoped to attract a wider audience, and it thus prepared structures meant for a much larger movement than it ever became. The success of Luc Jouret, a gifted speaker who easily attracted hundreds to his lectures, could only add fuel to the fire of such hopes. The fact that Jouret was able to draw such large audiences to his lectures is proof that the topics he was dealing with were of interest to at least a part of the cultic milieu of the time. However, because of the seeker's mentality typical of the cultic milieu, most of those who came to Jouret's lectures did not want to commit themselves on a firm basis and, despite the lecturer's success, significant growth for the OTS in terms of committed membership never materialized.

The group's Templar activities had their roots in a 1952 "resurgence" in which the French esoteric author Jacques Breyer (1922-1996) played a central role. While reluctant to take upon himself any administrative responsibility in those Templar circles claiming some link with the "resurgence," Breyer enjoyed the role of an elder advisor to whom those groups turned at crucial times in order to ask his opinion. Di Mambro did so several times.

From 1984 forward, the movement had two centers of activity-French-speaking Europe and Québec. The presence in Canada was also meant to reach the English-speaking world, mainly the United States:

The Executive Council of this New Order decided that, in line with the historic destiny of the Order of the Temple, the headquarters of the Order should be located somewhere on the North American continent. The reason for this decision is simple. North America has become the source of most of the new impulses which determine the way life evolves on this planet. It is therefore fitting that the modern Knight Templar of the old continent should play his part in the Age of Aquarius by adding his inspiration to that which his counterparts in the New World will bring to the planet.

However, despite the beginning of a translation project designed to make certain rules and ritual texts available to English-speaking audiences, the order never had more than a handful of isolated members in the United States. In January 1989, at the height of its development and before internal turmoil took its toll on membership, OTS had 442 members, of which 90 were in Switzerland (monthly revenues: $12,600), 187 in France ($12,700), 53 in Martinique ($3,400), 16 in the United States ($1,125), 86 in Canada ($7,000) and 10 in Spain.

In addition to these revenues, several well-endowed members donated large sums that amounted to hundreds of thousands (and up to millions) of U.S. dollars over the years. These donors hoped that their generosity would permit the financing of "life centers" on farms acquired in Canada and in Cheiry, Switzerland, in 1990. But the group's leaders diverted part of these donations into other areas, including their own travel expenses and living costs for community members with no external means of support. The constant need for funds led to financial problems, which were perhaps not entirely unrelated to the events of 1994.

Beginning in the 1990s, several members began distancing themselves from the order. Important donors among these members wanted to recoup at least some of their money, and the group's revenues began to decline. Di Mambro had long pretended (since at least the late 1970s) to represent the "Mother Lodge" and to receive his orders from mysterious "Masters" in Zurich. The theme of "Unknown Superiors" is a commonplace of occult movements such as Rosicrucianism, Theosophy, and the I AM Activity. However, around 1990, Di Mambro's son Elie (1969-1994) began seriously to doubt the existence of the "Masters" of Zurich and discovered that fakery had been practiced by his father to produce the illusion of spiritual phenomena during the ceremonies celebrated in the order's sanctuaries. These phenomena – which included apparitions of spiritual entities – had been a major reason why several members had accepted Di Mambro as what he claimed to be. Even today, several leading former members remain convinced that, notwithstanding occasional fakery, some of the phenomena were authentic. Elie spoke openly about what he had discovered, which led to the departure of fifteen members. In 1993, there was a wave of resignations of French members who saw that their donations ended up as home improvements for their leader's residence. In February 1994, two members from Geneva sent an open letter to announce their decision to leave the movement, because "real fraternity [did] not exist in this structure, as extolled in the teachings." They were also worried about what happened to their contributions, observing the absence of the "life centers" which were supposed to be created. And these were not the only examples of defections.

Throughout the years, according to explanations provided by former members, Di Mambro had grown more authoritarian. He no longer helped with the daily chores, as he had in the original community. He wanted to gather bright people around him, but probably was also afraid of potential competitors. There was never any attempt at a takeover, but there were rivalries among Di Mambro's underlings, and some people felt that he was playing a game of divide and rule while expecting unconditional obedience from all members. When speaking to the police, a Canadian member who broke with the Solar Temple in 1993 summarized the feelings of many defectors: "I did not feel that the people were living what they preached. And I was tired of the infighting and never being able to find out what was going on, so I left."

A report on the organization's situation in Europe written to Di Mambro on 10 December 1993 by a Swiss OTS officer reflects the growing dissent that was affecting the group at this time. The document also shows how a longtime follower who had developed serious doubts about Di Mambro's honesty nevertheless wanted to persevere in serving the ideal he had dedicated his life to for so many years. This loyalty had tragic consequences, as he was murdered in October 1994 as he was about to leave the farm where he lived with other members. The report states,

> Rumors about embezzlement and various [forms of]skullduggery are propagated by influential ex-members. Many members . . . have left or are leaving. They feel their ideals have been betrayed. . . . It is even said that you have fallen because of money and women, and you're no longer credible. This is very serious for the Order's mission. There are even more serious grumblings, and you know them. Here they are: everything that we saw and heard in certain places has been a trick. I have known this for some time. Tony [Dutoit] has been talking about this for years already. I have always refused to pay attention to these rumors, but the evidence is growing, and questions are being asked. This calls into question many things I've seen, and messages. I would be really upset if I had to conclude that I had sincerely prostrated myself in front of an illusion!!! There is enough stuff here to send less committed people packing. And all the resignations and departures of recent times just confirm it.

> I don't want to analyze the reasons that could lead to such trickery, which was motivated by good intentions no doubt, but which transgressed the rules of common sense, when we see the mess we're in now. It's also been said that Zurich has never existed, that it's pure fantasy.

> As for myself, I believe in the cosmic law. I believe in the message received 2000 years ago by which I

aim to live. I believe in the life ethic which my parents taught me and which I aim to apply. I believe in a conscience which I aim to find within myself. If I go down this path, I cannot be wrong. And no rumor, true or false, could deter me from what I have to do. I will continue to work in the Order and for the mission as long as you need me and as long as I can do it.

These controversies were not confined to the OTS sanctuaries. During the 1980s, the Solar Temple had more or less escaped anti-cult polemics. Jouret had two lines written about him in an entry on the ORT in a booklet put out by a French anti-cult group in 1984, but in the 1987 edition, both he and the ORT were left unmentioned. Oddly enough, in the end critical coverage did not come from Europe or Canada, but from the island of Martinique: on 10 September 1991, Lucien Zécler, president of the local branch of the Association for the Defense of Families and Individuals (ADFI), the leading anti-cult movement in France, sent a letter to several associations and centers in Québec, asking for information on the OTS. The request followed the decision of several citizens of Martinique to sell their worldly goods, leave their families, and move to Canada to escape coming disasters. At the end of 1992, a former member of the OTS went to Martinique to publicly denounce the Solar Temple, which provoked local media coverage.

Not long after, Luc Jouret ran afoul of law enforcement officials in Québec after he encouraged trusted members to buy guns illegally. The police were investigating anonymous threats from an unknown terrorist group at the time and, when tipped off by an informer about the attempt by an inexperienced OTS member to get three guns with silencers, began to watch several members of the group. The members were arrested in March 1993. The Canadian media reported the story and published extracts from police wiretaps revealing the homeopath's unusual interest in fire arms. This gave the OTS more unwanted publicity and cooled the enthusiasm of several members, even though Jouret and two of his followers' were given the relatively mild sentence of one year of unsupervised probation and a fine of one thousand Canadian dollars (to be paid to the Red Cross) for buying prohibited arms.

These problems, internal and external, are crucial in understanding the OTS's gradual distortion and disintegration. Di Mambro had gathered around him a group that lent an appearance of reality to the fictions he created. And now this imaginary universe began to come under critical scrutiny. The head of the Solar Temple apparently decided to respond by taking himself and his followers away from the scene altogether.

Throughout the 1980s, the Solar Temple's doctrine had grown increasingly apocalyptic. Even in his public meetings, Luc Jouret frequently alluded to cataclysmic upheavals that threatened the planet with imminent destruction. The apocalyptic thinking of the Solar Temple had clear ecological connotations, and Jouret's lectures often described the earth as a holistic living entity who could no longer endure what humankind was inflicting on her.

The concern of the leaders for the environmental situation seems to have been a sincere one: Di Mambro kept several video recordings of TV reports about ecological problems; in his home, investigators also found a testament showing that Di Mambro and his wife had considered listing ecological organizations in their will. The Solar Temple's message was survivalist as well. We have already seen that this had caused the group to establish a base in Canada, which was considered to be a safer place. In 1986, the temple published in Toronto two volumes under the title, *Survivre à l'An 2000* (*Survival beyond the Year 2000*). The first volume was mostly doctrinal. The second dealt with the subject in a very practical way, establishing guidelines as to what provisions to store in order to survive a disaster that would destroy all essential technologies and what to do to survive atomic, bacteriological, or chemical warfare. In addition, it provided a detailed first aid manual. Nothing in these volumes would lead one to suspect suicidal tendencies; to the contrary, it seemed as if the adepts hoped to find themselves among those who survived the apocalypse unscathed.

How, then, can one explain the reversal that led a core of members to choose collective self-immolation? Besides survivalism, there were other latent themes, always on the same apocalyptic foundation, which had the potential to encourage somewhat different pursuits in the group. In a certain way, the Solar Temple's goals were classically gnostic in that they ultimately aimed at "the release of the 'inner man' from the bonds of the world and his return to his native realm of light." The manifesto-testaments sent just prior to the events of October 1994 echo such feelings: "We, Servants of the Rosy Cross, forcefully reaffirm that we are not of this world and we know perfectly well the coordinates of our Origins and our Future." "Always belonging to the Reign of the Spirit, incarnating the subtle link between Creature and Creator, we rejoin our Home." The most devoted Solar Temple adepts would push this reasoning to its extreme logical consequences.

According to several testimonies gathered by the investigators, the theme of "transit" began to be evoked by Di Mambro in 1990 or 1991. It meant a voluntary departure or a consent to bring the germ of life to another planet. It was necessary to be ready to leave at any time in response to the call. Di Mambro said he did not yet know what the mode of transit would be: he presented the metaphor of a passage across a mirror and evoked the possibility of the coming of a flying saucer to take faithful members to another world. On this last point, it is worth noting that, at some of Luc Jouret's seminars which I attended in 1987, a comic strip called Timeless Voyage was on sale. This strip tells the story of a group of UFO believers who, before the imminent "great mutation," are brought on board a "cosmic vessel" to "Vessel-Earth." Solar Temple members were thus already familiar with this type of scenario well before 1990. An ex-member explained to the investigators that talks about transit never implied suicide, but rather the idea of being saved from disasters. Perhaps the theme of "transit," rather than marking a break with survivalism, should be interpreted as a reorientation towards a survival in other dimensions following the irreversible worsening of the situation on this planet.

If we believe their declarations to the police after the events of 1994, most of those members who had heard about the idea of "departure" or "transit" considered it as rather nebulous or interpreted it innocuously as a departure to other geographical locations (for example, leaving Geneva). When members wanted to know more, they sometimes received evasive answers:

"Transit was the return to the Father, the return to the Unity, after having left Earth," said one ex-member. "Two or three years before October 1994, I discussed with our leader what was meant by the concept. She told me that I shouldn't worry, that I wouldn't realize, that we would all leave together, as one. At the time, naively, I never thought that meant collective suicide."

Some members had known a little more precisely how things would happen. One remembers that Di Mambro "started talking about transit to another world. He said that this would be accomplished by shift in consciousness and we wouldn't be aware of it." But this operation presupposed a certain degree of preparation:

"[Di Mambro] explained to us that one day we'd all
be called to a meeting at which a transit would be
accomplished. It had to do with a mission, with a

departure towards Jupiter. He said to his listeners that they had to be on call twenty-four hours a day so as not to miss the departure and that once the order was given, we would have to move quickly.

This helps to explain the speed with which some of the victims suddenly abandoned everything to head to their mysterious demise. But if this confirms the emergence of the idea of "transit" well before October 1994, it does not explain the reasoning that led Di Mambro toward this plan of action. Outside of possible explanations linked to Di Mambro's mental state, it seems likely that criticism by ex-members, episodic public exposure in Martinique and Québec, and disappointed hopes for success led the Solar Temple's leadership to revise their view of the future. In addition, the wiretaps of Luc Jouret made by the police in Québec during the 1993 investigation reveal that the charismatic physician was in a depressed mood, constantly complaining about feeling tired and expressing eagerness to leave the world. Still, no one factor is sufficient in and of itself, especially since the collective self-immolation involved not just one individual but the order's entire core group. We can not rule out the possibility that some elements in the decision still remain unknown to us.

It no doubt took a great deal of persuasion to convince a nucleus of members to accept such a radical step. Some documents reflect the hesitation that was probably expressed and the arguments used to reassure and maintain adherence to the plan. A few of these arguments were in keeping with classic themes of millenarian literature not otherwise found in the group's teachings:

"The idea of the passage from one world to another might worry some of you. I assure you that you are going towards a marvelous world which could not be, in any case, any worse than the one you are leaving.

"Know from now on that after the passage, you will have a body of glory but you will still be recognizable. You will no longer need to eat but if you want to eat, you will be able to do it without earning your bread with the sweat of your brow. Your eternal body will be subject neither to aging nor to pain nor to sickness."

According to Solar Temple beliefs, the departure was only possible because on 6 January 1994 the mysterious "Elder Brothers of the Rosy Cross" "effected their Transit for an Elsewhere that only the initiates know and serve." Taking off towards superior dimensions, the "Brothers" in some way carried Solar Temple members in their wake, allowing those who were worthy to ascend to a higher level. Significant allusions to this subject can be read in notes found on a diskette in one of the chalets in Salvan (Switzerland): "Take the place of the E[lder] B[rothers] on Venus, so that later on J[upiter?], we will be reunited. They will precede us, make room for us, show us the way and we will follow them." According to the declarations of a witness who later perished during the second "transit" in December 1995, Jouret, at a small gathering just before the events of October 1994, explained that if the leadership would cross a new step in effecting a passage from matter to essence, all the subsequent levels would automatically progress one degree.

Even within this perspective of escape from worldly catastrophes and transit to a better world, however, the order's leaders deemed it fitting to leave something behind for posterity. Only this desire to leave a legacy can explain why the leadership continued to be as active as ever while making preparations for their exit. The exact date of "departure" was probably decided on short notice: the outline of the internal monthly instructions meant for distribution to the members, which was found by police in the chalets in Salvan, continued until May 1995. These instructions were prepared by Jocelyne Di Mambro, who knew about the self-destruction project. If the day or the month had been set a long time in advance, she would certainly not have taken the time to prepare instructions for the period after the set date. The will to leave a legacy and a following behind after the "transit" also shows itself in the initiative of summer 1994 (and up to the eve of the events) to start up a new organization, the Rosicrucian Alliance (*Alliance Rose-Croix*, ARC).

At a first meeting in Avignon on 9 July 1994, ninety-five out of the one hundred eighteen people present responded positively to the proposition to create a new association. The ARC's constituent assembly, a purely administrative operation, met with a few people present in Montreux on 13 August 1994. Of the four committee members elected that day, two were found dead in October. The real launching of the ARC took place at a second meeting in Avignon on 24 September 1994, with the theme "The new mission of the Rosy Cross"; the invitation described the new order as "the natural successor to the OTS." One hundred people were present including eighty-eight dues-paying members plus some of Di Mambro's entourage. The documents revealed a desire to simplify the organizational structure. Participants had the feeling of a new beginning; the notebook of one of the participants had listed under 24 September, "Meeting of the New Alliance in Avignon."

Many of those present on 24 September 1994 were not aware that the hour of the "departure" was approaching. Joseph Di Mambro and those close to him were becoming more and more discouraged, as an audio cassette from spring 1994 in which several core members of the group discussed their "departure" demonstrates. Di Mambro is heard saying,

> "We are rejected by the whole world. First by the people, the people can no longer withstand us. And our Earth, fortunately she rejects us. How would we leave [otherwise]? We also reject this planet. We wait for the day we can leave life for me is intolerable, intolerable, I can't go on. So think about the dynamic that will get us to go elsewhere."

Compared with other controversial groups, the Solar Temple encountered very modest opposition; it would be excessive to use the term "persecution," despite what the group's spiritual testament would have us believe. In fact, Di Mambro's loss of a sense of reality made any opposition or criticism intolerable. The legal problems encountered by Jouret and others in Québec in 1993 did nothing to assuage his growing sense of paranoia. After all, the press had reported that several members of the group had been subjected to official surveillance and wiretapping. This led the core leadership to believe themselves the object of omnipresent police control and the victims of traitors who had infiltrated the movement.

Jocelyne Di Mambro's difficulties in getting her passport renewed only exacerbated these suspicions. This and the fact that Di Mambro sent a posthumous letter to Charles Pasqua (then French minister of the Interior) gave rise to speculation concerning a mysterious political or criminal background for the OTS's leader.

The explanation is simpler. Di Mambro had traveled several times to Australia, where he attempted to create a "life center." Suspicious international monetary transfers drew the attention of the Australian police: during the month of October 1993, Di Mambro received on three separate occasions 100,000 dollars from Switzerland, money which was then deposited into bank accounts he had opened in Sydney. Canberra Interpol asked the French police for information regarding Di Mambro, who had no known resources. The French police squad in charge of financial improprieties wondered if it might be a case of illegal trafficking in foreign currency.

The French consulate in Montreal also became suspicious of the Di Mambros. In March 1994, the French Ministry of Foreign Affairs asked the Ministry of the Interior to advise whether it should extend Jocelyne Di Mambro's passport, as the family was unable to provide proof of their residence in Canada and had changed residence five times in five years. Even stranger, Joseph Di Mambro had obtained no less than five passports in seven years, and his visas showed he had made numerous short international trips, including several to Malaysia. By October 1994, the inquiry headed by the financial squad of the French judicial police was still ongoing. As for Jocelyne Di Mambro's passport, the French embassy in Ottawa finally renewed it, but only for three months, and this gave rise to a strange incident. Jocelyne Di Mambro hired a Montreal lawyer to defend her interests in the passport renewal affair. Through an unknown channel (perhaps simply the French consulate?), the lawyer heard about the investigation of his client and her husband and seems to have become reluctant to be associated with the couple and their possibly questionable business affairs. He wrote to Jocelyne Di Mambro on 25 August 1994 to explain to her that the affair had implications that were "political as much as they were legal," and that the non-renewal decision came from the French Ministry of the Interior and was linked "to a police investigation of a criminal matter." Even as he told his client that he would no longer be representing her interests, he advised her to "take very seriously the results of the investigation by the French authorities."

In point of fact, during the investigations following the events of October 1994, nothing came to light confirming a surveillance of the group during this period. Not only did the financial invest-igations squad of the French police likely have more urgent business to attend to, but the matter appears to have been related only to unexplained financial transfers by an individual French citizen and not by the leader of a small apocalyptic order. The police in Québec ceased their surveillance of the Solar Temple after the incident with the illegal gun purchase in 1993, and the French Renseignements généraux (political police), which also keep an eye on religions and "cults," knew little about the Solar Temple. But one can imagine what the lawyer's statement could have meant for an increasingly paranoid leadership, which now believed that its worst suspicions were confirmed. It is significant that the document sent in October 1994 to Charles Pasqua (enclosed with the Di Mambro's passports) was written on a computer at Salvan on 30 August 1994-just after the Di Mambros received the letter from their Montreal lawyer. As Minister of the Interior, Pasqua was held personally responsible for the problems they encountered: "We accuse you of deliberately wanting to destroy our Order and having done so for reasons of state." Such writings confirm the Di Mambros' growing persecution paranoia, but lend no credibility to the theories linking the letter to Pasqua with mysterious underworld connections.

Another text found on Jocelyne Di Mambro's computer and written after a conversation with an unknown speaker adds further evidence of a growing sense of persecution:

"We don't know when they might close the trap on us – a few days? a few weeks?

"We are being followed and spied upon in our every move. All the cars are equipped with tracing and listening devices.

"All of their most sophisticated techniques are being used on us. While in the house, beware of surveillance cameras, lasers, and infra-red. Our file is the hottest on the planet, the most important of the last ten years, if not of the century.

"However that may be, as it turns out, the concentration of hate against us will give us enough energy to leave."

The alleged surveillance was construed as one more proof that the group was really what it claimed to be, the vehicle of a mission of cosmic magnitude. The previous document also mentions two members (one of whom died in Switzerland and the other a year later in France) suspected of infiltrating the movement. Several texts written during that period warn against "traitors," and the group believed in the right of applying "justice and sentence" to those who showed disloyalty. In a videotape dated September 1994, Di Mambro explains that "justice and sentence" are the equivalent of "vengeance," but in an impersonal sense. In the spring 1994 audio track about the "departure," Di Mambro talks about those "who had committed themselves and then no longer wanted to remain involved. That changes nothing about their commitment.

"You'll see, you'll see how things will go for them." The letter to Charles Pasqua is explicit:

214

"If we must apply our justice ourselves, it is because of the fact that yours is rotten and corrupt. It behooves us, before we leave these stinking terrestrial planes, to reduce certain traitors to silence, which you and your agencies have directly or indirectly manipulated to destroy our honor and our actions."

While it cannot be doubted that the external opposition encountered by the Solar Temple strengthened the resolve of its leaders to depart for a higher plane of existence, the root of Di Mambro's decision to launch the process which led to the "transit" is most closely connected to internal dissent (the theoretical idea of the possibility of having to "depart" having already been present longer in the ideology of the group, as we have seen). Di Mambro nourished a deep resentment toward critical members and former members, although these dissidents had kept their criticism within the confines of the group and had not gone public-except for the ex-member who spoke with the media in Martinique in December 1992 and who had repeated her accusations to the Canadian media in March 1993. In the important tape recording (mentioned earlier) of a discussion within the core group in spring 1994, Di Mambro declared to his most trusted disciples,

"There are people who claim that I have taken everything for me – what I have taken, I haven't taken it for me, since I leave everything behind. But I will leave nothing, I will leave ashes, I will leave nothing to the bastards who have betrayed us. The harm they have done to the Rosy Cross, that I cannot forgive; what they have done to me, it doesn't matter. But the harm they have done to the Rosy Cross, I won't forgive it. I cannot."

Di Mambro still harbored feelings of betrayal and resentment during the final hours of his life. On 3 October 1994, when the "transit" had begun and a number of victims had in all likelihood already lost their lives, Di Mambro (or one of his assistants) wrote two drafts of letters to a general attorney which accused two former members of blackmailing him and of tarnishing the Temple's reputation.

As already asserted, however, it was not just a matter of "leaving" and punishing "traitors," but of accomplishing these ends in such a manner as to leave behind an enduring legend. The group was convinced that it belonged to "the pivotal elite" which "has been removed from the collective by superhuman effort." The temple "did not recognize" itself "as belonging to the human world, but to the race of Gods."

The leaders of the Solar Temple explained their actions in the texts sent to the media from a Geneva post office on 5 October 1994, and in three videocassettes which were shipped to a French OTS member by another trusted member at the same time. Two of these cassettes are titled "Testament of the Rosy Cross," and the third is titled "Joseph of Arimathea-Messages."

The lengthy recording of the "Testament of the Rosy Cross" opens with the symbol of ARC (a double-headed eagle behind a rose with a cross). On the screen a seated woman appears who reads a text; in the background, a rose emerges from a misty landscape; as background music, the Grail theme from Richard Wagner's opera Lohengrin plays throughout the entire lecture. The lengthy "testament" is read with a growing exaltation; there are several mentions of "departure." This "Testament of the Rosy Cross" is most interesting because of its synthesis of Solar Temple beliefs on the eve of the group's self-immolation.

The testament first underlines man's mission as mediator between God and the Earth: "We are the focalization on which the Creator rests. Today, we are in the final cycle of conscious creation; we must be able to control these bodies and, with full maturity, to leave the mother [i.e. the Earth]. We must not bring back consciousness to the state before the fall, but become aware of this state, enrich it with the painful experience of the fall and redeem our being, so that we could continue after the fall with a capital of enriched consciousness-energy-love." In this way, the spirit is able to follow its route across the sublimation of matter and, enriched by its experience in matter, "start up a superior cycle of evolution."

According to the testament, 26,000 years ago the Blue Star (related to Sirius' energy) left on the earth "Sons of the One"; it appears in the sky every time its help is needed and responds to magnetization when humanity undergoes its crises of transmutation. The years 1950 to 1960 saw a growing change in the consciousness of human beings. Humanity is passing through periods of preparation called "tribulations," successive cycles of seven years which end in 1998. The circumstances of the "departure" are then explained:

In the 1980s, the Sons of the One called the Blue Star. With man's consciousness still too fragmented, it was asked of the spiritual forces to intervene and to allot an additional period of time to move back the date, to slow down the irrevocable changes on Earth. The Earth was given an additional seven years to prepare. This delay acts like a rubber band which, when stretched to its limit, becomes unstable and too powerful. This limit has been reached and we still need more time. But this delay given to us has nonetheless allowed beings to hear the message, to prepare and to participate with full consciousness in this unique event which we call the passage. The passage, which is also the gathering of the Sons of the One. The Blue Star has come to magnetize the last workers and bring them back towards those of the first hour. The time of return is at hand and the astrological influences are affecting all the physical and non-physical planes. They work on the hearts and spirits of all those who accept their divine origin and are ready to play their part until the end. At the moment of passage, the Blue Star will instantly transform in a flash the carriers of life and of the consciousness.

The Star will unleash its influence on the earth, and there man, the unbeliever, remaining on Earth, will hope for death. The Blue Star will leave, he will feel abandoned and he will be right, but it will be too late. The radiant Star will be gone, bringing with it every chance at redemption. Yet, if man had wanted to remember, wanted to hear, wanted to see. Why did he not seize his last chance, brought by the Blue Star?

The third cassette is a composite of four elements: three messages received from above by one of the members and a strange sequence that Di Mambro wanted to leave to posterity. In a room that looks like a church crypt, we see through a doorway, in front of a large pillar, people's profiles, one by one, whom it is not possible to identify because they are dressed in ample capuchin capes pulled around their faces. They process in a slow and untiring march, each holding in both hands a lit candle. This mysterious procession is commented on by the voice of Joseph Di Mambro and a member of the fraternity:

> JDM: Space is curved, time comes to an end . . . Our cycle is over, these images tell all.
> F: On 6 January 1994, at 0h15m, the Elder Brothers of the Rosy Cross left their terrestrial planes, preceded by entities from the Great Pyramid who have gone back to their original planes. Programmed for all eternity, this unique event in history confirms the truth and the actualization of the prophecies that warned man that one day, because of [mankind's]

217

disdain for the Word, the Gods would leave the earth. A unique time is coming to an end as these knights, anonymous by choice, last carriers of the original fire, prepare in their turn to proceed, by their own means, with the liberation of the capital of energy-consciousness which the Rosy Cross bequeathed to them until the completion of the work.

JDM: The good-hearted man can live in this precise second, a sublime event: the passage of the cycle of Adamic man towards a new cycle of evolution, programmed on another earth, an earth prepared to receive the stored vibrations enriched by the authentic servants of the Rosy Cross.

This solemn scene is meant to symbolize the final procession of the Knights of the Solar Temple, who are leaving this Earth: "Noble travelers, we are of no era, of no place." If there were still a need to demonstrate that Di Mambro planned to create and leave behind a grand legend concerning his order's transit, this "choreography" offers persuasive evidence.

On 4 October 1994, at 1:40 P.M. (Swiss time), Canadian police intervened at a fire in Morin Heights and discovered two adult corpses. On 6 October, the corpses of two parents who had been savagely murdered were found with their baby child hidden in a closet. It was later discovered that the murders had occurred on 30 September and that the perpetrators had subsequently flown back to Switzerland. Also on 4 October, a little before midnight, residents of the small Swiss village of Cheiry noticed that a fire had started at the La Rochette farm in the heights around the village. On Wednesday, 5 October, around 3 A.M., three chalets were in flames at another place in Switzerland, Granges-sur-Salvan. Twenty-three corpses were discovered at Cheiry, twenty-five at Salvan. In Cheiry, most of the victims had apparently been called to a meeting on Sunday and were probably already dead on Monday, 3 October. A total of sixty-five bullets were found in their heads, and most of the victims had absorbed a strong soporific before being shot. No firearm had been used at Salvan, where only members of the core group lived; they had been injected with a poisonous substance provided by Jouret.

It has been clearly established that some of the fifty-three victims were murdered, while others submitted to execution voluntarily. However, even if their deaths were technically

218

assassinations (bullets in the head), we will never know with absolute certainty how many victims volunteered for their "departure" or how many realized beforehand that the fabulous voyage to another planet they had been hoping for would take such brutal form.

The fact that members who were fully cognizant of the macabre details of this "departure" and who were deeply affected by the loss of long-standing friends nevertheless decided, in December 1995, to themselves "leave" (again using firearms) in a clearing in French Vercors left many observers in such a state of incredulity that a number of journalists advanced the hypothesis of external intervention. But no such trace has been found (which would have been easy, since the area was snowy), and without ruling out the possibility that some victims did not fully consent or wanted to back out at the last minute, the deeds of these members are explicable without the intervention of a third party. It is true that several OTS survivors (including victims of the December 1995 "transit") were troubled over the methods used in October 1994. However, this discomfort did not stop a few of them from recognizing that they would have responded to the call if it had been addressed to them, or indeed from feeling a little disappointed not to have been invited to participate.

Several testimonies collected by the Swiss police after the event of December 1995 show that a process of reinterpretation was quickly elaborated among the core of the surviving believers, leading to the conclusion that what happened was in fact positive and that those who departed had sacrificed to save the consciousness of the planet and to pave the way for others. In their eyes, the "departure" conjoined the horrible and the sublime in a strange harmony. They came to the decision to follow the same path, probably convinced that the first group was waiting for them. The death of five more persons in Québec in March 1997 follows the same pattern, and the letter sent to the media by this handful of hard-liners articulates their doubts that there remain other people ready to follow the same path after them.

Scholarly observers have advanced varied interpretations of the Solar Temple's saga. Whatever the primary cause of the "transit," it was not a hasty decision, and the core group took time and care to legitimate ideologically the suicides and murders. This process probably also helped them reinforce each other in their choices, which had to be agreed upon collectively. Moreover, they likely celebrated ceremonies that ritualized their beliefs concerning the act they were about to commit near the time of the final departure. Texts detailing these ceremonies were discovered at Di Mambro's residence at Salvan. They strikingly illustrate the mind-set of the core group with regard to the coming transit:

> Brothers and Sisters of the First and of the Last Hour...
> Today... as we are gathered here in this Holy Place...
> The Great Terrestrial Cycle is closing in on itself.
> Alpha and Omega are fusing [to initiate] a new Creation.
> The Time of the Great Gathering is proclaiming the Departure of the Sons of Heaven.
> In the Name of a Will above mine
> I am handing the seed of our Immortality and of our Transcendent Nature to the Infinite Worlds
> At this Supreme Moment
> The ruby power of the Work should free itself and rejoin the Levels of the Future
> So that, engendered by ourselves
> Like the Phoenix
> We might be reborn from our ashes
> Through the Sword of Light
> Raised toward the Levels Above, what is refined should depart from the world of density
> And ascend toward its Point of Origin
> Our Terrestrial Journey is coming to an end
> The Work is being completed
> Everyone must return to their position on the Great Celestial Chessboard.

We have to consider seriously the OTS's beliefs. Di Mambro acted at times like a common swindler, but he very likely remained convinced of his message and mission until the end. Certainly, internal dissent and outside criticism helped to convince hesitant members of the core group that radical methods were needed in order to leave Earth. But, although we will never know for sure, it seems doubtful that a lesser degree of public exposure would have prevented the "transit." Even if he was able to hide such feelings when it was needed, Di Mambro had reached the point that he could no longer accept questioning of or disagreement with his views. Convinced of their own superiority and insulated psychologically from countervailing perspectives, the leadership came to view any dissonant voice as unbearable.

Finally, the transit presented an attractive response to the movement's decline: the temple needed to be "re-dynamized" periodically. The transit also allowed the group to escape from perceived threats and offered a way to assert dramatically its claims before the entire world. Creators of their own legend, the core members of the Solar Temple considered themselves as an elect circle, heirs to an uncommon destiny who were invested with a cosmic task to fulfill. Believing that they would become gods, they followed the flute player in a dance of death and paid the ultimate price.

•

On Jan. 7, 2005, 29-year-old Ricky Rodriguez recorded his final thoughts as he prepared to embark on a violent rampage of revenge. "Some of the things I'm going to try to do are rather shocking, and maybe not right in a lot of people's books," he said on a chilling videotape. "I'm just loading my mags here. Hope you guys don't mind if I do that while I talk."

Raised to be a prophet and a savior, Ricky was about to become an executioner, and a grim lesson in religious fanaticism.

"There is this need that I have," he said on the tape. "This need. It's not a want. And I wish it wasn't. But it is. It's a need for revenge. It's a need for justice. Because I can't go on like this."

His attempt to exact justice led to two violent deaths, including his own.

Rodriguez was once in line to be the next holy prince in the infamous Christian sect Children of God, now known as the Family International.

San-Francisco-based reporter Don Lattin has been reporting on the sect since the early 1970s, and Rodriguez's chilling video pushed him to spend the last two years investigating the motives behind Rodriguez's violent legacy. The result is his just-released book "Jesus Freaks."

Lattin says he was intrigued by the video of Rodriguez, "the drama of loading the bullets and sharpening his knife. He loved action movies so, you think, he almost saw this as a movie. I just had to get to the bottom of this. What was really behind this?"

"What could turn a kid, who was raised to be prophet in this group that claimed to be Christian, claimed to have love and compassion for mankind. What could turn him into a kind of raging monster?" said Lattin.

In the late 1960s David Berg – the self-proclaimed prophet and Children of God founder – began preaching a bizarre brew of sex

221

and scripture. In writings and preaching, Berg advocated free love among his disciples, including adult-child sex.

"Berg was actually a genius because he would test drive these bizarre theologies, bizarre teachings, within his own inner circle," said Lattin. "So very early on, still in the late '60s, he would start having these sharing parties where he would go around naked with a bottle of the wine saying all things are pure and they'd have these orgies but no one knew that outside of the inner circle."

"These guys don't just drop out of the sky," Lattin said of Berg's appeal. "So why are people following this guy if he's a monster and a drunk and a maniac? [Because] Berg came directly out of the Christian evangelical tradition."

Though that notion infuriates most evangelicals, Lattin points to Berg's own mother, Virginia Brandt Berg, who was one of the first famous radio evangelists. Berg failed in the pulpit early on, spending years on the road as an itinerant minister. But when the tumultuous 1960s rolled in, Berg finally found his voice.

"There were these two very strong social forces going on," said Lattin. "There was the countercultural, the youth movement. All these people living on the street, in the road with backpacks, lot of drugs. And there was the beginnings of this evangelical revival in the country."

By the 1970s, Berg's following grew into the tens of thousands. His so-called "law of love" urged young women to win converts to the group by prostituting themselves, something he called "flirty fishing."

Ricky Rodriguez's mother was Karen Zerby, a close confidante of Berg's, and together they anointed Rodriguez "Davidito" – the future prophet of the sect.

Other children in the inner circle were given their own roles, including ex-member Davida Kelley, who became the princess to Rodriguez' prince.

"We were both raised and nurtured to be the future leaders of the Family or the End Time prophets, so to speak," Kelley said. "We were programmed to believe that."

"Going way back, I think we could refer to my generation as the second generation and I would say we were experimental, test-tube kind of babies so to speak," she said.

Kelley says Berg was "obviously very inspired, very possessed and very fanatical, but he was also a pedophile."

In fact, provocative adult-child photos and stories lace the pages of group's manual, entitled "The Book of Davidito." And according to Kelley, sexual interaction between adults and children was not just an expectation, it was a commandment.

"At that time, myself or other young girls who were in the Unit at the time as apprentices, so to speak, would be required to crawl into bed and interact with David Berg," said Kelley. "I lived with David Berg from the time I was born till age 13."

When asked if she ever witnessed Ricky being sexually abused, Kelley said "Oh yes, of course by all the adult women. Most of them, at least, in the Unit."

Kelley says she even witnessed Karen Zerby, Rodriguez' mother, abusing him.

In 1986, after a series of official investigations and lawsuits, the Family International officially renounced sexual contact between adults and children.

In 1994 Berg died, and Zerby took over as leader, and as the second generation grew up, critics says the years in The Family left many scarred.

"There have been dozens of people who have committed suicide, and the family disputes this and says, 'well, some were drug overdoses.' Well that's another way of killing yourself, a drug overdose," said Lattin.

Despite that claim, most current members of the family, including some young people ABC News interviewed in 2005, insist stories of abuse and second-generation suicides are overblown.

"If it was categorical, if it was widespread, how come I never suffered abuse," a member named Anna asked . "How come I who have over 100 friends in the Family International all over the world, how come none of them ever told me they witnessed abuse or experienced abuse?"

After years of struggling with his faith, Rodriguez left the sect in 2001 but never came to terms with his past. He sought to bring his mother to justic.

The night after recording the videotape, Rodriguez went searching for his mother, who had long ago gone underground. Seeking a clue to her wherabouts, Rodriguez arranged a meeting with Angela Smith at his Tuscon, Ariz., apartment. Smith had been a trusted assistant to his mother.

Rodriguez killed Smith, and then he drove several hours into California. Sometime after midnight, he pulled into a parking lot in the city of Blythe and fired a single round, ending his life.

"Ricky was a combination of emotions that he was feeling," said Lattin. "He was incredibly angry at his mother and his leaders.

He was also very guilty – he blamed himself for a lot of the abuse that went on. He was just a time bomb waiting to go off."

"Man, if I don't get to her – I'm going to keep hunting her in the next life, let me tell you," Rodriguez said on the tape. "And I'm going to keep going until somebody gets her or I get her – justice will be done. Believe me."

Lattin says Zerby has never been brought to justice.

"No leaders of the family have been brought to justice for this, for what they acknowledge was child abuse. People say, 'why? How could that be?' Well, there's a statute of limitations. A lot of this happened a long time ago and almost all of it happened outside of the U.S. by people who kept constantly changing their names," he said. "So even the victims, the kids themselves, often don't know who abused them."

Zerby remains the spiritual leader of the Family International, though the group refuses or is unable to report her whereabouts. They also continue to deny that Rodriguez suffered any abuse as a child and take no responsibility for his suicide.

Family International spokeswoman said in an interview two years ago to ABC News, just after Rodriguez' death:

> Jay Schadler: *Why do you think Karen Zerby is nowhere to be found?*
> Borowik: *We don't look on it as nowhere to be found. She's very present in her writings.*
> Schadler: *Do you know where she is?*
> Borowik: *Do I know where, no. Not necessarily, no.*
> Schadler: *You don't? The Pope is a spiritual lead. We know where he is. Karen is a spiritual leader. And we don't know where she is. And her son just committed suicide.*
> Borowik: *I'm aware of that.*
> Jay: *So why don't we know where she is?*
> Borowik: *That's her policy. That's all I can tell you.*

Borowik also sent a written statement in response to Lattin's book. It reads, in part,

"Lattin's effort to analyze the life and motives of Ricky Rodriguez and the murder/suicide he committed in 2005 was undoubtedly a challenging task. Although Lattin's book does contain some sound research and factual information, it is laced with inaccuracies, misconceptions and erroneous conclusions lacking a factual base – not to mention, sketchy research. Information provided by a handful of apostates with a clearly delineated agenda to demonize the Family is deemed credible, whereas information proceeding from current Family members is deemed questionable, at best."

With the group's leader still in hiding, the story of the children of the Children of God remains unfinished. Each child will have to write his or her own ending.

•

On September 13, 1993, motorists driving on the Massachusetts Turnpike witnessed an unusual sight: A highway billboard for the Museum of Science in Boston had been covered by a ten-foot-by-ten-foot black banner with the words "Save the Planet—Kill Yourself" painted in white.

It would be the first high-profile action by the newly formed Church of Euthanasia, featuring the group's most enduring slogan.

Throughout the 1990s the church orchestrated several similarly outrageous public actions — including an appearance on the *Jerry Springer Show* — seeking to draw attention to the environmental dangers of overpopulation.

Today the Church of Euthanasia website still functions and serves as an archive, although the church itself is gone. Its aggressive campaign against the existence of humanity never caught on, but you can say this for the group: In falling apart, at least they practiced what they preached.

Filmmaker Stephen Onderick chronicled the church's mostly forgotten history in his documentary, *Save the Planet, Kill Yourself.* "To some, the Church of Euthanasia was a heroic organization calling attention to important ecological issues,to others it was an elaborate series of pranks," Onderick said, "to still others it was a genuinely dangerous cult."

The documentary is a compelling retrospective on a movement that was likely the most controversial pseudo-religion of the 1990s. Onderick obtained access to several hours of never-before-seen footage, as well as 12 hours of interviews with the key players.

The Church of Euthanasia was founded in 1992 by software developer and DJ Chris Korda. Korda was inspired by the ideals of Dadaism, an artistic movement that emerged during Word War I out of a desire to, as one artist put it, "to destroy the hoaxes of reason and to discover an unreasoned order." According to poet Tristan Tzara, the beginnings of Dada "were not the beginnings of art, but of disgust."

On the church's site, Korda says this inspiration came to her in a dream, during which she was "confronted [by] an alien intelligence known as The Being who speaks for the inhabitants of

Earth in other dimensions. The Being warned that our planet's ecosystem is failing, and that our leaders deny this. The Being asked why our leaders lie to us, and why so many of us believe these lies." She was also heavily influenced by news of global climate change, a view she claims to have begun forming as early as age 10 after reading a *New York Times* headline about the irreversibility of global warming.

For this reason, the church — and Korda is adamant that she perceives it as a religion first and foremost — has one commandment: "Thou shalt not procreate."

When asked if there had ever been members who had to be expelled for violating it. "Regrettably yes," she told me. "There have been a number of excommunications, and it's been my unpleasant duty to enforce them. Since we only have one commandment, there's zero tolerance for failure to uphold it."

There are also four pillars, which are voluntary: suicide ("optional but encouraged"), abortion ("may be required to avoid procreation"), cannibalism ("mandatory if you insist on eating flesh," but only if someone is already dead), and sodomy ("optional, but strongly encouraged").

"Save the Planet, Kill Yourself" emerged as a succinct way to express alarm at the destruction of the environment, as well as a pathway to the only viable remedy Korda could identify, which was voluntary population reduction.

The first effort Korda made at popularizing this phrase was at the 1992 Democratic National Convention in New York City, where she passed out stickers with the slogan to other convention delegates. A few months after that, she began applying the stickers on police vehicles. The slogan would become a staple of the church's abrasive banners and signs at public events for years to come. It was also the name of Korda's 1994 EP—released, fittingly, on the label Kevorkian Records.

In 1994, the church was recognized by the state of Delaware; 501(c)(3) tax exempt status would follow a year later. A journal called *Snuvv It* was published and mailed to members along with Korda's "e-sermons." On September 10 of that year, the church held its first public march as part of Boston's Population Awareness Day event. Korda led a contingent of about a dozen members while carrying a stick with a bloody baby doll and a torn strip of an American flag tied to it—a pro-abortion symbol. Other props included a large fake RU 486 abortifacient pill that was rolled around while everyone chanted "Save the planet! Kill yourself!" The church was promptly ejected from the festivities.

The church's pro-suicide advocacy began in 1995 with the purchase of a billboard with a 900 number for a "Suicide Assistance Hot-Line" and the message: "Helping you every step of the way! Thousands helped! How about you?" The idea was to play callers pre-recorded messages with suicide instructions, but the phone company, recognizing these intentions, never activated the line.

The church's website would go on to feature explicit suicide instructions. This was back in the days when Jack Kevorkian was actively assisting people in ending their lives, and Korda figured the legal risk of advocating suicide was low. She would openly tout the instructions on the site as a way to get publicity, telling "Shovel in 1999" that it was "a disappointment to me that no one's actually killed themselves and then had their parents sue us. That would actually punch through the media shield."

That was a dark bit of foreshadowing, it turned out: In 2003 a woman in Missouri was found dead lying next to a printout from the Church of Euthanasia site. Jennifer Joyce, the top prosecutor for the city of St. Louis, publicly threatened the church with voluntary manslaughter charges, and the instructions were promptly removed. When asked, Korda, who is generally verbose and fast-talking, if there had ever been any follow-up by the courts, she paused, then said rather slowly, "I am unaware of any such activity, nor would I be disposed to comment on or discuss such an activity if it did in fact exist."

In 1996, the church began counter-protests against anti-abortion activists in the Boston area. The first weekend, church members stood outside a Boston clinic carrying signs to provoke demonstrators with messages like "Fuck Breeding," "Sperm-Free Cunts for the Earth," "Fetuses are for Scraping," "Depressed? Commit Spermicide," "Make Love, Not Babies," "No Kid, No Labor," "Love the Earth, Tie Your Tubes," and "Feeling Maternal? Adopt!"

The following weekend, they visited a clinic that had been the site of a shooting a year earlier and had attracted a large group of protesters from the anti-abortion group Operation Rescue. This time they showed up with the same signs plus a new 15-by-six-foot banner that said "Eat a Queer Fetus for Jesus." The carnivorous babies on sticks made a reappearance "just in case there was trouble," except now they had blood-red fake skulls on top. A month later the church was antagonizing anti-abortion demonstrators outside a different clinic, led by a member dressed as a Catholic priest and carrying signs for "Pedophile Priests for Life."

In 1997 the church upped the ante by creating a fake organization called the Boston Fertility Task Force. Onderick described the operation in an email: "[They] proceeded to use it to draw real pro-life protesters out to a completely invented protest of fetal trafficking at a sperm bank in Boston. They also put up posters around town claiming that Courtney Love would be at the Sperm Bank to be inseminated on the day of the protest, and they showed up to find nuns fingering rosary beads and teens waiting around to see Courtney Love outside of the building, at which point they unveiled a two-story tall penis puppet that ran through traffic toward the building and ejaculated pseudo-sperm in front of the building."

"We went toe-to-toe with some very dangerous people," Korda said. "We were on the Operation Rescue list of official enemies. We discovered that when we did the Walk for Life and they had a book full of their official enemies. They had a whole page devoted to the Church of Euthanasia, with pictures. They hated us. They wanted us dead, and these were not guys to be messed around with."

The same year, Korda and other church members were on the *Jerry Springer Show* in what is their most widely-viewed media appearance. The episode, called "I Want to Join a Suicide Cult," was framed in typical Jerry Springer fashion as a plea to "Grace Petro" (actually church member Nina Paley) to not join the Church of Euthanasia. She appeared alongside an alleged ex-boyfriend, who broke up with her due to her desire to not have children, and radical anti-abortion activist Neal Horsley. At the time, Horsley was preparing a website called the "Nuremberg Files," which would list the names and personal information of abortion doctors. Doctors that had been killed would remain on the list with a line drawn through their name.

While agreeing with much of the church's platform, Springer took Korda to task for statements suggesting that a depressed teenager contemplating suicide should be offered assistance, rather than talked out of it. He also repeatedly expressed disgust at the calls for cannibalism and brought attention to the church's literature that provides explicit instructions on "butchering a human carcass."

Korda spent much of the following year making appearances in Europe in support of her techno album *Six Billion Humans Can't Be Wrong*. In 1999, the church turned its sights on the environmental movement with a homemade raft that traversed the Charles River during Boston's WBOS Earthfest festival. The raft had an 18-by-five-foot "Save the Planet, Kill Yourself" banner and struggled to stay afloat, but managed to play music from Korda's CD loudly enough to draw crowds. Eventually the police escorted the raft to shore and told the activists to turn the music off.

The next year, the church attempted to join the environ-mentalists outside Boston's Bio 2000 conference. While most protesters were there to oppose genetic engineering and other activities that were part of the conference, the church wanted to show its *support* for the conference, on the grounds that destroying mankind was a desirable outcome. They carried a banner that said "Human Extinction While We Still Can." According to Korda, the protest organizers cut the cables to the group's sound system and then proceeded to beat them up. It would be the last of the group's public demonstrations.

"What we were doing was extremely dangerous," Korda said. "I got tired not just of the hate and the death threats, of which I have boxes, but I got tired of nearly being beaten to death. A lot of these actions took place in the street, and by the time the police showed up we were happy to see them. Usually by that point we were just about to go to the hospital. It's fair to say that most of the most formidable opposition didn't come from Christians, whether of the Catholic or Baptist variety, but from leftists, because they believe in 'direct action.' They don't like the police. They'd much rather beat us up. You can imagine why we might get tired of that."

In December 2001, Korda would court controversy one last time, by releasing a music video called "I Like to Watch." The video was a mashup of amateurish techno with clips of porn, sports, and the 9/11 attacks. Korda told me that it accurately captured her "perverse fascination and sexual arousal" at watching the attacks on television.

"Politically, it felt good to see Americans dying for a change. There was a sense of justice, of the 'chickens coming home to roost,'" she said. "In gender terms, the huge gash made by the plane was obviously female. I had witnessed a Freudian drama on a national scale: America's penis had been turned into a vagina."

Comments like that, coupled with the church's penchant for big, over-the-top displays of crude, vicious misanthropy, might make some wonder if the Church of Euthanasia was, wholly or partially, a huge performance art piece, or a decade-long prank.

If so, neither Korda nor her disciples ever broke kayfabe, and even today—the group is dormant, its 501(c)(3) status lapsed because it's not bringing in any money—she seems deadly earnest, eager to discuss the church and in particular her "Antihumanism manifesto."

In the 6,000-plus-word document — the last bits of which are just bullet-points — Korda says that "humans are making a conscious choice to place their interests above the well-being of life, and this is not merely foolish or misguided, it is shameful and criminal. If humans are unable — for whatever reason — to exist in a way that supports life, then humans are unfit, and must be eliminated." She points out that "unlike mere misanthropy, anti-humanism is distinguished by reverence for nonhuman life." A section called "Solutions" outlines ideas for how human elimination might play out, as well as thoughts on "behavior modification" strategies that might avert mass human extinction. (That bit contains a disclaimer in the end stating these are all hypotheticals and not calls for violence.)

Korda's manifesto is filled with scientific concepts like the Fermi paradox and the ideas of thinkers like E.O. Wilson and Richard Dawkins. It makes for an odd juxtaposition against the "church-approved" list of resources on HIV/AIDS denialism, for which there is no scientific justification whatsoever. If not completely nihilistic — Korda expresses some sympathy for nonhuman animals — her worldview is bleak to the point of absurdity, and the philosophy behind it is a hodgepodge of strands of radical thought seemingly snatched at random. If the church is a joke, it's not a very funny one.

•

Born Adolfo de Jesus Constanzo in Miami, Florida, on November 1, 1962, to 15-year-old Cuban immigrant Delia Aurora Gonzalez del Valle, Adolfo was the oldest of three children, all of whom had different fathers.

At six months old, Gonzalez had her son blessed by a Haitian priest who observed "palo mayombe," an offshoot of mainstream West African religions. The practice, which involves drinking a liquid in which human bones have been boiled, is often used for casting spells of wealth or power. Gonzalez and her first husband believed their son was "a chosen one" who was "destined for great power."

Constanzo was still an infant when his father died, and he and his widowed mother moved to San Juan, Puerto Rico. Gonzalez soon remarried and had Constanzo baptized in the Catholic Church to please her second husband. Adolfo even served briefly as an altar boy.

Gonzalez and Constanzo kept their true faith a secret, often traveling to San Juan and Haiti for Constanzo's religious education. In 1972, the family returned to Miami, Florida. His stepfather died soon after, leaving Gonzalez with some money. His mother married yet again, this time to a man involved with the local drug trade and the occult.

Free to worship as he wished, Adolfo started an apprenticeship with a Haitian priest, who taught him the skills he needed to "profit from evil." Constanzo, now in his teens, cruised gay bars committing petty crimes and robbing graves to stock his priest's cauldron. By 1976, Constanzo believed he was developing psychic powers, supposedly predicting the 1981 shooting of President Ronald Reagan.

In early 1983, Constanzo pledged himself to Kadiempembe, his religion's version of Satan. That same year, Constanzo traveled to Mexico City, where recruited his first disciples: Martin Quintana Rodriguez and Omar Orea Ochoa. Constanzo seduced both Quintana and Orea, and a year later he moved in with them.

Adolfo started offering his fortune telling and ritual cleansing services to the community, and word of his "abilities" began to spread. He claimed to harness magical powers that would make gangsters and their bodyguards invisible to police, and bulletproof against their enemies. He also helped drug dealers schedule their shipments based on his premonitions. At the height of his career, Constanzo had more than 30 devoted clients, including illegal narcotics dealers, organized crime bosses, and high-ranking law enforcement officials.

By 1986 Constanzo had amassed considerable wealth; he was able to buy a fleet of luxury cars and a $60,000 condominium in Mexico City. During this time, police believe Constanzo began to feed his cauldron with human offerings. According to their records, authorities say he and his cult were responsible for at least 23 ritual murders around Mexico City.

On April 30, 1987, Constanzo and his cult murdered seven members of the Calzada crime family after they denied the religious leader full partnership in their syndicate. The family was tortured and mutilated, their body parts removed to feed Constanzo's cauldron. Police found the remains over the course of a week, but were unable to link the evidence to a suspect.

Buoyed by the killings, Constanzo expanded the cult's headquarters, moving 20 miles outside Matamoros to Rancho Santa Elena. At the ranch, Constanzo began a deeper involvement in the illegal drug trade, and pursued his ritualistic killings in earnest. That year, on May 28, 1988, Constanzo shot drug dealer Hector de la Fuente and a farmer named Moises Castillo. Dissatisfied with the sacrifices of the two men, he supervised the torture and dismemberment of Raul Paz Esquivel two months later, during a trip to Mexico City. The remains were dumped on a public street and found by local children.

A month later, after a two of his followers were kidnapped during a drug war, Constanzo sacrificed and tortured a stranger to death, chanting prayers for the safe release of his two cult members. In November of that same year, he sacrificed cult member Jorge Valente de Fierro Gomez after the man violated Constanzo's ban on drug use.

On Feburary 14, 1989, Constanzo had drug dealers Ezequiel Rodriguez Luna, Ruben Vela Garza, and Ernesto Rivas Diaz tortured to death at the ranch. Nine days later, the cult kidnapped another stranger, who they had to shoot in the ensuing struggle. Unable to complete their ritual, the cultists decided to find another victim. The group accidentally murdered the cousin of a cult member before realizing his identity.

Constanzo scheduled another ritual killing for March 13, 1989, in order to ensure the safe passage of a shipment of illegal drugs. The victim's suffering, however, wasn't sufficient for Constanzo. "They must die screaming," he insisted, telling the cult members that he wanted an American student for his next ritual. The group lured 21-year-old Mark Kilroy, an affluent American student, to their van. When the young man tried to escape, the group bludgeoned him in the back of the head with a machete. The group was elated by the sacrifice. Kilroy's death, however, would turn out to be a fatal error for Adolfo Constanzo.

The pressure on Mexican police to find Kilroy was immediate and intense. American officials kept a close eye on the case, and the victim's family offered a $15,000 reward for any information leading to their son's safe return. Matamoros police interrogated 127 known criminals about Kilroy's possible whereabouts. During their investigation, they stumbled onto drug dealer Serafin Hernandez Garcia, a frequent visitor to Constanza's ranch.

On April 1, 1989, after Garcia refused to stop at a police checkpoint, officers followed the petty criminal to Rancho Santa

Elena. After a quick search of the property revealed illegal narcotics, the police arrested Hernandez and another drug dealer, David Serna Valdez. In custody, Hernandez freely admitted to Kilroy's abduction and murder. He also confessed to participation in 14 other murders over a nine-month period.

On April 11, 1989, Hernandez took police to the ranch, unearthing the remains of 15 victims. One of the bodies was Mark Kilroy's — his brain was missing, and his body dismembered. Garcia told law enforcement officials about the group's religious leader, Adolfo Constanzo, and proudly described his involvement in the ritual sacrifices.

Constanzo had disappeared by this time, hiding out in the houses of various cult members, and making plans to flee Mexico. More and more of the cult's members were arrested until May 6, 1989. While police were going door-to-door on an unrelated case, they stumbled on Constanzo and four of his followers, two of whom were his lovers. He panicked and began shooting at police. Within moments, 180 policemen surrounded the apartment. The shootout lasted 45 minutes, with only one officer wounded.

When Constanzo realized he would not be able to escape, he ordered a follower to shoot he and his lover, Martin Quintana. By the time police entered the apartment, Constanzo and Quintana were dead.

The survivors of the shootout, along with 12 other cult members, were indicted on various charges, including multiple murder, weapons and narcotics violations, conspiracy and obstruction of justice. American authorities stand ready to prosecute the convicted cult members for Mark Kilroy's murder, should they ever be released from Mexican custody.

•

Robin Gecht had worked for John Wayne Gacy, the infamous Serial Killer Clown. After Gacy was arrested and incarcerated, Robin formed his own cult, with Edward Spreitzer, Andrew Kokoraleis and Thomas Kokoraleis. Obsessed with Satanic rituals, Heavy Metal music and murder, the Crew engaged in cannibalism and necromutilomania. The Crew abducted prostitutes and performed butchered mastectomies. They committed sexual acts with the mutilated body and the severed mammary. The Crew saved the gore for masturbation and consumption, chopping and masticating the meat during unholy Crew communions.

"Well, in answer to your question on obsession with breasts, it is a thing with my entire family going back as I'm told to great

233

grandfather. Each of us men have married large breasted women. My ex-wife is a 39D and yes she was very satisfying to me," said Robin Gecht on one occasion when asked about why he amputated women's breasts.

The arrest, trial and conviction of John Wayne Gacy sent shock waves through the community. The crimes received international media attention. John was a successful businessman, involved with the Democratic Party and community charities. He had his picture taken with First Lady Rosalynn Carter, he was even allowed a "special clearance" status with the Secret Service. John dressed as a clown for charitable functions, his "Pogo the Clown" personality was a member of the Jolly Jokers, a group of Chicago area clowns involved in charitable works for community children. The revelations of rape and murder shook Chicago, Illinois and America, to the core. John began his homicidal house of horrors in 1972, his trial concluded in 1980. Robin was watching and waiting. John Wayne Gacy often had his young employees perform work on his house, usually digging the dirt from the crawl spaces under his floor. The boys did not understand the reason for John needing such deep crawl spaces, however, they performed their labors, as instructed. Several employees remember being returned to the home, to shovel concrete over certain areas in the basement and garage. Again, even to a young construction laborer, the tasks did not make sense. The boys had been told to spread lime in the areas they were working, an unusual request. Robin was employed at PDM Contractors, owned by John Wayne Gacy, the Killer Clown. John employed boys, he murdered some of his young employees. John claimed he did not murder all of his victims alone, he cited an accomplice. When evidence indicated John was not in the city and could not have committed the murder of a young man connected with his business, John alleged the crime was committed by this accomplice, without his knowledge.

Women involved with Robin described a man obsessed with nipples and breasts. Robin would stick pins their areolas. He would slice the nipple, transfixed by the laceration. After the blood had clotted, he would explore the wound. Robin explained that he wanted to "see how the nipple worked" and his fascination ended relationships. These limited mutilations led to infections, the women subjected to his cravings suffered pain and discomfort, from his sexual desires. They feared Robin, he was a man lusting to perform a vivisection on a female breast. Edward alleged Robin had amputated the nipples of his wife. After Robin was apprehended for the Chicago Ripper Crew homicides, women came forward and accused him of these alleged crimes. If the women, the mutilated survivors, had contacted authorities when the crimes occurred, Robin's mission of mayhem may have been aborted. Then again, the women exposed to Robin, early in his developing ghoulishness, were possibly too terrified to contact the law. They would have been afraid to testify against him, as he would have been released on bail, pending trial. Robin had a strange power over people.

Robin converted his apartment into a Satanic temple. Robin read verses from the "Satanic Bible" aloud and adorned the walls with inverted crosses. This is strange, as Saint Peter was crucified on an inverted cross; Robin was decorating his wicked chapel with memorial symbols honoring a martyr. Robin listened to Heavy Metal music, ignoring the real motivation behind the obvious marketing strategies of bands. He attempted to ascertain spiritual meaning in the music and lyrics, a la Charles Manson discovering messages in the "White Album" from The Beatles. Robin was becoming a cult leader, he only lacked devoted followers.

Black Sabbath began a revolution in music. The sound, themes and vocals of this Heavy Metal band became an instant target of televangelists. Although Ozzy Osbourne often sang of finding love in God and delivered vocals comparing war pigs to witches at black masses, the fundamentalist evangelical movement seized this opportunity to create the Satanic Panic. A modern day witch hunt in the USA. Some people found fear and fled to churches led by distress mongering preachers. Some people loved Metal music and found the sound and lyrics thought provoking and challenging. An ideal form of art to express emotions and ideas regarding social, governmental and religious institutions. A way to explore everything between birth and death, and beyond, with a new musical philosophy. Some people found a muse for their insanity. They began to plan awful horrors never dreamt of, in the most horrible nightmares of Hell.

Edward, Andrew and Thomas were followers, of below average intelligence, they would have followed anyone, anywhere. They were the type of boys that enable bullies, by participating in the abuse of a weak, solitary, vulnerable victim. Followers are everywhere. They love government jobs, churches, schools, cults and clubs. Followers enjoy groups and they thrive in the company of their team. They will tolerate child molestation and rape, as they value their organization to the utmost. They will sacrifice their individuality for the feeling of belonging to something. Followers are the people of Penn State University, followers are the adherents of the Roman Catholic Church. They are the people that watch crimes being committed and they rationalize their cowardice with any argument, to assuage their conscience and deflect their guilt. In the bitter end, they are always betrayed by their masters, they always betray their masters. As they betrayed their very own selves, when they capitulated to a power greater than their own minds.

Chicago is the Midwestern version of New York City. The Second City is a vast metropolis, with a unique culture and environment. The Windy City is famous for deep dish pizza and The Chicago Bears, the Al Capone mafia era and the Sears Tower. Chicago is The Museum of Modern Art and the poverty and crime ridden South Side. The Skyway expressway and elevated public transportation by train. Hyde Park and the University of Chicago. Specialized restaurants, family owned and operated small businesses, in every neighborhood. Chi-Town is industry and commerce, with ports on the Great Lake Michigan, gigantic rail switch yards and interstates for transportation by truck. Chicago is the sinister home of H.H. Holmes and John Wayne Gacy, Shy-town is a human conglomerate of crime and dark alleys and bad neighborhoods. In Chicagoland, people watch the Cubs play baseball, from parties on the rooves of nearby buildings. In Chicago, cheap motels and prostitutes and guns abound. Chicago is a place with abundant opportunity and plentiful peril. The Chicago Ripper Crew cruised the streets in a van. Robin would identify the target, the Crew would violently overpower and abduct the woman. They would take the woman to the Satanic chapel, or a cheap motel room, for gang rape. Robin would read verses from the Satanic Bible, while the Crew would ravage and savage the victim. When they had taken their turns at terror, they severed a breast, with wire. After the amputation, Robin would commit sexual acts with the open wound, on the body of the victim. He would masturbate, using the breast as a gruesome sex toy, in his hand. They would use the flesh in rituals, carving the soft meat with knives, while the suffering victim was killed with blunt force trauma, delivered with a hatchet to the head. After the body was dumped, usually in a garbage strewn area, or a cemetery, the Ripper Crew cult would consume the breast, chopping the mammary into pieces and chewing the bloody breast bits, raw.

Angel York survived the Chicago Ripper Crew. She said a red van was cruising and stopped near her, as she was walking on the sidewalk. She was taken captive by men, suddenly. She was handcuffed, in the van. She was repeatedly raped. She was told to cut her own soft breast, with a sharp knife, in exchange for mercy. She testified that when her shaking hand slashed her own breast, with the blade, one man went into a frantic frenzy. He grasped her hand, plunging the knife into her chest. He mutilated her breast. He masturbated into the gaping, bleeding wound. Sated with his butchery, he duct taped the wound and the Crew released their hold on her limbs, pushing her out, off into the gutter. Angel had suffered abject misery by a crew of men dedicated to torment and torture. She had been given grievous wounds by a ghoulish cult addicted to gore. Yet, she noticed a roach clip, adorned with feathers, hanging from the rear view mirror of the rape van.

The Crew may have been abused as children. They may have taken animal sacrifice from the Old Testament scriptures and converted the barbaric practice into a modern day ritual of ridiculous cruelty. They may have lived hopeless lives in a depressing big city, cold and battered by prophetic winds of a futile future. The Crew may have known life would end with death, as we are all condemned to die, eventually. They did not need to do these things, to strangers attempting to live their lives, in the same circumstances and situations, as the members of the Crew may have found themselves. They could have controlled themselves. They could have begun a band, they could have written books together, they could have painted atrocities on the walls of buildings. The worst aspect of the Chicago Ripper Crew crimes is that they were so successful.

In 1982, contemporary advances in forensic science had not been made. Police were unable to determine the time of death, in many Ripper Crew cases. The drastic wounds to the chests of many victims gave insects and animals access to the interior of the corpses. Many of the women killed by the Ripper Crew were in an advanced state of decomposition when recovered, making identification difficult. Even if semen samples from the Ripper Crew had been recovered from the body cavities of the victims, DNA science had not advanced to the point of having the ability to establish the identity of possible suspects. The Chicago Police Department knew they had killers lurking in the midst of the population they were sworn to protect. They did not have the technological capabilities to retrieve viable evidence. They were giving a growing number of mutilated bodies to the coroner, while they were watching and waiting for the Crew to make a mistake.

Cult member Edwaard Spreitzer later testified, "A black female was picked up, blindfolded and gagged. Robin shot her point blank in the head. Put chains around her neck and legs, attached two bowling balls and threw her in the water. I understand her body was not found."

Edward described Robin as being in a state of utter blood lust, during this period. He recalled a particular attack, the Crew had wrestled a victim into an alley, from the street. Robin hacked at the breast of the struggling woman with a knife, he immediately began having necromutilomania sex with the gaping laceration, in the alley. The woman was screaming and the wound was pouring blood. Robin finished his perversion and he finished the woman, beating her head to a pulp, with an axe. Victims were found with pulverized skulls. Victims had been tortured with ice picks. A victim was found in a pool of blood that had leaked from the anus of the ruined remains, as the victim slowly expired, the internal injuries to the colon and large intestine exsanguinated the body. A victim was slashed from head to toe with a razor, leaving the skin in bloody tatters.

Beverly Washington lost her left breast to the Ripper Crew on October 6, 1982. Beverly was abducted off the street, she was gang raped in the van. She was tortured with a knife, Robin slashed her breasts, amputating the left breast and mutilating the right breast. She was found bleeding, dumped next to train tracks in the chilly October weather. Beverly described a scene of extreme sadistic cruelty. The van was a mobile torture chamber, the men were crude and intent on inflicting agonizing injuries. They uttered Satanic slogans while they tormented her. When they were finally done with her, they discarded her. They kept her breast, she later learned, for masturbation and consumption. The breast flesh that remained, after their cannibal feast, was kept in a trophy container.

This is an incomplete list of the women that suffered death and mutilation at the hands of the Chicago Ripper Crew: Linda Sutton, prostitute and mother of two children. Hispanic woman with engagement ring. Lorraine Burrowski, abducted from place of employment. Shui Mak, mutilated remains undiscovered for months. Angel York, survived and provided information. Sondra Delaware, discovered on a river bank. Rose Davis, discovered in an alley. Carol Pappas, married to a Chicago Cubs player. Beverly Washington, survived and provided information. Rose Beck, she fought hard against her attackers. Susan Baker, found after the Ripper Crew arrests. We will never know the true body count. The

Ripper Crew is believed to have claimed the lives of, at least, twenty women. Robin critiqued John Wayne Gacy, saying he should have disposed of his victims by dumping them, instead of keeping them under the crawl spaces of his home. In fact, John Wayne Gacy dumped four victims near the Des Plaines River, as he had run out of space, at his home.

The Ripper Crew was also involved in a drive-by shooting that left local drug dealer Rafael Torado dead, injuring another man at the phone booth. If the Ripper Crew had not been apprehended, a mass murder was likely, as the Crew had escalated their level of violence from serial killing for pleasure to murder for profit. Eventually, Robin would have found a reason to attack a group of people, perhaps a public gathering, such as a church, or a school. The serial killing was not the ultimate aim of the Ripper Crew, they were arrested in the beginning of their campaign. The testimony of Angel and Beverly gave the police a description of the rape van. The roach clip hanging from the rear view mirror, with feathers attached, was a unique detail. When patrolmen noticed the vehicle, they found Edward driving, alone. He was detained and inter-rogated. Edward betrayed Robin, immediately. Edward was sick of the memory of witnessing Robin beating a victim with a hammer. He confessed he was forced to perform sexual acts by Robin, although I am sure he did not have an explanation for his arousal and ability to perform. Edward explained the ritualistic sacrifices to Satan. However, when Robin was arrested and brought to the interrogation area, Edward immediately recanted his confessions. Andrew and Thomas corroborated the recanted confessions of Edward. As detectives read the litany of lunacy, Andrew and Thomas knew the police had the information needed for conviction, they cooperated enough to seal the fate of the Crew. Due to the confusion and chaos in court, with four different constantly changing accounts of the crimes, prosecutors were unable to charge Robin with murder.

Andrew Kokoraleis was executed on March 17, 1999. He was the last man executed by the state of Illinois, before the moratorium on execution was imposed. He was praying, while he lay on the gurney. As the lethal injection was begun, he asked for forgiveness and stated: "The Kingdom of God is at hand." Edward Spreitzer was given the death penalty, his sentence was commuted to life in prison, due to the moratorium on execution in Illinois. Thomas Kokoraleis was sentenced to seventy years, he is currently incarcerated. Thomas is remembered for saying, "That's the girl

Eddie and I killed in the cemetery," when he saw a photograph of Lorraine Borowski, while detectives were showing him pictures of missing women. Robin is serving one hundred and twenty years for the mutilation of Beverly Washington. He will be eligible for parole in the year 2020. The Chicago Ripper Crew should have been executed as a crew, hung from the gallows at the same moment, four necks snapping together.

The Chicago Ripper Crew contributed to the 1980's Satanic Panic in America. Thousands of innocent citizens were persecuted for fictitious crimes, based on coerced testimony. Men and women were arrested, convicted and incar-cerated, based on untrue allegations by hysterical crusaders. If the serial killers don't get you, the religious fanatics will.

•

We will never know to what degree the crimes of cults are prompted by religious concepts. The fanaticism associated with the cults are obvious and usually they are led by a charismatic person with the ability to sway and control followers. But to what degree can he sway them? Charles Manson ordered them to kill – and they killed. Others kidnapped, raped, confined and abused – all on the orders of a dominant cult leader. It was typically a Bible-spouting character claiming some divine preference and teaching fear as much as goodness.

In condemnation of the cults, however, we should not ignore the inquisitions, witch hunts, child abuses, the Magdalena houses, the cloistered nuns prohibited to speak, self-flagellation and a host of other practices that spell part of Christian history.

DR. KING AND HIS FRIENDS ON VENUS

Interestingly enough, there has been little to no criticism of The Aetherius Society. While most who've ever heard of it consider it utterly ridiculous bollocks, and others note that before setting up the society, "Dr." King was a mere taxi driver, intent on berating and challenging passengers about their spiritual health, they seem quite nice people, and there has still never been a major event nor criminal action that can be attributed to The Aetherius Society. Though most people, no doubt, think it's pretty bloody weird. Despite the small number of actual members, they are quite active on Meetup.com promoting talks related to Aetherian topics.

The society preaches an easily-recognizable melange of New Ageish philosophy. Their blend of 1950s era anti-nuclear campaigning and yoga makes the group's message increasingly plausible in a post-Fukushima age where you can't swing a dead, irradiated Hello Kitty and not hit someone carrying a yoga mat.

George King was born in Wellington, Shropshire to George and Mary King. His mother was said to be psychic and his family was "imbued with occult inclinations". In the 1930s, King belonged to a number of occult groups.

King was big on meditation. Really big. In fact he studied yoga for 10 years and up to 12 hours a day until he became so in tune with terrestrial knowledge that he became a "Knower".

As King tells it, he was sitting alone in his London apartment one day, fooling around with god knows what, when suddenly out of the blue a voice, using the pseudonym "Master Aetherius", commanded, *"Prepare yourself! You are to become the voice of Interplanetary Parliament"'*. He states that although he was initially shocked by this statement, coming from thin air and all, he knew he had heard it due to his mastery of all terrestrial phenomena.

Several days later an unnamed yoga master, whom King knew was alive and well in India, appeared by walking through the locked door of his apartment and taught King exercises in order to bring him closer in touch with the Cosmic Masters who would soon use King as the "Primary Terrestrial Mental Channel." Followers of King refer to him as Dr. George King. Followers also claim him as Reverend George King and Sir George King. There seems to be no evidence this former taxi driver ever received an accredited degree that would allow him to properly call himself "doctor." Randi notes "none of the three titles are verified".

The official Aetherius Society seems to have dropped most title claims (notably Sir) except for the doctor title. The society does not document the source of King's doctorate, despite claiming to have carefully archived King's transmissions. David Barrett, in *A Brief Guide to Secret Religions*, states King received his doctorate from "the International Theological Seminary of California, a degree mill with no accreditation". An early version of the Wikipedia entry on King offers the unreferenced claim that "His followers address him as Dr. George King but the doctor's title was conferred to him not by any university on earth but by spiritual sources." For a time, King also seems to have claimed to have received a Doctor of Letters (D.Litt.) degree. In the USA, this is generally an honorary degree. However, in the U.K. it's usually considered a degree above Ph.D.

A look at the society's site from the Wayback Machine has a rather richer list of titles and honours. The Society appears to have stopped making claims of knighthoods and princeships around 2005.

Many online non-Aetherius Society sources still refer to King's official biography from the 1990s and early 2000s. The Aetherius Society page at The World Religions & Spirituality Project at Virginia Commonwealth University lists him as:

"Sir George King, OSP, PhD, ThD, DD, Metropolitan Archbishop of the Aetherius Churches, Founder President of the Aetherius Society." He also boasted other honorary titles, including Prince Grand Master of the Mystical Order of St. Peter, HRH Prince George King De Santori, and Knight of Malta. Certificates of these various degrees and titles are displayed at the Society's Temple in Hollywood, California.

His Prince Grand Master title was awarded from the Mystical Order of St. Peter, which "was set up by Dr. George King after a Mystical Communion he had with no less a Being than Saint Peter." The Mystical Order of Saint Peter has a cherished past stretching back to the mystical epoch of 1981.

A UFO wiki claims "In 1980, King was also dubbed 'Sir George King' by His Royal and Imperial Highness Prince Robert Khimchiachvili, the 74th Grand Master of the Sovereign Order of Saint John of Jerusalem, Knights of Malta."[According to the New York *Sun*, "From 1970, Prince Robert M.N.G. Bassaraba de Branco-van-Khimchiachvili-Dadiani ran a bogus Order of St. John of Jerusalem, Knights of Malta from his faux-marble apartment (filled with equally genuine Louis XV furniture) at 116 Central Park South. If you had a passage fee, he had a gong for you, and hundreds of

242

men and women with more money than sense each paid him up to $30,000 for his phony knighthoods." Khimchiachvili and two associates were later convicted of wire fraud.

The Aetherius Society claims King won the "Prize of Peace and Justice" from The International Union of Christian Chivalry. The society notes "previous recipients of this prize include Albert Einstein, Mother Teresa, and Albert Schweitzer." This group does not appear to exist; only one other person in a Google search makes any claim of membership with the union. Richard Quezada claims "Member of the International Union of Christian Chivalry" and also lists himself as "A Mentor of The Aetherius Society".

The official Aetherius Society notes King received a "Grant of Arms by Her Majesty's College of Arms in London, England." The talk section of the Wikipedia article on King a user notes that a "Grant of Arms - is something you apply for, not conferred on you." Another user comments (on the "grant of arms" as well as some Freedom of the City title claim):

The Aetherius Society journal *Cosmic Voices* claims in 1986 "Freedom Of The City of London and Freeman of England - High Honors Bestowed upon Our Master". Another researcher on King's Freedom of the City of London award notes:

"A photograph of Dr Sir George with other Society members: Commander Sir Watkiss, Dame Iris Lawrence et al standing outside the Guildhall bears witness to this. Curiously, like their Master, none of these dignitaries is listed in the current edition of Who's Who. And the nature of Dr King's services to humanity is least. What could he have done to have been made a Freeman of the City of London? A telephone call to a City librarian solved this mystery: not a lot. In fact, the charming young lady behind the information desk in the Guildhall Library informed the author that she too is a Freeman of the City of London, as no doubt is the local barber, the man behind the counter in the sandwich bar and Uncle Torn Cobbley and all.

Freemen apply for the Freedom themselves (and about 1800 per year so do) and usually pay a 'fine' for this. There is a Freeman title that can be bestowed and is considered an honor. However, it is not clear if King simply applied for the designation or it was given to him as an honor.

Diana G. Tumminia's *Alien worlds: social and religious dimensions of extraterrestrial contact* provides much additional insight into the grandiose titles and honors followers claim were conferred upon King. Amusingly: King was crowned by His Royal and Imperial Highness Prince Henri III Paleologue (apparently King's cousin), who bestowed upon him additional orders and titles.

King claims in his book *The Age of Aetherius* that he received the 1981 "Minister of the Year" award from the International Evangelism Crusades. This group was started by the late Frank E. Stranges, who also wrote *The UFO Conspiracy* — a UFO believing preacher would award "Minister of the Year" to another UFO believing preacher. In 2006 the group awarded Minister of the Year to Julie Stranges, Frank Stranges' wife. International Evangelism Crusades' standing in the US religious community seems to be lacking. Stranges was also the president of the International Theological Seminary of California, the diploma mill insitution that awarded King his Ph.D.

The society's current King biography notes King was a Chaplain of the American Federation of Police. The organization's full name is "American Federation of Police and Concerned Citizens". Anyone who is a concerned citizen appears to be able to become a member for $45. Charity Navigator gives this organization its lowest ranking (1 star). Several police organizations have warned that solicitations by the American Federation of Police are possible scams: in 2004, it raised $3.2 million from donations, spending $2.25 million on their own expenses and $521,803 on actual charitable services.

The site does not appear to have any official way to apply for a position as a chaplain and does not provide any list of official chaplains. The late Stranges, who awarded King the 1981 "Minister of the Year", appears to be one of the few people besides King to claim to be a Chaplain of the AFP. The AFP does have a National Chaplain position on its advisory board. According to private email correspondence with a spokesperson for the AFP "we only appoint and utilize one Chaplain". There is no chaplain title awarded other than National Chaplain. The National Chaplain serves for one year and this position is automatically renewed until either party agrees to terminate the relationship. The last two national chaplains were Catholic priests. While it's possible that, at some point, the American Federation of Police decided a UFO cult leader would be make an excellent National Chaplain, it does seem implausible given their known track record of appointing Catholic priests. In correspondence, the AFP spokesperson indicated they did not maintain a list of past National Chaplains and the original founder had died, and institutional memory died with him.

The organisation did, however, operate a diploma mill:

"The [American Federation of Police] was a really sleazy outfit," says Nelson, now the Times's Washington bureau chief. "They had this thing, the National Law Enforcement Academy. They were giving out phony degrees all over the country. You'd pay some money, do some token course work, and be presented with this thing that was represented as some sort of great academic achievement. It was just bogus."

The Cosmic Masters are a group of spiritual beings from higher planes of existence on other planets. Only King may speak with them – which is unfortunate given he died in 1997. Buddha, Mohammed and Jesus (who now, according to the society, lives happily on Venus) were all connected to the Cosmic Masters. The Cosmic Masters tell us that the Earth is soon to go through a great transition. The following are quotes from Cosmic Master Mars Sector 6:

"Today you stand in the valley of decision. The Goddess, Terra, must shortly take Her rightful Place in the Cosmic Scheme of evolution. This will mean a reduction in the intensity of the ionosphere around Terra and a resultant high rise in the potency of Cosmic Rays actually reaching the surface of this Planet. This will mean that only those of sufficient development will be able to withstand this Cosmic bombardment."

"Therefore it is obvious that Terrestrial man must sort the wheat from the involved chaff. This is logic."

"Terrestrial man faces many problems in the interim period. He faces the possibility of war brought about by the scheming few, who have successfully trapped the unthinking majority by their insidious conditioning campaign."

"He faces disease which is now prevalent upon the Planet."

"He faces the direct result of another's greed, another's lust for power, another's wrongful control."

"These things do men face this night."

"These things can all be put right by man if he decides, this night, to throw his God given Energies into the channels of construction, away from the channels of destruction."

"Service and co-operation are the keynotes which will enable mankind to put right these conditions. Indeed, mankind upon Terra has the greatest opportunities ever offered to any other lifestreams in the whole Solar System at any time since its inception; for man upon Terra has fallen so low that the climb back could be far more glorious than any yet accomplished since the inception of this Solar System."

245

This is damning information straight from the ceiling and into King's frontal lobe. When asked about why the Cosmic Masters do not land openly and all of humanity can bathe in their collective intelligent, peace and wit King has a message, received from the Cosmic Masters, that explains all that away so there'll be no more questions, OK?

A prayer team member directs prayer energy into a spiritual energy battery during Operation Prayer Power.

King has stated his cult religion is focused on the improvement of mankind. As the Cosmic Masters give him information about current events, upcoming disasters and whether he left the iron on or not, he is in a prime position to develop mankind's spirituality. Before it's too late. The three main operations the society is involved in are called:

- Operation Starlight
- Operation Sunbeam
- Operation Prayer Power This operation was directed to King in 1958 and took three years to complete. King was commanded to climb 18 peaks so he could act as a channel in order to charge these peaks with spiritual energy using his elevated yogic state. These mountains are now free for all to climb and send out their own energies. However which peaks he actually climbed are not listed on the website.

Operation Sunbeam had grand design. The "logic" of this mission was that the energy already put into the 19 mountains of Operation Starlight (that is not a typo by the way, Operation Starlight states 18 while Operation Sunbeam says 19. Go figure, eh). and shield it from Mother Earth so as mankind can take it for itself. King created a battery in which to store this energy and release at times of global trouble.

Operation Prayer Power is "truly Love in action" according to the society. After managing to modify the prayer battery from Operation Starlight, King was able to create a prayer battery. Every week, hundreds of people charge the prayer battery using powerful prayers and mantras. This collective energy is able to solve all the worlds ills.

- Holdstone Down, North Devon, England, charged by Master Jesus
- Brown Willy, Cornwall
- Ben Hope, Sutherland, Scotland
- Creag-an-leth-choin, Strathspey, Scotland

246

- Old Man, Cumbria, England
- Pen-Y-Fan, South Wales
- Carnedd Llywelyn, Gwynedd, Wales
- Kinderscout, Derbyshire,England
- Yes Tor, Devon, England
- Mount Baldy, California, USA
- Mount Tallac, Northern California, USA
- Mount Adams, New Hapshire, USA
- Castle Peak, Colorado, USA
- Mount Kosciusko, New South Wales, Australia
- Mount Ramshead, New South Wales, Australia
- Mount Wakefield, New Zealand
- Mount Madrigerfluh, Switzerland
- Le Nid D'Aigle, France
- Mount Kilimanjaro, Africa, charged by Saint Goo-Ling

Total 19, 17 charged by Dr George King

Members of the Aetherius Society will occasionally give public talks where they claim to have irrefutable evidence of George King's claims. The so-called irrefutable evidence consists mostly of claims that King knew X before it was public knowledge. Since he could not have learned this from any conventional means, he must have learned it from space aliens. His alien sources ("cosmic intelligences") are variously called Mars Sector Six and Aetherius (a kind of cosmic Gandalf the White). Four incidents are typically put forward:

In October of 1957, England's first nuclear power plant (Windscale) had a fire. The government claimed the accident was not serious. King, however, claimed the Cosmic Intelligences told him (on October 29, 1957) "the scientists were not in any way giving a true account of the results of the accident". Documents released in 1989 showed the government, in fact, did not give a true account of the accident. The government's 1957 secret report was prepared the day before King's Cosmic Intelligences report. How could King have known the accident was worse? The report was secret. He must have gotten it via an alien transmission!

First, a bit of history. In the late 1950s, the UK wanted the US to see it as a responsible nuclear partner. It did not want to seem like a nation that doesn't know what it's doing with nuclear technology. And it wanted access to US research instead of having to recreate it from the ground up. It's key that all the Aetherius Society claims is King claims the government wasn't giving a true account. You don't need to be in contact with all-seeing space aliens to suggest any government in any nuclear disaster, especially relating to a weapons program, isn't going to tell the full story. Water is wet.

Was King (a decidedly anti-nuclear campaigner) the only one questioning the veracity of government claims? Would the British tabloid press not question the government account during the course of the accident?

The Whitehaven News on October 11 reported some troubling findings (18 days before King's "transmission"). The paper reported there "...came disturbing reports from the monitoring vans which were touring the district testing vegetation and air." This was 18 days before King's supposed message from the Cosmic Intelligences. It certainly sounds like there was enough alarming news to make anyone with a strong anti-nuclear stance consider the reality on the ground wasn't matching the government account. King could easily have been repeating what he read in the newspaper. There is zero evidence King had special knowledge that was not being floated in the local press.

Members like to note the timing of King's revelation and the government document seemed too close to be mere coincidence. King's cosmic transmission came one day after the government report was secretly released. Unfortunately, members do not consider how many degrees of freedom are involved in suggesting a "hit" is too improbable to be coincidence. If King came up with it three days before or a month after, would they still be calling this a hit? If the publication date of the document wasn't a good match, maybe the date the government experts first convened the panel is a hit. Or when they adjourned is a hit. It's very easy, retro-spectively, to find any two data points that correlate in some loose fashion.

On April 18, 1958, aliens called Mars Sector 6 and Aetherius informed King that there was a nuclear accident in the Soviet Union and hundreds of people were killed. It would have been worse but the aliens used some kind of technology to suck up large amounts of the radiation (enough to kill 17 million people). Below is the complete text of the transmissions from King's *You Are Responsible!*
'Mars Sector 6'
> "Owing to an atomic accident just recently in the USSR, a great amount of radioactivity in the shape of radio-active iodine, strontium 90, radio-active nitrogen and radio-active sodium have been released into the atmosphere of Terra."
'The Master Aetherius, from Venus:'

248

"All forms of reception from Interplanetary sources will become a little more difficult during the next few weeks because of the foolish actions of Russia.

"They have not yet declared to the world as a whole, exactly what happened in one of their atomic research establishments. Neither have they declared how many people were killed there. Neither have they declared that they were really frightened by the tremendous release of radio-active materials from this particular establishment during the accident.

"Because this accident took place, we will most certainly have to use a tremendous amount of energy, which should be used in a very different way. We should not really have to expend this amount of energy clearing away dangerous radio-active clouds from the atmosphere of Terra.

"However, because of Divine Intervention, we are able to use enough energy in this direction to save about 17,000,000 lives, which otherwise would have been forced to vacate their physical bodies.

"Such were the far-reaching repercussions from this accident that we were given permission by the Lords of Karma to intervene! However, although we are at the moment intervening on behalf of Terra, in this direction, certain damage has already been done to large land and water masses!"[

No one but those in the Soviet Union knew about the accident. The world did not find out until Zhores Medvedev defected to the west and exposed the story in the *New Scientist* in 1976. As it turns out in September of 1957 there was a nuclear accident in the Soviet Urals. How could King have known about something the world was clueless about until a couple decades later?

You will note that in the two transmissions the society claims are remarkable hits no dates, times, or locations are given beyond an undated accident in the USSR. The USSR was a pretty big place. Is getting a hit on "at some point the Soviets had an accident" really a remarkable hit? It's a pretty safe bet the Soviets had a few nuclear disasters as they entered the atomic age.

The major problem is the *New York Times* and other papers carrying UP stories were abuzz on April 13-14, 1958 about a possible nuclear accident in the USSR:

Soviet Catastrophe Reported

Copenhagen, Denmark, April 13 UP — Berlingske Tidende, Denmark's biggest newspaper, said today the recent Soviet nuclear tests had to be broken off because of a "catastrophic accident". The newspaper, quoting information reaching Copenhagen through diplomatic channels from Moscow, did not define the nature of the reported accident, but said it caused radioactive fallout over the Soviet and many neighboring states to increase to the danger point.

King made his prediction April 18, 1958 (four or five days later). It seems plausible that King was simply able to read the day's headlines about such speculation. Did King get this information from an alien or newspapers?

In April 1986, King was ostensibly told by the Cosmic Intelligences to take some unprecedented action in preparation for a disaster. He was told to activate a "special radionic apparatus" a bit less than 5 hours before the Chernobyl disaster began on April 26, 1986. Devotees operated these radionic devices at "an unprecedented level for several days".

The argument here seems to be "We were doing something we've never done before and something unusual happened in the USSR. So our unusual activity is evidence we knew that disaster was coming."

This is classic post-hoc reasoning. Something odd happened. So we look for something odd we might have done before, find something, and then make a connection. But we forget all the other times we were doing other odd things and nothing odd happened within some undefined space of time.

And, sure, doing something with this radionic device five hours before the accident seems like a hit but the society gives us no information how often they ran this device. Do they do it every other day? Every week at a regular schedule? One needs a lot more information before one can call it a "hit".

The society also seems to be impressed the device was used for an unprecedented length of time. More than a day was never done. Unfortunately, the times don't really add up. They started running the device two days before the Soviet announcement. However it was a day before the April 28 announcement that there were reports of unusual radiation that many assumed at first was a Swedish nuclear accident. So it seems they were not into their record activity until they knew about a possible nuclear disaster (day 2 people assumed Sweden, day 3 the USSR fessed up). Since they believed it would help, they'd keep it going.

One should also note the claimed transmission did not specifically mention a nuclear disaster or a specific time frame. Followers claims the transmission warned to "prepare for an imminent catastrophe" and "an emergency situation was about to occur upon Earth". King claims the transmission came 8:30 am PST on April 25th, 1986 while he was in Utah. Between April 24 and April 25, US newspapers like the *NY Times* carried worrying reports of volcanic eruptions in Alaska. Was King's vague transmission claim a guess that the Alaska volcano might be a repeat of the Mount St. Helens (1980) disaster?

The Aetherius society claims King knew about the dangers of the depletion of ozone layer two decades before the problem was recognized in the 1980s. On an LA TV show on July 19th, 1960 King made the following "prediction":

"The ionosphere unit now surrounding your world which normally absorbs a large percentage of cosmic rays, will gradually be taken down so that the cosmic and ultra violet rays may bombard this earth in their full potency."

Members of the Aetherius society interpret this to be a prediction about the depletion of the ozone layer, which was detected in the 1970s (not the 1980s as alleged) However, the problem with this "prediction" is the cosmic intelligences that allegedly supplied King with advanced knowledge do not seem to know where the ozone layer is located. It's actually located in the stratosphere, about 40km below the start of the ionosphere. As well, the ozone layer only protects us from UV rays, not cosmic rays. Given King's stance against nuclear weapons, it's not difficult to believe King was expressing fears about high-altitude nuclear tests the USA began in 1958, two years previous to King's "prediction".

In short, if you want to call this a prediction, you have to accept:

- It makes no actual mention of the ozone layer, despite it being known and monitored since 1928·
- It gets the location of the ozone layer wrong.
- It gets the function of the ozone layer wrong.
- It makes no mention of the danger CFCs posed to the ozone layer.

If you want to call this a prediction, you ultimately have to accept the cosmic intelligences have a very, very poor understanding of the Earth's atmosphere and were actually unwilling to tell King what industrial chemical humans should curtail production of. Odd, given they were happy to tell King to curtail nuclear power.

What will strike many as the most unbelievable claim made by the Aetherius Society is their belief that there are intelligent aliens on Venus and Mars (with Jesus being one of the more prominent citizens of Venus). The idea that planets within our solar system support advanced intelligent life seems quaint today. We know Venus is hot enough to melt lead and is not a jungle planet. Mars is not a Dune-like world with sword-wielding Amazons riding lizards. But in the 1950s, intelligent life within our solar system was a feature of sci fi literature, TV shows, and movies. The contactee movements of King and George Adamski well parroted it.

King and Adamski both had the same message: nuclear energy is bad, Venusian reincarnation, and both claimed to have been flown around the solar system on space ships. Adamski's contactee story, however, preceded King's by two years (1952 vs 1954). Both had a message contemporaneous with the times and, oddly, the plot of *The Day the Earth Stood Still* which came out in 1951. *The Day the Earth Stood Still* was about a representative sent by a parliament of different aliens to warn earth of the dangers of nuclear technology. King's claim is he met a representative sent by a parliament of different aliens to warn earth of the dangers of nuclear technology. Ufology has largely moved beyond the contactee movement, probably somewhat embarrassed by their unsophisticated claims later proven false by real space exploration. Adamski today is the poster child for the silliness of the times. Modern contactees are largely shunned by "serious" ufologists. Even as early as 1965, ufologists Jacques Vallee commented "No serious investigator has ever been very worried by the claims of the 'contactees'."

In light of data obtained by actual space exploration (versus fabrications made up sitting in the lotus position) Aetherius Society members have had to somewhat retcon King's fanciful ideas about physical civilizations on Mars and Venus. They're kind of spirit beings now. They live on a different "vibrational" plane of existence.

Examining King's book *You Are Responsible!* (1961) where he records many supposed conversations with these Martians and Venusians we see passages like:

> "What is the temperature of those on Venus who use a physical body?"
>
> "On Venus...some of our younger ones eat and drink the juice from certain berries and the juice that's given off by certain trees."

The reader would be forgiven if he/she came away with the idea King claims Venus has aliens in physical bodies and there were trees and other plant life.

In *You Are Responsible!* King also claims to have traveled to Mars and described buildings, "longitudinal vegetation belts", and Martian soil to be radioactive. No lander has found radioactive regolith on Mars. Astronomer Stuart Robbins has spent over five years staring at high resolution images of Mars and he's never mentioned seeing vegetation. Or buildings. None of the physical evidence from exploration of Mars or Venus supports King's claims of what he saw on these planets. King probably never went to Mars or Venus.

The Aetherius Society believes humans came to earth from another planet that we destroyed with runaway nuclear technology. The planet was known as Maldek and became the asteroid belt after exploding. The idea that the asteroid belt was a destroyed planet (from a collision) was an early hypothesis about its origins but that hypothesis was abandoned as it is not supported by the evidence. The objects in the asteroid belt largely just accreted in place. The lines of evidence for this run:

> 1) The matter in the asteroid belt is about 4% of the moon's mass. Nowhere near a planet's size.
>
> 2) There's not enough mass to have accreted into a planet.
>
> 3) The gravity from Jupiter prevents the matter from further accretion.
>
> 4) Asteroid chemistry is inconsistent with having once been part of a planet.

Society members point to the work of the late Canadian astronomer Michael Ovenden as support for their claims of Maldek. Ovenden hypothesized in 1972 the asteroid belt is the remains of a planet. However, Ovenden's idea hasn't gained any traction in forty years and is not supported by the evidence.

King's Maldek claim oddly parallels the plot of a 1957 Japanese sci fi movie called *The Mysterians*. The movie is about aliens who came from a planet that was in the current asteroid belt but destroyed by nuclear weapons! Familiar? The Maldek "revelation" was transmitted to King on April 7, 1960. The Mysterians had its US release May 1959. King moved to America in June 1959. It is possible he either saw this movie or was made aware of the plot by an adherent in the USA and this was the inspiration for the claimed April 7, 1960 transmission.

King claims to have been told by his Cosmic Intelligences there is a 10th planet in the solar system. The Cosmic Intelligences seem not have been able to predict Pluto's demotion. This undiscovered planet will be a place for the "sorting of the wheat from the chaff". It's a way station for people not quite ready to enter Aetherian heaven. The head of the Toronto Aetherius society claims this Planet X has a "mass of about 5 times that of the Earth" and "is orbiting the Sun at a right angle to the known planets." This claim seems at odds with King's description in his book *The Nine Freedoms* where he states "this young primitive world is in the Solar System, orbiting behind the Sun following exactly the same trajectory as Earth and is thereby not visible."

King's notion that another planet can hide from us in an orbit that always places it behind the sun ignores the planet's gravity would have noticeable and unexplainable effects on the orbits of Venus and Mercury. The unseeable planet Vulcan was hypothesized as an explanation for the peculiarities of Mercury's orbit, which did not jibe with Newtonian mechanics. Einstein's theory of relativity solved the problem. If there was such a planet as King claimed, even if always exactly opposite the sun, astronomers would still be struggling today to explain the orbits of Mercury and Venus. These orbits are fully explained, however.

Aetherius society seem to take harbor in the notion of a 10th planet further out and the notion that the "irregularities in the orbits of Uranus and Neptune" give credence to the claim that such a planet exists. This is based on out of date knowledge. Measuring the mass of a distant planet isn't easy. A small error in the mass can lead to incorrect orbits. The Voyager 2 mission eventually gave us a better measure of Neptune's mass and therefore the orbits of Neptune and Uranus. This has been in the literature since 1993. Their orbits are fully explained. One does not have to invoke a Planet X.

It would seem, unfortunately, that society members think they found scientific evidence to support their astronomy claims but failed to consider checking to see, thirty years later, if current data has overthrown previous hypotheses.

What the e-meter is to Scientology, the Radionic Pendulum is to the Aetherius Society. The society claims the pendulum was designed by King and he was "a world renowned expert in the field of radionics". The society supplies nothing to back that claim. If you are wondering how the devices works, King explains in an amazingly dull 82 minute lecture.

The society's official page on the pendulum does not make it clear what the device is used for other than wiggling it on the end of a string and getting yes/no answers. In 2010 the society published a flyer for the Mind, Body & Spirit festival in London[that made claims that the pendulum was for use in:

1. Heath diagnosis
2. Finding allergies
3. Selecting remedies and dosages
4. Dietary requirements
5. Developing intuition

A November 27, 2011 London meetup event listing offers a photograph that suggests how the device might be used to "Choose vitamin and mineral supplements". It would appear to be simple pendulum dowsing. The society does not explain how its $16.95 dollar pendulum is superior to one you can buy in a dollar store for, well, a dollar or just dangling a paperclip on the end of a string. The product page does note their pendulum is first lathed in the UK and then shipped to the other side of the world to be further lathed in New Zealand. That has to add some cost. It's not explained why this two step, multi country lathing arrangement is necessary.

The New Zealand branch has a workshop on its use. They proclaim the pendulum is a "great tool for health diagnosis". The society likens its operation to dowsing rods. At their $50 a head workshop you can "learn to diagnose vitamin and mineral requirements" with the radionic device.

You Are Responsible! is a book by King, based on his experiences in the late 1950s and early '60s as an alleged UFO contactee. The book contains many messages, which King claimed were telepathically transmitted to him from alien life on Mars and Venus.

The book is in two parts. Part 1 details King's claims of traveling to Venus and Mars and witnessing advanced civilizations on both planets as well as foliage and vegetation belts. King reveals Jesus was from Venus. Part 1 also touches on the subjects of Yoga and telepathy. The final chapter of part 1 recounts a claim by King that he took part in a space war between Martians and evil aquatic aliens on a world called "Garouche". King claims Garouche is located on the opposite side of the galaxy.

Part 2 King recounts alleged "transmissions" he claims he received from space aliens, notably "Aetherius" and a space alien called "Mars Sector 6". Through recounting these supposed "transmission", King alleges space aliens warned him about the dangerous of nuclear technology, the need to educate Christians about the supposed truth of reincarnation, karma and reincarnation. Some of these transmissions followers have interpreted as prophetic and have attempted to match them with events known post hoc.

As always, there are hundreds of people believing this BS, buying the magic pendulum and waiting for the ultimate disaster. They are the Aetherius Society, a special brand of looneys that seem harmless but propagate to the world a new brand of religious /cosmic insanity.

WILL THE REAL JOHN FRUM PLEASE STAND UP?

In the morning heat on a tropical island halfway across the world from the United States, several dark-skinned men — clad in what look to be U.S. Army uniforms — appear on a mound overlooking a bamboo-hut village. One reverently carries Old Glory, precisely folded to reveal only the stars. On the command of a bearded "drill sergeant," the flag is raised on a pole hacked from a tall tree trunk. As the huge banner billows in the wind, hundreds of watching villagers clap and cheer.

Chief Isaac Wan, a slight, bearded man in a blue suit and ceremonial sash, leads the uniformed men down to open ground in the middle of the village. Some 40 barefoot "G.I.'s" suddenly emerge from behind the huts to more cheering, marching in perfect step and ranks of two past Chief Isaac. They tote bamboo "rifles" on their shoulders, the scarlet tips sharpened to represent bloody bayonets, and sport the letters "USA," painted in red on their bare chests and backs.

This is February 15, John Frum Day, on the remote island of Tanna in the South Pacific nation of Vanuatu. On this holiest of days, devotees have descended on the village of Lamakara from all over the island to honor a ghostly American messiah, John Frum. "John promised he'll bring planeloads and shiploads of cargo to us from America if we pray to him," a village elder says as he salutes the Stars and Stripes. "Radios, TVs, trucks, boats, watches, iceboxes, medicine, Coca-Cola and many other wonderful things."

The island's John Frum movement is a classic example of what anthropologists have called a "cargo cult"—many of which sprang up in villages in the South Pacific during World War II, when hundreds of thousands of American troops poured into the islands from the skies and seas. As anthropologist Kirk Huffman, who spent 17 years in Vanuatu, explains: "You get cargo cults when the outside world, with all its material wealth, suddenly descends on remote, indigenous tribes." The locals don't know where the foreigners' endless supplies come from and so suspect they were summoned by magic, sent from the spirit world. To entice the Americans back after the war, islanders throughout the region constructed piers and carved airstrips from their fields. They prayed for ships and planes to once again come out of nowhere, bearing all kinds of treasures: jeeps and washing machines, radios and motorcycles, canned meat and candy.

257

But the venerated Americans never came back, except as a dribble of tourists and veterans eager to revisit the faraway islands where they went to war in their youth. And although almost all the cargo cults have disappeared over the decades, the John Frum movement has endured, based on the worship of an American god no sober man has ever seen.

Many Americans know Vanuatu from the reality TV series "Survivor," though the episodes shot there hardly touched on the Melanesian island nation's spectacular natural wonders and fascinating, age-old cultures. Set between Fiji and New Guinea, Vanuatu is a Y-shaped scattering of more than 80 islands, several of which include active volcanoes. The islands were once home to fierce warriors, among them cannibals. Many inhabitants still revere village sorcerers, who use spirit-possessed stones in magic rituals that can lure a new lover, fatten a pig or kill an enemy.

Americans with longer memories remember Vanuatu as the New Hebrides—its name until its independence from joint British and French colonial rule in 1980. James Michener's book Tales of the South Pacific, which spawned the musical South Pacific, grew out of his experiences as an American sailor in the New Hebrides in World War II.

To join the search of John Frum and his devotees, one must board a small plane in Vanuatu's capital, Port-Vila. Forty minutes later, coral reefs, sandy beaches and green hills announce Tanna Island, about 20 miles long and 16 miles at its widest point, with a population of around 28,000. You would have to climb into an ancient jeep for the drive to Lamakara, which overlooks Sulphur Bay, and wait while the driver starts the vehicle by touching together two wires sticking out from a hole under the dashboard.

The jeep rattles up a steep slope, the narrow trail slicing through the jungle's dense green weave of trees and bushes, intensely beautiful and primitive. One visitor reported that his driver said that he is the brother-in-law of one of the cult's most important leaders, Prophet Fred—who, he added proudly, "raised his wife from the dead two weeks ago."

Reaching the crest of a hill, the land ahead falls away to reveal Yasur, Tanna's sacred volcano, a few miles to the south, its ash-coated slopes nudging the shoreline at Sulphur Bay. dark smoke belches from its cone. 'Yasur' means God in the island's language. The squat, stubby volcano is the house of John Frum.

"If he's an American, why does he live in your volcano?" some tourists wonder aloud.

"Ask Chief Isaac," the driver says. "He knows everything."

Dotting the dirt road are small villages where women with curly, bubble-shaped hair squat over bundles of mud-coated roots called kava, a species of pepper plant and a middling narcotic that is the South Pacific's traditional drug of choice. Connoisseurs say that Tanna's kava is the strongest of all.

For as long as Tanna's inhabitants can remember, island men have downed kava at sunset each day in a place off-limits to women. Christian missionaries, mostly Presbyterians from Scotland, put a temporary stop to the practice in the early 20th century, also banning other traditional practices, or "kastom," that locals had followed faithfully for millennia: dancing, penis wrapping and polygamy. The missionaries also forbade working and amusement on Sundays, swearing and adultery. In the absence of a strong colonial administrative presence, they set up their own courts to punish miscreants, sentencing them to forced labor. The Tannese seethed under the missionaries' rules for three decades. Then, John Frum appeared.

Daniel Yamya has the soft-focus eyes and nearly toothless smile of a kava devotee. Daniel was once a member of Vanuatu's Parliament in Port-Vila, and his constituents included John Frum followers from what was then the movement's stronghold, Ipikil, on Sulphur Bay. "I'm now a Christian, but like most people on Tanna, I still have John Frum in my heart," he says. "If we keep praying to John, he'll come back with plenty of cargo."

The village nakamal is the open ground where the men drink kava. Two young boys bend over the kava roots, chewing chunks of them into a stringy pulp. "Only circumcised boys who've never touched a girl's body can make kava," Daniel says. "That ensures that their hands are not dirty."

Other boys mix water with the pulp and twist the mixture through a cloth, producing a dirty-looking liquid. The welcome ritual has tourists handed a half-coconut shell filled to the brim. "Drink it in one go," they are told. It tastes vile, like muddy water. Moments later their mouth and tongue turn numb.

The men split into small groups or sit by themselves, crouching in the darkness, whispering to each other or lost in thought. Those brave enough to toss back a second shell of the muddy mix soon sense that their head tugs at its mooring, seeking to drift away into the night.

Yasur rumbles like distant thunder, a couple of miles over the ridge, and through the trees one gains a glimpse an eerie red glow at its cone. In 1774, Capt. James Cook was lured ashore by that same glow. He was the first European to see the volcano, but local leaders banned him from climbing to the cone because it was taboo. The taboo is no longer enforced.

After one drinks their third shell of kava, they dance unsteadily to the rhythm of the waves and try to pluck the shimmering moon from the sky and kiss it.

Surrounded by an eerie doomsday moonscape of volcanic ash, Yasur looms behind the village. But at only 1,184 feet high, the sacred volcano has none of the majesty of, say, Mount Fuji; instead, its squat shape remindful of a pugnacious bulldog standing guard before its master's house. Taxo drivers always point at the cone. "Haus blong John Frum," they say in pidgin English. It's John Frum's house.

In the village dozens of cane huts, some with rusting tin roofs, encircle an open ceremonial dancing ground of impacted ash and the mound where the American flag flies each day, flanked by the much smaller flags of Vanuatu, ex-colonial ruler France and the Australian Aborigines, whose push for racial equality the villagers admire. Clearly, John Frum has yet to return with his promised cargo because Lamakara is dirt poor in consumer goods. But island men, wrapped in cloth known as lava-lava, women in large flowered dresses and mostly barefoot children in T-shirts appear healthy and seem happy. That's no surprise: like many South Pacific coastal villages, it's a place where coconuts drop by your side as you snooze. Yams, taro, and pineapples and other fruit thrive in the fertile volcanic soil, and plump pigs sniff around the village for scraps. Tasty fruit bats cling upside down in nearby trees.

Chief Isaac, in an open-neck shirt, green slacks and cloth shoes, greets visitors on the mound and leads them into a hut behind the flagpoles: the John Frum inner sanctum, off-limits to all but the cult's senior leaders and male visitors from abroad.

The hut is dominated by a round table displaying a small U.S. flag on a pedestal, a carved bald eagle and imitation U.S. military uniforms neatly folded and placed in a circle, ready for use on John Frum Day in a little more than a week. Above, suspended by vine from a beam, hangs a globe, a stone ax and a pair of green stones carved into circles the size of a silver dollar. "Very powerful magic," the chief says as he points to the stones. "The gods made them a long time ago."

Written on a pair of blackboards is a plea that John Frum's followers lead a kastom life and that they refrain from violence against each other. One of the blackboards bears a chalked red cross, probably copied from U.S. military ambulances and now an important symbol for the cult.

"John Frum came to help us get back our traditional customs, our kava drinking, our dancing, because the missionaries and colonial government were deliberately destroying our culture," Chief Isaac says in his pidgin English.

But if John Frum, an American, is going to bring you modern goods, how does that sit with his wish that you lead a kastom life? is the most obvious question.

"John is a spirit. He knows everything," the chief says, slipping past the contradiction with the poise of a skilled politician. "He's even more powerful than Jesus."

"Have you ever seen him?"

"Yes, John comes very often from Yasur to advise me, or I go there to speak with John."

"What does he look like?"

"An American!"

"Then why does he live in Yasur?"

"John moves from America to Yasur and back, going down through the volcano and under the sea."

If one mentions Prophet Fred, anger flares in Chief Isaac's eyes. "He's a devil," he snarls. "I won't talk about him."

Chief Isaac and other local leaders say that John Frum first appeared one night in the late 1930s, after a group of elders had downed many shells of kava as a prelude to receiving messages from the spirit world. "He was a white man who spoke our language, but he didn't tell us then he was an American," says Chief Kahuwya, leader of Yakel village. John Frum told them he had come to rescue them from the missionaries and colonial officials. "John told us that all Tanna's people should stop following the white man's ways," Chief Kahuwya says. "He said we should throw away their money and clothes, take our children from their schools, stop going to church and go back to living as kastom people. We should drink kava, worship the magic stones and perform our ritual dances."

Perhaps the chieftains in their kava reveries actually experienced a spontaneous vision of John Frum. Or perhaps the apparition has more practical roots. It's possible that local leaders conceived of John Frum as a powerful white-skinned ally in the fight against the colonials, who were attempting to crush much of the islanders' culture and prod them into Christianity. In fact, that

261

view of the origins of the cult gained credence in 1949, when the island administrator, Alexander Rentoul, noting that "frum" is the Tannese pronunciation of "broom," wrote that the object of the John Frum movement "was to sweep (or broom) the white people off the island of Tanna."

Whatever the truth, John Frum's message struck a chord. Villagers on Tanna began throwing their money into the sea and killing their pigs for grand feasts to welcome their new messiah. Colonial authorities eventually struck back, arresting the movement's leaders—including Chief Isaac's father, Chief Nikiau. They were shipped to a prison at Port-Vila in 1941, their subsequent years behind bars earning them status as the John Frum movement's first martyrs.

The cult got its biggest boost the following year, when American troops by the thousands were dispatched to the New Hebrides, where they built large military bases at Port-Vila and on the island of Espíritu Santo. The bases included hospitals, airstrips, jetties, roads, bridges and corrugated-steel Quonset huts, many erected with the help of more than a thousand men recruited as laborers from Tanna and other parts of the New Hebrides — among them Chief Kahuwya.

Where the U.S. armed forces go, so go the legendary PXs, with their seemingly endless supply of chocolate, cigarettes and Coca-Cola. For men who lived in huts and farmed yams, the Americans' wealth was a revelation. The troops paid them 25 cents a day for their work and handed out generous amounts of goodies.

The Americans' munificence dazzled the men from Tanna, as did the sight of dark-skinned soldiers eating the same food, wearing the same clothes, living in similar huts and tents and operating the same high-tech equipment as white soldiers. "In kastom, people sit together to eat," says Kirk Huffman, who was the curator of Vanuatu's cultural center during his years in the island nation. "The missionaries had angered the Tannese by always eating separately." It seems this is when the legend of John Frum took on a decidedly American character. "John Frum appeared to us in Port-Vila," Chief Kahuwya says, "and stayed with us throughout the war. John was dressed in all white, like American Navy men, and it was then we knew John was an American. John said that when the war was over, he'd come to us in Tanna with ships and planes bringing much cargo, like the Americans had in Vila."

In 1943, the U.S. command, concerned about the movement's growth, sent the USS *Echo* to Tanna with Maj. Samuel Patten on board. His mission was to convince John Frum followers that, as his report put it, "the American forces had no connection with John Frum." He failed. At war's end, the U.S. military unwittingly enhanced the legend of their endless supply of cargo when they bulldozed tons of equipment—trucks, jeeps, aircraft engines, supplies—off the coast of Espíritu Santo. During six decades in the shallows, coral and sand have obscured much of the watery grave of war surplus, but snorkelers can still see tires, bulldozers and even full Coke bottles. The locals wryly named the place Million Dollar Point.

After the war, when they returned home from Port-Vila to their huts, the Tanna men were convinced that John Frum would soon join them, and hacked a primitive airstrip out of the jungle in the island's north to tempt the expected American planes from the skies. Across the South Pacific, thousands of other cargo cult followers began devising similar plans—even building bamboo control towers strung with rope and bamboo aerials to guide in the planes. In 1964, one cargo cult on New Hanover Island in Papua New Guinea offered the U.S. government $1,000 for Lyndon Johnson to come and be their paramount chief. But as the years passed with empty skies and seas, almost all the cargo cults disappeared, the devotees' hopes crushed.

At Sulphur Bay the faithful never wavered. Each Friday afternoon, hundreds of believers stream across the ash plain below Yasur, coming to Lamaraka from villages all over Tanna. After the sun goes down and the men have drunk kava, the congregation gathers in and around an open hut on the ceremonial ground. As light from kerosene lamps flickers across their faces, they strum guitars and homemade ukuleles, singing hymns of John Frum's prophecies and the struggles of the cult's martyrs. Many carry the same plea: "We're waiting in our village for you, John. When are you coming with all the cargo you promised us?"

The John Frum movement is following the classic pattern of new religions," says anthropologist Huffman. Schisms split clumps of faithful from the main body, as apostates proclaim a new vision leading to sacrilegious variants on the creed's core beliefs.

Which explains Prophet Fred, whose village, Ipikil, is nestled on Sulphur Bay. Daniel says that Prophet Fred split with Chief Isaac in 1999 and led half of the believer villages into his new version of the John Frum cult. "He had a vision while working on a Korean fishing boat in the ocean," Daniel says. "God's light came down on him, and God told him to come home and preach a new way."

People believed that Fred could talk to God after he predicted, six years ago, that Lake Siwi would break its natural dam and flood into the ocean. "The people living around the lake [on the beach beneath the volcano] moved to other places," says Daniel. "Six months later, it happened."

Then, almost two years ago, Prophet Fred's rivalry with Chief Isaac exploded. More than 400 young men from the competing camps clashed with axes, bows and arrows and slingshots, burning down a thatched church and several houses. Twenty-five men were seriously injured. "They wanted to kill us, and we wanted to kill them," a Chief Isaac loyalist says.

Maliwan Tarawai, a barefoot pastor carrying a well-thumbed Bible stated, "Prophet Fred has called his movement Unity, and he's woven kastom, Christianity and John Frum together." The American messiah is little more than a figurehead in Fred's version, which bans the display of foreign flags, including Old Glory, and forbids any talk of cargo.

In the morning vocalists with a string band sing hymns about Prophet Fred while several wild-eyed women stumble around in what appears to be a trance. They faith-heal the sick by clutching the ailing area of the body and praying silently to the heavens, casting out demons. Now and then they pause to clutch with bony fingers at the sky. "They do this every Wednesday, our holy day," Tarawai explains. "The Holy Spirit has possessed them, and they get their healing powers from him and from the sun."

Back in Lamakara, John Frum Day dawns warm and sticky. After the flag raising, Chief Isaac and other cult leaders sit on benches shaded by palm fronds as several hundred followers take turns performing traditional dances or modern improvisations. Men and boys clad in stringy bark skirts stride onto the dancing ground clutching replicas of chain saws carved from jungle boughs. As they thump their feet in time to their own singing, they slash at the air with the make-believe chain saws. "We've come from America to cut down all the trees," they sing, "so we can build factories."

The chief tells about his trip to the United States in 1995, and shows faded pictures of himself in Los Angeles, outside the White House and with a drill sergeant at a military base. He says he was astonished by the wealth of the United States, but surprised and saddened by the poverty he saw among white and black Americans alike, and by the prevalence of guns, drugs and pollution. He says he returned happily to Sulphur Bay. "Americans never show smiling

264

faces," he adds, "and so it seems they always think that death is never far away."

When asked what he most wants from America, the simplicity of his request is moving: "A 25-horsepower outboard motor for the village boat. Then we can catch much fish in the sea and sell them in the market so that my people can have a better life."

As one looks down into John Frum's fiery Tanna home, they are reminded that not only does he not have an outboard motor from America, but that all the devotees' other prayers have been, so far, in vain. "John promised you much cargo more than 60 years ago, and none has come," someone asks. "So why do you keep faith with him? Why do you still believe in him?"

Chief Isaac shoots an amused look. "You Christians have been waiting 2,000 years for Jesus to return to earth," he says, "and you haven't given up hope."

RESPECTING THEIR BELIEFS

Not long ago there was a story that went viral about an ultra-orthodox Jewish rabbi who covered himself head-to-toe in clear plastic during a commercial flight and apparently remained that way for the entire trip. Speculation was that the self-Saran Wrapping was done to uphold the orthodox tenet requiring men to keep themselves completely separated from women.

The very simple quote in response to the image of a man sitting on a crowded airplane, covered entirely in transparent plastic?

"Respect his beliefs."

Now I want you to join me in a little thought experiment. I want you to imagine that the guy under the plastic wasn't dressed in the familiar vestures of an orthodox Jew but is instead wearing soiled, beat-up jeans and a dirty shirt while sporting a ratty, unkempt beard and long hair. In other words, what if the man on the plane *hadn't* been expressing an extremist religious belief but was just, you know, nuts? Would anyone really be cavalierly demanding that people, particularly the people stuck next to this guy on the plane, "respect his beliefs" and not regard him as a run-of-the-mill whack-job?

I've made the argument plenty of times but this is such a perfect example of what I often complain about. Basically what I'd like to know is this: Why are we expected to respect beliefs that are clearly outlandish and completely divorced from reality simply because those beliefs happen to be the foundation of one faith or another? The simple answer, of course, is that as a society we've decided that certain kinds of crazy aren't crazy at all, and that there's sanity in numbers. You can get away with just about any kind of behavior that would otherwise be considered unacceptable in civilized society as long as you're doing it in the name of your god and absolutely if your god happens to be one of the three or four most popular gods on the planet, the ones who won a few rounds of the Mr. Universe Pageant a couple of millennia ago.

But again, why is it necessary, even in the opinion of some self-professed nonbelievers, that the general public show respect and deference to the thought processes that would lead a man to wrap himself in plastic, presumably to avoid touching women and therefore offending God? How about this for a change: It's not. It's not necessary at all.

With the exception of those who allow their faith to lead them to do despicable things – those whose behavior isn't simply eccentric but dangerous – I do my best to respect people who claim to be religious. I respect the *people* themselves. That doesn't mean I respect their beliefs, because I don't. I don't feel the need to show one ounce of deference to the beliefs of someone who thinks that God listens to his entreaties any more than I would feel the need to show deference to the beliefs of a guy talking to a telephone pole on a street corner who thinks the same thing. Neither of the two has evidence to back up his claims and the only difference between them, really, is that one probably has a roof over his head and *isn't* considered crazy by most of society.

The fact is that when you peel away the culturally sanctioned rationale for not eating meat on a Friday, or sitting on a box and covering the mirrors after someone dies, or making sure that a woman's body is clothed almost completely, what you're left with is just plain old nuts. And what's worse is that the rules and restrictions adhered to by the faithful all too often negatively affect people who should be well beyond the jurisdiction of any one particular religion. It's one thing for someone to make a personal decision not to work on Sunday because he believes his god demands it – it's another thing entirely for a pharmacist not to dispense the morning after pill for the same reason.

I quite frankly don't give a damn what your god wants; the rights, privileges, and even whims of living, breathing human beings supersede the requirement you've imposed upon yourself not to offend the entity you talk to before you go to bed every night. The rights of a gay person to get married or of a woman to have an abortion should at no point be considered equal to the "rights" of the faithful to adhere to the regulations imposed by Jesus, Yahweh, Muhammad and so on. Yes, you're allowed to believe what you want, but when that belief collides with reality, reality shouldn't be the one forced to submit. In the game of chicken between what's proven and what can't be, guess which one has to veer off.

No, a religious belief doesn't need to be respected just because it's a religious belief.

Because if you stripped away the religion, guess what a guy wrapped head-to-toe in plastic on an airplane would be?

Just plain, old crazy.

And the guy in plastic isn't alone. There's Ken Ham building his $130 million replica of the ark – never considering that the ark and the tale of Noah might just be an ancient folk tale – and that the

$130 million would feed and provide housing to thousands. But the money must to be spent to support his pathetic belief that the earth is only 6,000 years old in some wild egocentric trip bordering on true lunacy. And I am to respect his beliefs?

I am supposed to respect those who truly believe that Joe Smith put a rock in his hat and through it translated a mysterious language written on plates of gold that were returned to the angel Moroni? I am supposed to dignify a story like that by respecting those who believe it? Unfortunately, I can't. But I can respect the cancerous power of an indoctrination instilled by parents delivering their children to be sacrificed on the altar of ignorance.

I cannot respect parents rejoicing in the praise of fellow-believers because they held true to their faith and permitted their child to die for the lack of a blood transfusion.

I cannot respect the beliefs of the door knockers victimized by the Watchtower and led to believe only they will see heaven. I can only sympathize with their vulnerability and ignorance. I cannot give my respect to a group of uneducated, inept men who corrupted a Bible and called it true to the original.

I cannot respect the guiles and crimes of Benny Hinn and his lot. To prey upon the sick and desperate, to defraud and imitate a cure is as criminal as any offense heard in a court. These are the predators at the pulpit, weaving their deceits and pretenses to steal from the weak their final hope. And when their "cures" rest in graves and their crimes exposed multiple times, there will yet be thousands rushing to their crusades like lemmings to the slaughter. And once again, we will recognize the meaning of Stupidism.

STUPIDISM

ABOUT THE AUTHOR

David Ellsworth lives in a quite village in Mexico but frequently visits his favorite haunts in Europe. He is the author of 27 books, many of which found their place on bestseller lists. He is married to Magdalena Juarez Ibarra, formerly one of the nation's top officials in the Hacienda, Mexico's equivalent of the IRS. They share their home with their two 12-year-old Schnauzers, Oliver and Olivia.

OTHER BOOKS BY
DAVID ELLSWORTH

Smith County Justice
The Wishing Tree
America Unknown
World War II Unknown
Promises Kept
A Letter for Alicia
What's Killing Us?
Los Vecinos del Norte (Spanish)
Cops (French)
Pilar
It's Over
Leaving Home / Going Home
Escape Plan
Short Stories
Christmas Stories Never Told
Sasha
Black
Selfism

Made in the USA
Las Vegas, NV
25 September 2021